MAY THE ODDS BE WITH US

Legal Segregation in America

The Sports Betting Profession
vs.
Corporate America

Paul Czuchra

Paul Czuchra

Published in the United States

ISBN-13: 978-1481256506
ISBN-10: 1481256505

DEDICATION

To Frances, Lois Ann, and Clarence.
Family kindles the inspiration to extend
"LIBERTY AND JUSTICE FOR ALL."

Paul Czuchra

ACKNOWLEDGMENTS

Thanks to Frank Weatherholt and Ray Lenzi.
Your insights and support made it possible for me to have a career in the business. ODDS-R would not have been possible without you. Neither would *MAY THE ODDS BE WITH US.*

Kudos to the late Lou Kopple and Jerry Porterfield for your help in my early years in the business.

A tip of the hat to John Avello, Johnny Spot, and Bob Gregorka for your assistance.

Also, to Chris Fenton at J & J Sports. You helped sustain my interest in the business through the work we do.

My gratitude to the personnel at the West Las Vegas, Rainbow, and UNLV libraries for help with the research and production of the book.

More thanks to Carol von Raesfeld (The von Raesfeld Agency) for help with editing and publishing that began with *THE ODDSMAKERS* and continues today with *MAY THE ODDS BE WITH US.*

The odds will always be with you, Meagan, for your contribution to the cover of this book.

"*Dzienkuje,*" Mike and Jim. Our friendship helped me stay focused on the completion of the book.

TABLE OF CONTENTS

TABLE OF CONTENTS - continued

TABLE OF CONTENTS - continued

MAY THE ODDS BE WITH US

PREFACE

The admonition "write what you know" begs the question "Why would others care about what you know?" Unless the story relates to what they might want to know, it might be best to keep it to yourself.

Is it possible for me to kindle an interest in others in the business of sports transactions? Besides an offer of a "New Haven special"[1] or a "lock of the century," the likelihood is that interest will be kindled by projections of the business into the big picture of America that binds all of us.

My qualifications make the odds favorable. I have worked in the business in Las Vegas for over thirty years. My graduate degrees confirm my ability to research topics that project the big picture. My novel *THE ODDSMAKERS* is evidence that I have honed skills to communicate through words that show rather than tell.

My commitment to speak truth to power will change the responses of skeptics from "so?" to "Ah, so...." This commitment is devoid of the biases embedded in the ideologies that have divided this nation. The commitment will be fulfilled by life experiences that encompass more than sixty decades on this planet. "Know thyself" is as near as it can be.

A faculty member in my graduate program suggested students undergo psychoanalysis in order to confront the biases and motives that might distort

---

[1] New Haven is the home of the Yale Lock Company. A "New Haven Special" is a "lock"—a guaranteed, can't lose prediction.

their work. The motive behind *MAY THE ODDS BE WITH US* is to speak the truth that reverberates into the big picture of life; otherwise, the title of this book would be *Sex, Lies, and Sports Betting at the Brothels in Nevada.*

—PAUL CZUCHRA

INTRODUCTION

"TO BET OR NOT TO BET"
Is that the question?

A sequel to Hamlet's dilemma "to be or not to be" would add the letter "t" for the sports betting profession. "To bet or not to bet—that is the question" for members of this profession.

The dilemma is that the profession must "be" in order for members to bet. Without the legal freedom to bet, the profession faces a dilemma even Shakespeare might not be able to pose.

The dilemma of whether the profession "can be" was created by those who control the freedom of choice over whether or not to bet. The people who have the power to determine whether members of the profession can bet have control over whether or not they can be. The legal segregation they created for members of the profession determines their possibility to be.

The coalition opposed to the business was forced to make an accommodation that allows members of the profession the freedom to bet in one state, but that coalition was able to do it in a way that leaves unanswered a resolution for the dilemma "to be." They created obstacles that make the odds against a challenge prohibitive.

Hamlet's dialogue captures this dilemma:

"Whether tis nobler in the mind to suffer
The slings and arrows of outrageous fortune
Or to take up arms against a sea of troubles..."

Skirmishes with the segregators in this "sea of troubles" have led to victories that amount to "grandfather clauses" that satisfy the tastes of the residents of one state at the expense of those in the other forty-nine. This "victory" created a situation in which it has become easier to accept the "crumb" that was tossed rather than to "take up arms against a sea of troubles."

The architects of this "sea of troubles" have had the power to define their portrait of the sports betting profession. They have been able to negate the words of Picasso that "it isn't up to them to define the symbols. The public who look at the work must interpret the symbols as they understand them." Picasso's words would be translated by baseball umpires into "It ain't nothin' til we call it."

Members of the sports betting profession have been the "nothin" in this picture. They have been excluded from "the public" who should define their profession with words that suit them.

The interpretation of the profession has been controlled by those who control the sounds of silence from the members. The power brokers own the pulpits from which they preach their gospel. But while they preach they also know that the people in the profession know "there is more to this picture than meets the eye."

Even in silence the people reject the attempt to force feed them the words from those in power who have attempted to turn "seeing is believing" into "hearing is believing." Members of the profession know the "public" does not believe what the segregators say about them. Those who have had that power to define the profession forget their methods are exposed by the methods employed by the public to expose the truth. Truth is in common sense.

Common sense refutes the distortions of the picture presented by the segregationists. Common sense is not bound by the interests of those who have attempted to portray the profession in ways that serve their businesses interests. Common sense portrays the picture as it is not the way they say it is.

This method needs to add the feeling that is necessary to describe the "sea of troubles" as the people in the business see it. The passion for freedom adds "feeling is believing" to the big picture. This feeling creates ties that bind expressed through words from the Civil Rights Movement—"free at last, free at last." Those feelings behind those words would not allow freedom to be restricted by those who have had the power to deny members of the profession their right "to be."

Legal Segregation

Legal segregation is the big picture for people in America who engage in the profession of sports transactions. This profession is the latest version of legal segregations that "lowlight" American history.

Segregation has been the business of Caucasians who had economic reasons to impose segregation on people of color. Their government "reserved" land for Native Americans so the "new" natives could occupy their lands without the nuisance of conflicts. The benefits attached to "Native" citizenship on reservations were incentives to keep Native Americans in their places. After they were no longer deemed to be a threat to the new "natives," the Indian Citizenship Act of 1924 granted them dual citizenship.

The internment of Japanese Americans in concentration camps expanded on the geographies that were part of previous segregations. Japanese Americans who lived on the west coast of America and in Hawaii were identified as threats to economic interests in those areas. World War II provided a reason for the Executive Order by President Franklin

3

D. Roosevelt to assign them to "War Relocation Camps. They remained in these concentration camps until the Supreme Court ruled the Executive Order could not be used to segregate them.

Citizenship was not part of the employment benefits for African Americans enslaved by their business owners in America. The Thirteenth Amendment, the Emancipation Proclamation, and the Civil War were used to begin the legal and military actions by the Federal Government to end segregation by state and local governments. Despite the passage of the Civil Rights Act of 1964, "the people" had to take action to challenge the residue left behind by their legal segregation.

The Civil Rights Act could declare an end to the segregation of the daily activities of individuals, but "the people" had to take action to implement that declaration of their independence. Resistance by individuals and groups had to accompany government action. People who refused to move to the back of the bus or from lunch counters that were designated for others or to remain in designated schools were responsible for the enactment of the legislation.

The legal segregation of our profession has expanded on what had been used to justify the segregation of African Americans. "Separate but equal" was replaced by "separate but unequal" to people who engage in sports transactions. What they do replaces race and ethnicity as the reason for segregation. Geography determined by federal law deems the same transaction as both legal and illegal.

Those who reside in Nevada can make legal transactions. Those who make sports transactions outside Nevada violate federal law. Members of the business outside Nevada are illegal aliens. As long as no one catches them, they can get away with what they do. If they move to their Nevada "reservation" they are legal, unless they try to make transactions outside the state. They can also become illegal if they cross the border from Nevada, but only to make sports transactions.

This picture has an element that binds with other segregations. Whether the laws are federal or local, they restrict people to a specific geographic area. Geography is the picture of where people are segregated.

None of "the people" who have been segregated have had the power to prevent the segregators. While the climate in which these segregations were enacted varies, economics has been a motivator. "Someone" profits from the segregation of those who do not have the power to stop them until the climate changes to open the door to the opportunity to do so.

People who engage in sports transactions can learn lessons about how do to it when the time comes from people who have suffered the pangs of legal segregation. Where there is a will there can be a way. The actors behind government can be made to change their tune when the climate becomes right for them to do so. In order to do so, we must examine what makes our profession the target of segregators.

Options to Gamble

Americans gamble on stocks, options, commodities, futures, derivatives, the weather, and even on their own lives through insurance policies. Wagers on these and other so-called investments are legal. They are regulated by federal and state agencies in order to maintain the integrity of the transactions for the players. Although there are laws that prohibit insider trading, by law no adult or group is prohibited from transactions on them. They are defined as "investments," not gambling.

But governments also sanction transactions that have been defined as "gambling." State-run lotteries are an imprimatur for so-called gambling by state governments. Governments extend the options to gamble through licenses for casinos. Games such as craps, bingo, poker, blackjack, and slots are some of the options for those who prefer those transactions. Casinos also offer pari-mutuel horse racing. Racinos offer their customers a menu of race and casino options. Nevada has approved more than 500 of these games defined as gambling.

State compacts with Indian tribes also extend the possibility to gamble to casinos on Indian reservations. States also offer the option to make wagers on horses across state lines. Wagers can be made by phone to a private company such as U.S. Off Track which is licensed by the State of Oregon. Those wagers are limited to states that legalized wagers on horses.

This multitude of options contrasts with the one option for people who prefer to engage in sports transactions. Nevada is the *only* State that offers the option to make sports transactions. The transaction can only be made at a licensed sportsbook within a casino in Nevada. There are no other options for a sports bettor to make a legal bet anywhere else in America. Illegal options exist to meet the demands of those who cannot make it to Nevada.

None of the other options to gamble are restricted by law the way laws restrict sports transactions. None of the other options are restricted by federal law to one state. No other option is in direct violation of federal law if the transaction does not take place in one state in America. No other option to gamble has forced people to create an illegal market to meet the demands of those who do not reside in Nevada. And no other option to gamble has created the need for laws that criminalize the illegal markets created by legal segregation.

This picture of the profession of sports transactions could be titled "Only in America." How can it be that that sports transactions have been singled out for this level of discrimination? The question can only be answered through an examination of why it could only happen in America.

What is illegal?

Both federal and state statutes address what is illegal. The Federal Wire Interstate Act of 1961 prohibits sports wagers that can be made across state lines.

The Organized Crime Control Act of 1970 prohibits wagers on sports in the context of "organized" crime. This law defines sports transactions as one of the agendas of organized crime.

The Professional and Amateur Sports Protection Act (PASPA), otherwise known as "the Bradley Bill" prohibits sports wagers in all states except Nevada and several states where sports pools had been made legal prior to the legislation. The Bradley Bill removed whatever doubt that may exist that sports transactions are illegal in any state that was not "grandfathered" by PASPA.

Federal laws address sports transactions as part of a big picture. They expand on state and local prohibitions. According to Federal laws, sports wagers are more than a bet between a player and a bookmaker. The reasons extend from the connections to organized crime to the evils of gambling in general, to the alleged corruption of the integrity of the game, to the corruption of "wholesomeness" of the individuals who participate in the games, to the patent rights of corporate sports monopolies. Federal legislation also added online wagers to the prohibition. The Internet Gambling Prohibition Act of 1997 (IGPA) is one example of the attempt to address the technology that can be used to circumvent statutes on the books. This legislation and other legislation that followed address

7

the way sports wagers can be made with online and offshore sportsbooks. How transactions are made has become as important as who makes them.

Several states have supplemented these efforts. There are as many laws that restrict sports transactions as there are states. States prohibit sports transactions as part of a general prohibition on gambling. Some states make a distinction between so-called recreational sports wagers and those that are a part of organized crime. There are laws that prohibit residents from transactions with online gambling sites. Other laws restrict sports transactions to state sanctioned lotteries.

Punishments vary according to the size of the bet as well as the context. But there are no state laws that would permit a sports bettor outside Nevada to make a legal bet the way it can be made in Nevada at a sportsbook.

Why is it illegal?

There's more to this picture than meets the eye. The laws are what they say but what is behind them? That question requires a "visit to the scenes" where the voices responsible for the laws try to explain what is behind them.

But the feelings of the people this picture attempts to portray have been excluded. The reasons that have been given to explain this picture excludes the voices of the people who are the subjects of the picture.

Their voices must be included to explain why members of their profession are segregated by law. They must have the opportunity to offer their explanation about why a transaction on the Super Bowl outside Nevada is illegal, but a wager on whether the Dow Jones goes up or down is legal anywhere in America.

They must be offered the opportunity to express themselves about the reasons that games such as craps and blackjack are offered in casinos throughout America while sportsbooks are an option only in Nevada casinos. They can add their two cents as to why a transaction on which horse may win a race does not meet with the objections as those on which team will win a game.

Their voices must be raised to ask how it is that those who crippled America through trades in derivatives can be in a legal profession while sports oddsmakers and handicappers are illegal aliens outside Nevada. They can ask why it is it that an investment in a sports franchise through the stock market is legal, but an "investment" by the same person on the games that team plays is illegal.

A Tie That Binds

Answers to these and other questions raised by the big picture will require more than a thousand words. Whether the picture is worth more than the thousand words depends on how it resonates with the viewers, the listeners, the readers, and the analysts who interpret this picture through the ties that bind us as people and as citizens of America.

This journey will weave through details that may appear to be of interest only to those in the profession of sports transactions. But what may appear to be details to those of you outside the industry is a part of the context of America that binds all of us.

Super Bowl is a name most of us know. Most of us have either watched or heard about this game. But a change in the name of that game from "Super Bowl" to the "Big Game" is the blow-up of the big picture from Nevada to America. Nevada sportsbooks must use the name "Big Game," not "Super Bowl." The reasons behind the need to change the name may not appear to have significance to those outside the sportsbook industry in Nevada, but the truth behind the need to change that name is one of the ties that bind. The need to use the name "Big Game" has significance for all Americans.

MAY THE ODDS BE WITH US is more than a wish. The truth can change the odds to where the profession of sports transactions has a chance to win this game against corporate America. Legalization of the sportsbook industry would also improve the odds for the future of America. The payoff for this parlay will be greater than the true odds for a two teamer.

CHAPTER ONE

BIG BANGS

"THE POINTSPREAD"
Change is inevitable

The pointspread changed the dialogue of the transaction. Pointspreads became the equalizer between the numbers used for football and basketball games with the numbers game of the business of sports transactions. The pointspread breathed action into a business that had been suffocated by the money line. Without the big bang from the pointspread, the technological "big bang" that later impacted the industry might have been more of a big burp.

Some historians use the term "invention" to describe this change. Others have used the term "innovation." There is a consensus among historians that Charles K. McNeil created the pointspread.[2] If the industry were legal, perhaps those who were responsible for the pointspread would have had the opportunity to apply for a patent that would have removed all doubt. But who could apply for a patent on an activity that is prohibited by law everywhere in America except Nevada? Patent rights are reserved for those who have the legal "right" to apply for a patent.

Historians have been able to document the names of some people in the business who helped propel the

---

[2] My alma mater, the University of Chicago, had the audacity to recognize the accomplishment of Mr. McNeil in their News for Alumni & Friends. They included "Chicago: Birthplace of the Point Spread" NBC Chicago, May 17, 2012.

11

industry to where it is today. They have also been able to document the time frame for the transition.[3] But the documentation of that nugget of history by itself has not conveyed its legacy for America; otherwise pictures of those pioneers, along with placards that recognize their achievement, would appear on the walls of the sportsbooks in Nevada. The industry would have supplemented these recognitions with "holidays" accompanied by special "props" to remind the people in the business today about their achievements. And, Nevada would have built a museum where landmarks of the business were acknowledged as they are in the "Mob Museum."

People in the business who have reaped the benefits of these achievements would be right to demand that Nevada pay tribute to those who helped pave the way for the corporations that now own them. The founders have been to this business what James Naismith and Alexander Graham Bell have been to theirs, but the business awaits a Rosa Parks to move it to the front seat of parity with others that have. Until then, disagreements about who was responsible for the pointspread and when the odds were first offered will be shelved in favor of an agreement about its impact. Without the pointspread, this industry would be pictured as a black hole rather than a big bang.

Older had not been better for the business. At one time, all transactions were in the form of money line bets. Money lines had worked for individual sports such as boxing, tennis, and golf because "by how much" did not accompany the transaction. Money lines are also suitable for team sports such as baseball, hockey, and soccer because the scoring systems for those games are not geared to "by how much." Goals and runs limit "by how much" to special

---

[3] See Chapter 5 "Betting the Line" by R. Davis and R. Abram for additional information about the invention of the pointspread.

propositions such as the run and a half-line in baseball and the goal and a half-line in hockey. The scoring systems that bind baseball, hockey, and soccer bind them to the money line.

But money lines are not as suitable for games such as basketball and football. The scoring systems and the number of points that can be put on the board can make the money line "blah" compared to the action generated by a pointspread. The accumulation of points during a game created with the drama attached to whether or not a team "covers" the number. This drama extends the drama of who will win the game to "by how much."

Pointspreads have also kindled interest from players because they are an equalizer for people who make the transaction. The money line could have an advantage for people on the other side because it can increase the juice attached to the transaction beyond the *11 to 10*.

"Books" are less able to fudge seven points with a commission larger than the *-11 to 10* "juice" that accompanies every transaction. Sportsbooks can make one side of the seven points *-120* and the other side even. The *11 to 10* commission or "vigorish" (vig) remains the same. A sportsbook would have more latitude to increase the 11 to10 vig with a money line comparable to the seven pointspread. Some sports-books in Las Vegas spread seven points as much as -*300* for the favorite to +*220* for the underdog. This commission or "vig" is better than *7 to 5* which increases the potential hold for the sportsbooks beyond the 11 to 10.

This leeway had been common until competition between sportsbooks forced them to make their money lines competitive for games with odds that are closer to "even." However, the ten cent line for teams that are more evenly matched in a game is still increased to as much as forty cents or more for matchups between the best and the worst of teams.

Complexities with the transaction, big favorites, and price fixing are just a few of the reasons why money lines were ready for a move to the back burner for football and basketball. Those games are suited for the front burner with pointspreads that could light the fire. "Action" from the "juice" embedded in "by how much" turned up the fire to full blast.

People on both sides of the counter could win and lose in more ways than the one tied to the money line. In addition to outright winners and losers, point-spreads opened the doors to "covers" and "back door covers." It added drams to scripts for the "oh woe is me soap opera that plays in every sportsbook morning, noon, and night that will never have a conclusion. They are a reminder that no one in the business has or ever will "see or hear it all."

Those unfamiliar with the business might nevertheless question why and how pointspreads have had the magnitude of a game changer for the business. Even if the pointspread is easier to use and understand, how could it have driven the need to invent a tool that would revolutionize the industry? What prompted the inventors to know there was a need for more than the money line?

Common business sense would be one answer. The language adds simplicity to its precision, especially for matchups that involve big favorites. It is easier to say and comprehend a situation in which the New Orleans Saints are twelve point favorites over the Detroit Lions. The translation to the money line could make the Saints -725 with a take back of +525 on the Lions. "Say what?" might be the response from customers to that money line if it had been posted for the opening week of the 2009 season. Or another response from potential players would have been to take a "pass" on the game because there was "no way" the Lions could win outright.

On the other hand, no customer would have asked, "How much is twelve points?" or "What do you mean by twelve points?" The pointspread enables players to tell bookmakers, "I want the Lions plus the 12 because they have a great chance to cover even if they don't win." Other players could counter that they would rather lay 12 points rather than put $725 to win $100. For both sides the pointspread adds the drama of "by how much" to who will win.

The patent on the pointspread could extend to the written word. The pointspread gave birth to what is known in the business as the "hook." The "hook" is shorthand for those in a hurry to write lines on games with slash marks beside a number rather than to write the half point. Half points were handwritten with a slash mark behind each number instead of the "½" after a number. "3/" became the abbreviation for "3½."

The lingo "hook" added to the language people in the business could use to describe an outcome. For those on the losing side of that kind of outcome it could add to the depth of the woe in their soap operas. They would add a slash mark across the throat that was delivered to them by "Captain Hook."

Not only did the pointspread add the drama of the "hook," it increased the opportunities to become a victim or beneficiary of the slash. Pointspreads made it possible for players to make more transactions. Players might have had to otherwise pass on a game because a transaction on the money line of a big favorite would cut into the bankroll for transactions on other games. A $725 bankroll would limit a player to one money line transaction on the Saints to win $100. With an additional $45, that player would have a bankroll to make wagers on the Saints as well as six more teams, each for $110 to win $100.

15

This ability to communicate through pointspreads opened the door for more options to include in the business. The language led to options that had been precluded by the money line. The pointspread increased the number of ways to make transactions as well as the size of the "boards."

Parlays and teasers for football and basketball became big business. The number of teams that could be parlayed or teased expanded to as many as double digits on parlay cards. Differences in the payouts on parlay cards stimulated competition on both sides of the counters. Players found it worthwhile to shop for the best odds while sportsbooks were forced to find ways to attract business.

"Pittsburgh Jack"[4] used the pointspread to help revolutionize payouts on parlay cards. Payouts of $100 for $1 on a ten team parlay card on which ties would lose that had been the standard were increased by him to as much as $850 for $1 at the Barbary Coast on a ten team half-point card which precluded ties. The half-point spreads with the larger payouts created a boom for parlay card business which, in turn, increased profits for sportsbooks all made possible by the pointspread.

Without pointspreads, teaser transactions would not be part of the language of the business. Teaser bets through money lines would have had to be configured through mathematical formulas that would cause more confusion that it would be worth. A money line seven team teaser would not be near the same ballpark as seven point teasers that entice customers to play with the pointspread. The teaser option for football and basketball has become an integral part of the business because of the pointspread.

The same is true for "over and under" transactions. Although Bill Dark, former owner of the

---

[4] A member of the Hall of Fame.

Del Mar Race and Sportsbook in North Las Vegas[5] created the over and under option for baseball, his invention reached a pinnacle after it was co-opted for basketball and football. The parlay of side to total has become one of the most popular transactions of the business. Most games now have totals to go along with the pointspread. That would not have been possible without the pointspread. Recognition of the popularity of the "over and under" wager reached a pinnacle when Al Michaels, the announcer for Monday Night Football, told his audience it was "over for the under" after the last score. Without the pointspread, it might have been over for both the over and the under.

Besides its impact on the number of ways transactions could be made, the popularity of the pointspread also contributed to the popularity of basketball and football. The move from back to front burner created the need for more burners. There was a demand for more action. Both professional and college football and basketball expanded their seasons to meet with the demands from fans and members of the business for more action. The demand was met with earlier starts and later finishes on days that later expanded into weeks and months that football and basketball games would be played. The pointspread was the necessity for what followed. While "necessity is the mother of invention," the invention of the pointspread bred necessity. What went around came around.

The "board" at the "Hole in the Wall" Sportsbook at the Castaways Hotel and Casino reflected this twist. When Sonny Reizner[6] opened the doors to the sportsbook, college basketball would not be posted until after January 1st—after the college football bowl season had ended. Teams on that board were limited

---

[5] Another member of the Hall of Fame.
[6] Another member of the Hall of Fame.

to the few major conferences. College teams such as St. Mary's of California and Wisconsin Green Bay were not "board teams." Odds are now posted on those schools as well as dozens of other teams Sonny would have never dreamed of posting on that board. Confidence in the pointspread, along with a demand for more action from customers on more teams helped to make possible what at one time would have been an impossible dream.

Sonny's invention of the Challenge was made possible because of the growth in the popularity of the business attributable to the pointspread. The "Challenge" was the first of the pro football handicapping contests that have become an indispensible part of the landscape of the industry.[7] Almost every sportsbook now includes football and basketball contests as part of their menus.

The impact of the pointspread extended beyond the ways and opportunities to wager. Companies that published schedules for football, basketball, and baseball were beneficiaries of this growth in the schedule. More was better for them. More teams, more games created the need to consolidate them in a book both players and sportsbooks would have to use to communicate.

Publishers of these books addressed this need with schedules that met the need for simplicity and expediency. Owners of these schedules could influence which games would be posted on the boards. A rotation for games on the schedule derived from the research with teams and leagues that identified when, where, and at what time their games would be played. This info became a traffic light that smoothed the way

---

[7] Sonny Reizner also was the first to give free drink tickets and t-shirts to customers. Frank Weatherholt is my source for this info. Frank was general manager at the time. He also managed the Sahara and other sportsbooks during his five decades in the industry.

for customers to reach the sportsbook counters. Without the schedules there would have been traffic jams at the counters, especially on Saturday and Sunday mornings during football and basketball seasons.

The need for a schedule for both players and sportsbooks led to competition among publishers. Revenue from advertisements generated profits from the publishers as well as for the advertisers. J.K., Jim Feist, and Don Best published schedules with advertisements from businesses who could sell their "two cents" for "big bucks." "Touts" would pay because there were few outlets for wisdom that could reach people who would pay for an opinion about the outcome of a game. Those businesses would have been "small potatoes" without the schedules that became necessary because of another consequence of the pointspread.

The pointspread also created power ratings for handicappers to use to compare their assessment of a game against what oddsmakers had posted on the board. Without a pointspread, both sides of the transactions would have lacked the tool that enabled them to play their numbers game.

The power rating of a handicapper might show a greater difference than the 12 points posted on the boards of Las Vegas sportsbooks for the matchup between the New Orleans Saints and the Detroit Lions. That power rating might establish New Orleans at 92 and Detroit at 78. That difference would be two points more than the line on the board. New Orleans might be a "play" in that power rating system, while it might be a "pass" for others. Whatever their conclusions, the dialogue was made possible by a comparison of "spreads" created by systems that established power ratings.

Pointspreads also impacted other "players" in and around the industry. Newspapers print pointspreads.

Sports programs on radio and television refer to point spreads. Announcers who don't dare mention a specific point spread during a game use the terms "favorite" and "underdog" to describe the teams. Some would go so far as to describe teams as big favorites or underdogs. They would not know which was which without a pointspread that makes sense to them and their viewers. The language of people in the business has also become lingo for people on the outside looking in.

This situation might not have been possible if courts had not decided that the pointspread is language protected by freedom of speech. Pat Burke, then President of Vegas One News, fought to establish the constitutionality of the language in the late 1970s.[8] Vegas One News sold pointspread information from Nevada sportsbooks to customers throughout America. A court supported his right to transmit that information by telephone across state lines. The court decided the pointspread is freedom of speech protected by the Constitution.

Vegas One News did not violate the Wire Act of 1961. The Court decided that the transmission of pointspread information is separate from the trans-action on that information. That decision led to the growth in the number of businesses that were needed to provide information that could be used by people in a business that had grown beyond the need for more than the information newspapers could print.

The pointspread also made it easier for oddsmakers to extend their creativity to propositions. First half and second half lines as well as in running propositions contributed to the explosion of interest in the business.

---

[8] Burke's challenge to the Courts would make him a member of the Hall of Fame.

But the best may be yet to come from the pointspread. The "big bang" in the business generated by the action from the transactions has expanded the universe of the business to the limits of America. Perhaps this expansion of interest might become the basis for a movement by people in the business to extend the impact of the pointspread to the Supreme Court. This invention made in America by Americans for Americans might then be accorded the respect it deserves instead of the denigration that accompanies its segregation by corporate America.

Television
Seeing is feeling

Television connected with the action from the transactions to juice the business. A pharmaceutical company would ensure its future if it were able to bottle the trip through a football season in Nevada sportsbooks.

That trip is one that goes from "I can't believe what I'm seeing" to "hang around, you ain't seen nothin' yet." The potion to spark the feeling is generated by seeing the pointspread in action on the screen.

Without television the kick from the pointspread would be short and wide. Without the kick from television casino corporations might have closed the doors on their unwanted stepchild. Television helped to keep the doors open.

Radio and Wire service reports might not have had enough action to keep the business alive. Written and spoken words could not connect with people in the business the way television could deliver their action home.

Before television opened the doors to telecasts of almost every game on the board, people in the business relied on reports from radio or the wire services to bring them closer to their action each and every day. The three television networks limited their coverage to weekends.

Sportsbooks could not add to what people in the business could see on television at home. Radio and the UPI Ticker filled the gaps, but the action generated by those reports would not keep customers glued to their seats in a casino. Casinos needed help from other pleasures to help customers get a kick from their wagers at sportsbooks.

Customers would have otherwise been at the mercy of radio announcers who read from ticker reports that recited what had happened with their teams on the road. Their raps with rulers on a desk attempted to replicate the sounds of bats on baseballs. An announcer would muffle sounds to convey a roar from a crowd that coordinated with the ruler to describe a wire report that a batter had flied out to left field. Announcers could embellish that description with hype that made it a "diving catch or a leaping catch over the wall" or whatever else could be conjured up to add drama to a mundane description of what had happened. Announcers also added to the atmosphere with sounds of vendors who huckstered "peanuts, popcorn, cracker jack" to fill the lulls in action. Few announcers had the audacity to holler "cold beer."

None would dare to mention the odds on the game, although at least one knew why some listeners had tuned in. Hall of Fame announcer Bob Elson would let his Chicago White Sox fans know which games he had bet through repeated updates on those games. The tone of his voice conveyed which team was his "side."[9] Mr. Elson was fortunate no one had the

---

[9] The late Lou Kopple is the source for this story. Lou began his career in the business in Chicago. He was the manager of the Silverbird and the Marina sportsbooks in Las Vegas. Lou was the proverbial "walking encyclopedia of the business." Lou should be a member of the Hall of Fame.

audacity to make the case that his wagers somehow influenced the outcome of the games he emphasized on the air, otherwise he might be standing alongside Pete Rose outside the door to the Hall of Fame.

Announcers were forced to change the way they had delivered reports on games. They had to be wherever the games were played to describe the action as they saw it, not from a ticker. Radio networks also changed their ways to meet the demands from listeners for more coverage. They expanded on the definition of "home" teams. The success of some teams generated national interest in how they would do during the season. The World Series and the NFL Championship and Bowl Games were broadcast from coast to coast. One network expanded on the principle of national interest. On Saturdays live reports were broadcast to America from all of the sites where the most important football games would be played.

However the UPI Ticker and the Western Union Sports Ticker remained the staple to keep customers at the sportsbooks. These services expanded coverage to include updates on most of the games on the boards of the sportsbooks. The reports could entice people to remain in the casinos to follow their transactions. Casino owners paid for this service with the hope that those who remained to read the wire would also play other casino games.

Casinos owners would even go so far as to turn their heads the other way to allow their players to call the sportsbooks for updates on scores in order to keep them as customers. Sportsbook managers would allow players who were around the counter to answer the calls. Players volunteered so they could be the first to have access to UPI play by play reports on their action. UPI reports were exclusive in casinos that competed to be first with the Western Union Sports Ticker featured elsewhere. Competition between wire services to be the first with updates helped to make a sportsbook the place to be for action on the transaction.[10]

Casinos owners would add money to their budgets to keep sportsbook customers in the casino. They paid for full time service from the sports television networks that expanded the coverage of games beyond those that had been limited to several on the weekends. Television added to the incentive for Nevada corporate casinos to fight to keep their monopoly on sportsbooks. One would go so far as to open 9,800 square feet of space with a 1,250 square foot Video Wall with 100 seats to watch the action.

Television coverage shortened the time and the distance for the action on the fields of play to become part of the action in the casinos. Visual coverage transformed communication from "prop" speed of the radio, wire services and newspapers to "jet speed." The closer players in the sportsbooks came to the action on the field, the closer they came to experience seeing with feeling.

Announcers were not necessary to show a "leaping catch over the wall." The visual of a leap with a glove extended into the seats where fans contended for a ball that extended three-quarters above the tip of a glove conveyed a feeling beyond what verbal and written descriptions could provide.

Words could not generate the feelings aroused by the picture of a one-handed catch in the back of an end zone where the toes of a receiver tipped behind the line beside a referee with extended hands curved upwards to indicate a touchdown.

A picture of a shot clock winding down from one second to zero while the shooter launched a

---

[10] Ray Lenzi is the source of this information. Ray managed sportsbooks at Churchill Downs Race and Sportsbook and the Stardust Hotel and Casino. Ray should be a member of the Hall of Fame because he is one of *the* historians of the business in Las Vegas.

turnaround three-pointer with the hand of a defender outstretched beside a referee whose hand was extended to indicate a three in a two-point game showed more than a thousand words could tell through the description of the action after it had happened. A wager on that action would be frosting on the cake for people in the business.

They could "feel their cake and eat it too"—even at home. "Home delivery" of the action created a class of its own for the business. Owners of the casinos had to compete for home field advantage. They offered "comps" that would keep customers where they would be able to expand their action to other venues. Owners bet their sportsbook customers would also wager on horses, slots, blackjack, craps, and other games while they watched their games on television. They could do both at the same time. Profits from games with a greater hold for casinos than sports would pay for the television sets throughout the casino that helped to keep customers at the tables.

Television networks responded to this growth of interest in the business. They added to their viewership in ways no other programming could do. They could charge casinos more for service if they had a lineup of sports, conferences, and teams that would attract customers. Competition among television networks reflected the difference between sports and other programming on television.

While events such as 9/11, hurricanes, tornadoes, and space junkets attract viewers, there is an end for them as newsmakers. Programs such as *The Sopranos* and *American Idol* can attract numbers of viewers that compete with those who watch the NFL. However, those programs cannot compete with the numbers that have watched the NFL over the decades. The passion for *The Sopranos* came to an end. So will the passion for *American Idol*. They were created by television networks for television.

The professional and amateur sports leagues have a life of their own. There is no end to the action they can make for television. While the business of sports transactions benefits from that partnership the business also contributes to the profits of the partnership, but its impact cannot be documented.

Any attempt to count viewers in the business would be as accurate as election vote counts in Afghanistan. The illegality of the business outside Nevada is tantamount to a "Jim Crow" law that keeps voters in the business from the polls. Even if a way were found to count them, the corporate television networks and the corporate sports leagues would prefer to keep the number in the dark.

The numbers might make a mockery of the "wholesomeness" of the product they propagate in commercials and self promotions. Corporations might cringe at numbers that describe the truth about how many of the viewers have action on their product. Those numbers might be "unwholesome" for the image they try to portray for the product they sell to the public as wholesome. Wholesomeness must compete with headlines about the "unwholesomeness" of the people in their product. They can spin those headlines, but in order to keep their product, the medium must comply with the dictates of the messengers. Television networks must accept the censorship imposed by the corporate sports leagues. The pointspread had to be added as the eighth word to George Carlin's list of "Seven Words You Can Never Say on Television."

Despite the censorship television networks have found ways to exploit a feature of our business that could appeal to everyone without stepping on the toes of their sponsors. Television networks have invented their version of so-called "handicapping" shows. As long as a so-called "analyst" does not advise viewers to put their money on Alabama, the "handicapper" can make a "prediction" that the Tide will win. Since the pointspread is a "no-no," they are under no obligation to mention to viewers that Alabama is a 30-point favorite. The scenarios allow the messenger to have its cake and eat it too.

Variations on this theme pervade the pre-game shows because the television executives understand the appeal of "celebrities" sticking their necks out "You did or did not 'nail' that one" can be music to the ears of listeners who get can get a charge from a plug that is not connected to the outlet.

One network reached the pinnacle of hypocrisy when it decided to titillate their viewers with hints of the business they censor. They employed former CBS college basketball announcer Billy Packer to work with former Indiana and Texas Tech head basketball coach Bob Knight to host a show that would add to the excitement of the NCAA College Basketball Tournament. The network expressed the hope that viewers would get a "feel" for the Tournament that only Las Vegas could provide. This feeling had to be different because sports transactions are illegal every-where in America except Nevada.

This "feel" would be transmitted from a show at the doorstep to the sportsbook in the Encore Casino, but the network did not mention in promos that the show would not mention pointspreads, nor would it include as guests professionals who are engaged in the business. Even those who never made it to the "fifth grade" might ask how the "feel" of the Tournament could be captured without the participation of the people who create it. This version of "feeling" amounted to what a man might get from watching commercials for Viagra or Cialis, not from the pills themselves.

Network executives lacked the integrity to create the feel that came from their forbidden territory of the sportsbook just steps away from the show. They did not have the integrity to reach out for the feeling that was in their grasp. The hypocrisy was compounded by the cooperation of the executives at the Encore who allowed them to get away with "murder" against their business.

Hypocrisy is the tip of an iceberg that punctures the integrity of corporate television networks. As long as they can have their share of the pie, they can live with the system that segregates viewers in the business in Nevada from those outside the State who use their product for illegal purposes.

This dream world does not require a warning about their product to people outside Nevada. The messenger does not have to add a disclaimer that they assume no responsibility for the repercussions that may come from the use of their program for illegal purposes.

If our business has the potential to be harmful to viewers, television networks should be forced to offer a disclaimer similar to those that accompany commercials for prescription drugs. This one would warn that "action from a transaction on this game might lead to serious consequences for the pocket-books of viewers."

The messenger caved in to demands from the sports networks to punish Las Vegas. While the messenger can televise the "Big Game" to Las Vegas, commercials to promote tourism to the city are prohibited outside Nevada. Perhaps censorship is their payback to the business in the city that takes them for all they are worth.

The Information Age extended the impact of the pointspread beyond what television delivered. New technology transported the business into uncharted waters off the shores of America. This bang expanded the sea of troubles for the business.

Offshore Sportsbooks and the Internet
What goes around comes around.

Technology changed the way transactions could be made. They had been made either face to face or over the telephone between people who had to meet in order to "settle." The Information Age made it possible to make and settle them without ever meeting after people in the business moved "offshore." Transactions with them from America extended the conflict between corporate sports leagues and the business of sports transactions into international relations.

The bang from the impact of the pointspread through television propelled the business into an orbit beyond the borders of America. Connections became available from the mainland to "offshore" sportsbooks through 800 telephone numbers and the Internet. Those connections would challenge the federal government to find ways to prohibit transactions that defied the borders of federal law.

New options to communicate met the demands for action by people in the business. Those demands could no longer be restrained by Government through the limitations of technology from another era. The Information Age had transported the sportsbook industry across the borders of America. 800 numbers made it possible to make connections from America with the world. They helped to distance callers in the business from the tactic of law enforcement that knew where, when, and how to be a "third party" to those calls. People in the business were no longer forced to "look over their shoulders" after every telephone transaction.

Although the Federal Interstate Wire Act prohibited transactions across state lines, 800 numbers and the Internet became alternatives for people in the business to circumvent that law. While the law prohibited the transmission of business via

29

telephone, it would not deter people from the use of 800 numbers and the Internet to make transactions with "offshore" sportsbooks.

But people who moved their businesses "offshore" were not free from the reach of America as several found out the hard way after their arrests in the Dominican Republic. That would not deter the expansion of "offshores" beyond the Caribbean to nations such as Costa Rica and Australia. "Offshore" came to mean all sportsbooks outside the boundaries of the United States except those in England. This version of "outsourcing" reflected the creativity of businessmen in the profession. Other professions might reward this creativity with accolades. Instead of accolades, America threatened these entrepreneurs with jail time if they returned to reclaim their citizenship.

The reasons behind the need to outsource were different than the economic motives of corporations that followed the example of people in the business. Owners of sportsbooks had to move to where it was legal for them to practice their business. Other American businesses outsource to lower costs in order to increase profits. The difference helps to define who owns America.

Nation-states such as Curacao and Costa Rica welcomed owners of sportsbooks. There was money to be made for both parties. Owners "paid" those governments through various forms of taxes that could have been revenue for America. Instead, the money was a form of protection for the owners from direct intervention by America to close their places of business. Owners paid through an unofficial renouncement of their citizenship. If they ever returned to America, they would be prosecuted as Jay Cohen would learn.

At the time America's bookmakers moved to the offshores with their 800 numbers, computer technology opened another door for people in the industry to communicate with them. The late Don Bessett began work with computers to transmit information. Tests for the system began with pay phones outside the Stardust Hotel to computers in his office on Las Vegas Boulevard across the street. Transmission of opening lines and moves on pointspreads had been limited to telephones. Public phones were located outside casino sportsbooks such as the Stardust. "Phone men" used this convenience to call people in the business that needed the information as it happened. Mr. Bessett experimented with ways to make the delivery of this information as it happened via computer.

Initially, technology restricted the computer service to input from calls from the phone men to Don Bessett's office. The pointspread information was then incorporated into the computer program. That information could then be transmitted to customers with computers.

Improvements in technology eliminated the need for phone men. Information could be transmitted directly from sportsbooks to Mr. Bessett's office. Opening lines and moves on pointspreads from several Las Vegas sportsbooks were transmitted as they happened. Las Vegas became the source of point-spread information for people in the business wherever they might be, even in offshore sportsbooks.

Mr. Bessett died before he could see the fruits of his labor. His wife sold the business to Mr. Al Corbo who renamed the business Don Best Sports. Don Best provided "line service" to people in the business who were in a "must know" situation about changes on the boards of Las Vegas sportsbooks as they happened.

Don Best added schedules of games to the computer service. The schedules enabled all of the customers in the business to be in the same rotation as the boards in the sportsbooks. Advertisements in the schedule connected readers to 800 numbers with offshores as well as to businesses that sold opinions on the outcomes of games. Everyone in the industry would be in sync through the Don Best schedule.

Technology extended the bang for the business beyond the borders of America into the battleground of international politics. The product America had criminalized everywhere except Nevada had few, if any, legal prohibitions in other countries around the world.

While transactions from America to offshores are prohibited by America, they are legal in the host countries for offshore sportsbooks. This divide is as clear as two sidelines of a football field. National sovereignty determines the rules of a playing field with few markers both sides accept.

In this sea of troubles America is unable to exercise absolute control over what it has deemed illegal. If sports betting were legal everywhere in America there would have been no need for people in the business to move offshore. Businessmen responded to the demand from people to do what their government told them they can and cannot do.

Additional laws would be necessary to extend the enforcement of the prohibition against the business beyond the borders of America. The Internet Gambling Prohibition Act (IGPA) of 1997 and the Unlawful Internet Enforcement Act of 2006 (UIGEA) were enacted to fill the gap. Both were designed to deter Americans from making sports transactions with offshores.

Enforcement of IGPA would depend on the cooperation of host nations for the offshore sports-books. The law ignored the reasons behind why these nations decided to accept offshore sportsbooks. The economic value of to them was worth a fight against whatever America might do to try to prohibit a business relationship between the owners of the sportsbooks and their customers. Nations that chose to license the sportsbooks decided the economic benefit for them was worth a fight against America in the playing field of international politics.

Antigua and Barbuda responded to attempts by America to curb sports wagering with a petition to the World Trade Organization (WTO). The WTO agreed that member nation United States was not in compliance with its treaty obligations because full access from America was denied to online gambling companies in Antigua and Barbados. The WTO ruled against the attempt by the U.S. to restrain what the Organization regarded as free trade. America chose to ignore the decision.

Opponents of the business in America decided to pursue other avenues to regulate online wagers. Enforcement of the prohibition against online wagering moved to the battleground where America could exercise control over the economics of the transaction between gamblers and online casinos. New legislation in the form of UIGEA attempted to curtail the ability of financial institutions to make credit card, electronic fund transfers, and check transactions with an internet gambling site.

Fines imposed by America against the online money transfer business NETELLER sent a message to other financial institutions that there would be penalties if they tried to circumvent the law. Funds seized by the U.S. Attorney's Office also sent more than a message to online gamblers. Their assets are now in the hands of the U.S. government.

The impact of UIGEA extended beyond the business of sports transactions. Directly or indirectly, the law included the businesses of poker, horse racing, and other casino games. The prohibitions that included these venues for online gambling and general dissatisfaction with other aspects of UIGEA prompted Representative Barney Frank (D-MA) to propose legislation that would address all of those concerns except for the business of sports transactions.

During the hearings on his Internet Gambling, Regulation, Consumer Protection Act (IGRCPEA) Congressman Frank said, "...the expression by the professional leagues of shock of the notion that people would actually bet on games was one of the least persuasive emotional outbursts I have encountered, but we acknowledge the reality of it." He had to accept the fact that the inclusion of sports transactions in his legislation would make it impossible to pass the Bill.[11]

Supporters and opponents of IGRCPEA are bound by complementary interests. Americans who engage in sports transactions are aligned with American offshore sportsbook owners who are aligned with the nations that allow them to conduct business there. The WTO is also part of this alliance which is united behind the principles of freedom of choice. This identical interest shared by members of the coalition is expressed in the belief that "We, the People" should have the freedom to choose whether or not to make transactions on sports.

Congressman Frank supports their position. Among his comments about all forms of gambling he said American citizens have become tired of being told "how to spend their time and money."[12]

Opposition to "We, the People" comes from a coalition of interests. Those who oppose gambling on moral grounds allied themselves with law enforcement agencies that enforce the prohibition against the business. This coalition lends support to the backbone of the alliance. Congressman Frank identified them as "the sports leagues such as the NFL and NCAA which lobbied heavily for the internet ban.[13]

---

[11] *Gaming Today* May 12-18, 2009 pp. 3-4 "Online bill leaves out sports betting."

[12] *Gaming Today* July 7-13, 2009, pp. 1-3 "Barney Frank online gambling will pass."

[13] *Gaming Today* July 7-13, 2009, pp. 1-3 "Barney Frank online gambling will pass."

This backbone has fought to protect their product from the business that according to them uses their product without consent and without compensation. They are joined by the casino corporations in Nevada that were "grandfathered" into a legal monopoly on that business by the Professional and Amateur Sports Protection Act. But casino corporations are not part of the backbone that also opposes the legalization of the business in other states. The twists the beneficiaries of States Rights would have to make on the same right for other states would require more than any of their spin merchants could manufacture.

Perhaps the sports leagues might be able to end this sea of troubles if they can redefine the conflict with the business as part of the "war on terror." Drones might then become available to back an ultimatum from America to offshore sportsbooks to "cease and desist" operations.

The odds on who is likely to win this conflict will come from the look into what is behind this picture. In the words of Picasso, "It's not just the picture, it's what's behind the picture." The words of jazz pianist McCoy Tyner will also help to tell a story in which "it's that feeling that tells the story." That story begins with the look behind the scene in Nevada.

CHAPTER TWO

NEVADA

"All States are equal under the Constitution."
But one State is more equal than the others.

"A Constitutional Right"

The Tenth Amendment to the Constitution states, "The powers not delegated to the United States by the Constitution nor prohibited by it to the States, are reserved to the States, or to the people." The Founding Fathers might not be able to reconcile this Amendment with a situation in which one State has the legal right to conduct a business that is prohibited in all of the other states.

"Waterboarding" might not extract an acknowledgment from the "guardians" of the Constitution that this contradiction requires an explanation. They might have to invoke their Fifth Amendment rights in order to avoid an explanation for why Nevada has been able to sanction and govern a business that is prohibited in other states by federal law. Sodium Pentothal might be necessary to extract from the "guardians" the answer to why there has not been a constitutional challenge to what has been Nevada's exclusive right to legalize the business of sports transactions. Those "guardians" might need double vision to excuse themselves from their inability to find provisions in the Constitution that permit one State to monopolize one business activity. An interrogation might relegate these "guardians" to detention centers

36

to mingle with others who also pose a threat to America.

This playing field for the business of sports transactions in America is pocketed with contradictions that mock the intent of the Founding Fathers to establish a separation of power that protects the rights of all. The playing field for the business has evolved to include the interests of all parties except the one explicitly included in the Tenth Amendment... namely, "the rights of the people." Those rights have been sent to the sidelines by the powers that shape this system.

Separation of power has evolved into a playing field that excludes "the power of the people." People in the business do not have the rights guaranteed by the Constitution. They do not have a voice in a battle-round that restricts their right to be legal. While the Supreme Court decision in *Brown vs. Board of Education* that helped to end the racial segregation of African Americans concluded that segregated educational facilities within a state were inherently unequal. Unfortunately there has been no court decision that concludes that the segregation to one state of people who practice a profession is inherently unequal.

Attempts by Delaware and Connecticut to legalize that profession in their states are the first legal challenges to the federal law that established this form of segregation. These attempts are regarded as an unwelcome intrusion into a status quo established by corporate America that abides by the motto "leave what is well enough for us alone."[14] Comments by Nevada Gaming Control Board member Randall Sayre at a Gaming Law Conference express a concern for

---

[14] *Las Vegas Sun* 11/6/2009 article "Threat seen to Nevada's sports betting monopoly" by Richard Velotta and Brian Wargo.

what might happen to Nevada's sportsbook industry if this possibility comes to fruition.[15]

Other states have not challenged the federal prohibition imposed on them. No one has forced those states to answer why they have not considered the legalizations of sports transaction in order to generate revenue as it does in Nevada. Even those states that legalized gambling before the Federal prohibition did not include the option of sports transactions.

For those states and others that legalized gambling after the federal prohibition, cooperation that keeps the status quo has been preferable to a confrontation with the coalition opposed to the business of sports transactions. Perhaps those states fear a challenge might result in a loss that might exceed the benefits of a legal decision that would open the door to the business. A challenge might result in their loss of a professional sports franchise.

Nevada has also become a member of the coalition that benefits from "leaving well enough alone." Nevada Regulators and Nevada corporate casinos have made accommodations with the opponents of sports transactions in order to preserve their monopoly on the business. But "leaving well enough alone" does not include the interests of the people in the business who are prohibited from the legal practice of their profession. Even though they created the business, they have not had a voice in the decision that made the practice of their profession illegal everywhere in America except Nevada.

A look back at the way sports betting began and evolved in Nevada will help uncover the reasons behind why it is the way it is. One step back will lead to two steps forward.

---

[15] "State regulator says need for new revenue will force other jurisdictions to turn to wagering on athletics."

The Origins of Our Universe

Nevada legalized gambling in 1931. New Jersey legalized gambling in 1978. Nevada had a monopoly on gambling for 47 years.[16] Nevada has retained its legal monopoly on the business of sports transactions since the first turf club was licensed by the State.

The Sierra Turf Club opened for business in Reno on January 23, 1952. The facility had 65 seats for the Race book and Sports pool. Between 1952 and 1975, eleven Race book and Sports pools opened throughout the State. They were restricted to a maximum of 75 seats. Santa Anita Turf and Sports Book Inc. was the first to open in Las Vegas on January 1, 1954 at Las Vegas Boulevard near Twain. The Turf Clubs remained open for business until March 31, 1989 when the GEM SPORTS CENTER in Winnemucca closed its doors. Del Mar Race and Sports Club was the last Turf Club to close operations in the Las Vegas area on June 30, 1988.[17]

Turf Clubs had been isolated from casinos. Nevada Regulation 5.020 was a response to the Kefauver Commission determination that the business was a part of organized crime. Section (1) of the Regulation stated "... race horse betting and sports pools are forms of gambling materially different from other types of gambling..."

Therefore, as stated in Section (2) of the Regulation "...operations shall be conducted only in a building wherein no other types of games are operated or intoxicating beverages dispensed..."

The reason behind the need for this isolation was stated in Section (1) of the Regulation. "...the public

---

[16] *Betting the Line* by Richard Davies and Richard Abram, pp. 115-118 captures the history of legalized gambling in Nevada.

The Silver State by James Hulse also captures that history.

[17] State of Nevada Gaming Control Board

health, safety, morals, good order and general welfare of the inhabitants of the State of Nevada require stringent controls and regulation of such activities."

The words of the Regulation created a stench that opponents of the business outside the state would embellish with their own words and actions. One faction of this coalition opposed all forms of gambling for moral and religious reasons. Transactions on sports were just one component of an activity they defined as gambling. They had to oppose gambling because it was immoral.

They were joined in their opposition to the business by Federal interests that enacted legislation to support the words of Nevada Regulation 5.020. In 1950 the Kefauver Commission imposed a ten percent tax on sports transactions in Nevada. The tax doubled the cost of the "juice" that turf clubs charged their customers who made transactions on sports. A transaction that had cost one dollar for every ten would cost two dollars because of the Tax. Customers could not live with price hike. Owners of the turf clubs were forced to find ways to avoid the imposition of the tax for their preferred customers.

Despite the ability of people in the business to circumvent the tax, it survived because the opponents of the business were able to sustain an atmosphere in which they linked transactions on sports to the integrity of the games. According to the Kefauver Commission, sports betting was a component of the business of "organized crime entwined in the legal gambling business in Nevada." The tax was a response to the perception of the threat of organized crime to the integrity of the game.

The Black Sox scandal was their headline "fix." It was the umbrella that embraced other "fixes" such as those that involved college basketball. Opponents of the business used these examples to make the argument that the people involved in sports transactions were a threat to the integrity of the game because they could buy athletes to fix outcomes of the games.

The containment of legal sports transactions to Turf Clubs in Nevada would not be enough for those who marched under the banner of the protection of the integrity of the game. The economic climate of the times helped to make their case. The best players who would have been able to influence the outcome of a game might have been tempted to consider the possibility to throw a game for compensation.

As the salaries of professional athletes rose to seven and eight figures there would be less incentive for them to fix a game. Those at the top of the pay scale were less willing to risk million dollar paychecks for the amount of money they might be paid by the "fixers." Marquee college players would not risk potential multi-million dollar paychecks for the chump change from a bet. The potential to fix games diminished because there were fewer players available who could determine an outcome.

The "Information Age" also helped refute the argument that sports transactions corrupted the integrity of the game. Performances of all athletes became a form of "public" property through television—replays and replays of instant replays that magnify every play. Public scrutiny weakened the argument that an athlete could get away with suspicious behavior. Marquee players in a position to control the outcome of a game could be scrutinized to the umpteenth degree to make sure that an outcome had not been compromised.

Games that might escape the scrutiny of television and instant replay were subject to the oversight of the sportsbooks in Nevada. They had to be on the alert for suspicious patterns of transactions in order to protect their pockets from being picked by "fixers."

But politicians behind the Kefauver Tax had their reasons to deny the business the opportunity to join them in the protection of the integrity of the games. Those reasons would become exposed as their attempts to control the business came into conflict with the business interests of casino corporations in Nevada.

The Ten Percent Tax deterred a movement to incorporate sportsbooks in Nevada hotel casinos. Operators of the casinos would have had to face the consequences if they defied the Ten Percent Tax the way owners of Turf Clubs had been able to do. Hotel casinos were content to leave the sportsbook business to the turf clubs.

The Ten Percent Tax had little impact on the industry outside Nevada. Neither side to the transaction would allow that Tax to influence the economics of their business. The federal government used the tax to cite people in the business for income tax violations.

After television helped transform the industry into big business, a coalition of interests in Nevada organized to take action to challenge the Tax. In 1974, Nevada Senator Howard Cannon sponsored legislation that reduced the federal Tax from ten percent to two percent. Turf clubs were able to pay the two percent Tax and make a profit.

This reduction in the tax spurred hotel casinos to open sportsbooks in order to compete for the dollars that had been wagered exclusively at the turf clubs. "Freedom" from this federal attack on the business came in 1983 when Senator Cannon was able to reduce the two percent tax to .025%. Removal of this obstacle opened the way for the enterprise to become big business. The State of Nevada was handed exclusive rights to a business that could generate revenue for its Treasury.

Elimination of the tax changed the playing field. Opponents of the business were confronted by a coalition of interests in the state that would challenge moral and political arguments against their business with facts. Government created institutions that certified the business with integrity. This integrity for the business that was certified by the state challenged arguments that sports transactions are incompatible with the integrity of the game.

Sportsbooks were liberated from the shackles imposed on the business by outsiders. The State of Nevada created an environment to make sportsbooks suitable for corporate business. A coalition of business and political interests had to establish the integrity of their game in order to refute the argument of their opponents outside Nevada that the business was incompatible with the integrity of their games.

The Nevada Commission and the Gaming Control Board

In 1949, the Nevada legislature enacted legislation that legalized transactions on horses and sports. In 1952, the Nevada Tax Commission began work on the formulation of Regulation 22 which would govern the operations of those who applied for licenses to operate race and sportsbooks. In 1959, the Nevada Gaming Control Act removed the Tax Commission from that role. The Nevada Gaming Commission assumed responsibility for the licensing and regulation of the industry. The Nevada Gaming Control Board was designated as the audit, investigative, and administrative arm of the Commission. After the Gaming Commission gave its approval to licensees, the Nevada Gaming Control Board was assigned the responsibility to establish regulations that governed the operations of those licensees.

These agencies were responsible for the creation a playing field that would unleash the business from the shackles of its "stone age." They had to respond to the opponents of the business outside the state by the creation of an environment within the state that certified Nevada with home field advantage.

The ten percent federal tax on sports transactions that was imposed by the Kefauver Commission stifled interest in the number of applicants for sportsbook licenses. In 1972, there were eleven Turf Clubs licensed to operate in the state. This albatross on the industry elicited dismay from the people involved in the development of Regulation 22 that would govern Race and Sports Pools. Paul Bible, an attorney for a law firm involved in the development of the Regulation, said in testimony before the Commission, "We have a tax that really forces people to go into illegal channels and causes people perhaps to indulge in an illegal activity."[18]

Commission Chairman Hannifan responded, "...we feel that perhaps we, as the enforcement agency, have a bit more responsibility to protect the state from the incursion into our affairs of the federal government."[19]

Commissioner Cox added, "I think we have too much federal government in here and even in my own office."[20]

While Commission members discussed how to deal with the ten percent tax, owners of the Turf Clubs had already improvised ways in which to circumvent the restriction. Preferred bettors were not charged ten percent on a $1,000 bet. Instead the bet might have been recorded for $10 with a note on the ticket that stipulated the real amount of the wager for $1,000. In that way, the bettor would only pay a tax of $1 on a $1,000 bet instead of $100.

---

[18] May 25, 1972 Hearings on Regulation 22, page 33 comments from Paul Bible attorney for a law firm that represented the Nevada Race and Sports Association.

[19] Ibid, page 37

[20] Ibid, page 38

Gaming Control Board members were aware of attempts by bookmakers to get around the Tax. One member said, "Knowledgeable people in the industry who have represented that there is really no way they (legal bookmakers) can collect the ten percent tax on all bets recorded and consequently, that ten percent tax forces them to not report all of them..."[21]

As long as sports tickets were handwritten, a coded language could be used that both the preferred customer and Turf Club owner understood, but the tax deterred the use of this method beyond the preferred bettors who were known to the owners. This limitation impacted the expansion of the industry in Nevada even though the pointspread and television had provided the impetus to move forward.

Section 22.010 (12) "Messenger"

Another intrusion from outside the State that had to be addressed was the Wire Act. The Nevada Gaming Commission had to address this federal law that prohibited sports wagers from other states into Nevada. The Commission addressed the impact of that law through the "smarts" they had acquired from people in the business about the ways they used to get around the ten percent tax.

The discussion of Regulation 22.010 Definitions (12) described the divide between federal law and the business. The Commission had to add the term "Messenger" to Regulation 22 in order to identify the customer who was the target of federal interests. Law enforcement defined that bettor as "a person engaged in the business or practice of running wagers; that is, placing wagers for others and collecting winnings for a monetary consideration."[22]

---

[21] Ibid, page 34

[22] Ibid, page 5

Testimony suggested that the onus for the enforcement of that prohibition be added through an amendment that would state "No licensee shall knowingly accept messenger bets." This amendment was proposed because "the purpose of this request would be to permit an individual who might be an immediate member of the family, might be a friend, to place a wager for a friend or a husband or a wife—whatever the case may be."[23]

Commission members responded with their concerns about enforcement. "...who is going to make the determination...you have situations where it would be impossible for the licensee to determine whether or not he is accepting a bet from a person whose money is being risked. I can see a serious problem there."[24] The source of the money for the wager, who paid the messenger and how much were not added to the definition. Gaming Commission members knew they could not require that sportsbooks make sure each customer was not also a messenger.

Even though federal law impacted discussions on Nevada Regulations, the Commission decided to leave the matter of enforcement to the Federal Government. Regulation 22.010 was approved as "Messenger bettor means a person who places a race book or sports pool wager for the benefit of another for compensation."

This definition reflected the insights of Commission members into how business was conducted at sportsbooks. They listened to customers and operators of the sportsbooks. Commission members had to acknowledge the fact the business operates in ways that can defy definitions and regulations. They knew "runners" not "messengers" were a part of the business that regulations would address but not regulate.

---

[23] Ibid, page 7
[24] Ibid page 9

Sportsbook owners dealt with "runners" as other businessman might have dealt with preferred customers who are essential to their business. A sportsbook owner might offer incentives to attract wagers from runners. Odds on a game that were unavailable to other bettors might entice a runner to wager enough to help a sportsbook balance the books on that game.

That favor might entice a runner to provide a sportsbook owner with the "inside info" behind the transaction. The owner could then use the info to "layoff" the money from the runner with other sportsbooks that might not be in the know.[25]

Sportsbook operators would have never dared to ask whether the money wagered by a runner came from out of state. Even though sportsbook operators might have known who was in back of the money from a runner that matter would be set aside for the sake of business. "Business is business. That's the way it is. Sometimes we needed their business. Sometimes they need us as an outlet. Runners are part of the business.[26]

Enforcement of the prohibition against wagers by "messengers" was left to the federal presence in and around Nevada sportsbooks. Federal agents roamed around inside the books. They and others were also assigned to patrol outside the sportsbooks around the public phones used by "phone men." Agents would try to eavesdrop on those conversations as well as those by runners who would "hang" in the sportsbooks to wait for instructions from their "money."

This tactic by the Feds became the proverbial double-edged sword. While agents could identify

---

[25] If a sportsbook was "buried" with action on one side of a game could try to find out why from a runner. The sportsbook owner would then be in a position to make a wager on that side with another sportsbook (layoff) in order to help balance the books on that game.

[26] Quote from Ray Lenzi manager at Churchill Downs Race and Sportsbook.

runners, the runners also identified them. Cat and mouse games between them forced changes in agents assigned to sportsbooks. Runners also moved to different sportsbooks in order to make detection of their business harder to follow.

"Guerilla" tactics on the part of runners and their "money" was an edge that helped establish the home field advantage for the industry in Nevada. These and other tactics raised the cost of enforcement beyond the benefits of an attempt to keep people from doing what they would find ways to do anyway.

Telephone Wagers

The Gaming Commission also had to address the problem of telephone wagers that were made directly into Nevada sportsbooks from out of state. Turf Clubs were known to take telephone wagers in their "backrooms" where detection was difficult by federal or state agents.

The Gaming Commission acknowledged this problem. "...we are speaking of this particular area of the industry should be a self-regulated sort of thing, but it hasn't been and this is the problem."[27]

One alternative "...was to permit telephone bets and let the bookmaker operate at his peril and hazard and if he violated federal law, then it is the risk he is going to take...the bookmakers within the association would be willing to post sufficient bond with the Commission...they would forfeit if they were found guilty of violating any federal law."[28]

A Commission member suggested, "...the best solution as far as the Commission is concerned would be to allow telephone bets and not place those

---

[27] Hearings on Regulation 22, p. 36
[28] Ibid, p. 33

tremendously complicated and very expensive In-WATTS Band 7s in the premises."[29]

Technology to allow a regulated system of telephone wagers into sportsbooks from within Nevada was not available. In 1972, In-WATTS Band 7's was the state of the art. But according to a Commission member, "This In-WATTS Band 7 doesn't prohibit it (illegal phone bets) at all."[30]

Telephone wagers for sports were not approved by the Gaming Commission until August 1985 after telephone technology had developed to the point where calls from outside Nevada could be prevented. Regulation 22 Section 130 Communications Technology specified that the telephone technology used for sports bets had to comply with the Requirements of Regulation 14.290.

In addition, local calls to sportsbooks were prohibited. Hotel operators might take it upon themselves to forward a question from a caller to the sportsbook. An answer from the sportsbook would then be channeled back to the caller by the hotel operator.

The Gaming Commission added to the control of telephone wagers through Section 22.140 Wagering Communications which described the procedures to be used by the sportsbook to open telephone accounts. Proof of the patron's identity and Nevada residency were among procedures that encompass almost two pages of details.

Despite the attempt to prevent wagers to sportsbooks through messengers, the door remained open for a Nevada resident to make wagers over the phone for a person or group outside Nevada whose money was in the account. People in the business would find the ways to do what they wanted to do.

---

[29] Ibid, p. 33
[30] Ibid, p 35

These attempts to secure Nevada's sovereignty from people in the business outside the state were as successful in principle as the attempts to secure America's sovereignty from illegal immigrants. In both cases, the "business" that dictated the need to circumvent the laws overwhelmed the capability of those who had to enforce them. Laws were reduced to selective enforcement if and when they could make a point that might deter others.

Nevada became "more sovereign" after offshore sportsbooks opened for business. Offshores expanded the opportunities for people in the business. They were no longer restricted to Nevada as an outlet to move money. The Nevada sportsbook industry became less important as the opportunities grew for people in the business to make transactions with the "offshores."

Corporate owners of the sportsbooks could live with a situation that directed the federal "hounds" elsewhere. The change in the climate for the business cast a cloud on the importance of all the work that had been done on the Nevada Regulations that addressed messengers and telephone wagers. They became part of a picture that faded from sight just as it had with the turf clubs.

In the meantime, more snapshots for the picture were in the process of development. These snapshots would add to what had been exposed by the others.

Sections 22.120 and 22.121 Prohibited and Suspicious Wagers

The Nevada Gaming Commission compromised Nevada's sovereignty after they included the arguments of opponents of sports betting in their Regulations. Section 22.120, Prohibited Wagers added a twist to the adage "you can't have your cake and eat it too." The Commission tried to prove otherwise.

Members offered this delicacy to the industry through Subsection (d) which prohibits wagers on "any event...involving a professional team whose home field, a court, or base is in Nevada, or any event played in Nevada involving a professional team, if not less than 30 days before an event or the beginning of a series of events, the team's governing body files with the commission a written request that wagers on the event or series of events be prohibited."

The Commission granted power to out-of-state sports corporations such as MLB and the NBA to determine whether sports wagers could be conducted on games they chose to be played in Nevada. Even though sports transactions are legal in Nevada, the Commission granted those Leagues the right to determine whether or not the sportsbook industry could conduct business on their product. The Commission "sold" the business right that is part of their industry to corporations outside Nevada.

Even though this Regulation states that the "commission approves the request" approval would be as automatic as a heartbeat. This subsection allows the Commission to relinquish Nevada's sovereignty to outside corporate interests who can dictate to the industry whether they can accept wagers on games played in Nevada. As a result Major League Baseball and the National Basketball Association have been able to give the sportsbook industry in Nevada the "finger" with prohibitions on the exhibition and regular season games they choose to play in Las Vegas.

Perhaps the Commission believes the revenue generated from those games is greater than the potential tax revenues that might be generated from wagers on them. Perhaps that is the reason behind the fact that the Commission fed the sportsbook industry a taste of "we can have our cake and eat it too" with a middle finger raised to the industry they had "toasted."

Through Subsection (b) of Regulation 22.120 the Commission relinquished sovereignty in another way. This clause states that wagers are prohibited on "any collegiate sport or athletic event which the licensee knows or reasonably should know is being placed by, or on behalf of a COACH OR PARTICIPANT IN THAT COLLEGIATE EVENT.[31]

In 1948, University of Nevada-Reno proposed the idea for the prohibition. There was no explanation why twelve years passed before this idea became part of the Regulations.[32]

Personnel at a sportsbook might recognize Pete Rose or Rick Pitino or Mike Krzyszewski if any of them tried to make a bet. But this clause makes them responsible for the detections of a coach at a junior college in Alaska or an assistant coach at Idaho State or Southwest Louisiana. And they are also responsible for friends of a big name coach such as Bob Knight who might make a wager based on "inside info" they might get from the coaching staff.

Commission members know their licensed sportsbooks are the only part of the industry that will be hurt if the integrity of the game is compromised by a participant in a game. No sportsbook owner has to be told by Regulators to enforce that type of rule. That responsibility comes with the turf.

But the Commission added this clause in order to allow the voices of those who are opposed to the business. They allowed outsiders dictate to the people in our business how to protect the "integrity of our game". This Subsection was dictated by people so distant from the realities of the world of the industry, that the Regulation could not be enforced.

---

[31] Capital letters added by author.
[32] Las Vegas *Review Journal* 9/30/2002 article by Royce Feour "Wagers on Nevada Banned in 1960"

However Commission members could be commended for their foresight when they added Subsection (c) of Regulation 22.120 which prohibits wagers on "The outcome of any election for any public office both within and without the State of Nevada." Perhaps Commission members were able to envision the need to protect the industry from the blame for the outcome of the 2000 Presidential election. But the Commission would not reconsider even after those who wagered on the election in Great Britain did not become part of the "fixed" outcome.

But Nevada politicians demonstrated their mettle through a gold medal flip-flop to save their unwanted stepchild from the pangs of Senator McCain's attempt to put an end to the sports betting industry in the State. No Nevada politician could afford to relinquish that degree of sovereignty in a State that prides itself on libertarian values.

Prior to this attempt by Senator McCain to ban all wagers on college sports in Nevada, the Nevada Gaming Commission had banned wagers only on Nevada college teams through Regulations approved in August 1961. The ban came without comment or discussion.

Subsection (10) of (then) Regulation 5.020 Race horse books and sports pools read, "No bets may be accepted on any amateur sports event held within the State of Nevada, nor any such event held outside the state when any participant in such event represents a public or private institution in the State of Nevada."[33]

That prohibition was restated in Regulation 22.120 Prohibited Wagers. Nevada sportsbooks could not accept wagers on "(b) any amateur sports event held in Nevada" or (c) any event held outside Nevada, if

---

[33] State of Nevada Regulations, 8/1/1961

any participant in the event represents a public or private institution located in Nevada."[34]

The wisdom behind this prohibition implied that college games played by Universities located in Nevada had a greater chance to be "fixed" than those played by Universities outside the State because sports betting is legal in Nevada. Those who added this prohibition suggested that proximity raised the odds that a game could be "fixed." According to Regulators, the closer the institutions were to the sportsbook industry, the greater the chance one of their games could be fixed.

Forty years later, Nevada Gaming Control Board Chairmen had to respond to Senator McCain's accusation that Nevada Regulations were hypocritical. Senator McCain argued that the ban should extend to all college teams because gambling on college sports was detrimental to the integrity of their games. Proximity did not matter to the Senator.

He proposed legislation that would prohibit the Nevada sportsbook industry from the acceptance of wagers on all college sports. He argued that since Nevada prohibited wagers on college games played by teams within the state, then there was tacit admission by Nevada regulators that those games were more likely to be fixed.

Brian Sandoval, then Chairman of the Nevada Gaming Commission, responded, "We are looking at this regardless of the outcome of Senator McCain's Bill. We have complete confidence in our ability to police the sports wagering industry."[35]

More than four decades after the Regulation was enacted to prevent what might "invite trouble and create the wrong impression"[36] the Commission

[34] State of Nevada Regulations, 1/1/1986
[35] Las Vegas Review Journal article by Steve Capp "Bets on Nevada urged" 6/30/2000
[36] Ibid

reversed itself in order to save the industry from what might have led to its extinction. Without wagers on college basketball and football casino corporations might have been receptive to the arguments that the sportsbooks might not be worth the cost in space and personnel. Added to those fears was the possibility that if there were prohibitions on college wagers that prohibitions on wagers on professional sports would follow.

Senator McCain's efforts to prohibit wagers on college sports were stymied by the ability of Nevada Senator Harry Reid to shelve the proposed legislation in Committee. His political acumen did not absolve Nevada's gaming regulators from the fact that by "bending over backwards" to accommodate opponents of the industry they jeopardized its existence within the state.

The Nevada Gaming Commission removed the restriction on wagers on UNLV and UNR in January 2001. Since the removal of that restriction there have been no reported violations of the integrity of UNLV or UNR games because of the wagers that were made on them. The industry proved it was able to police itself. Self- interest won over the restriction imposed by those unfamiliar with the way the business operates. Sportsbooks reaffirmed "the proof is in the puddin'."

Unfortunately the Gaming Control Board did not learn from this mistake. They compromised integrity once again with outside opponents of the industry through Regulation 22.135 "Use of communications devices prohibited." This Regulation stated, "...a book shall not allow a person to use a communications device within the premises of the book. The premises of a book shall be considered any area where race book or sports pool wagers are accepted." The Regulation added that persons who might use these devices "must be advised to immediately discontinue use of the device or be escorted off those premises. The devices included "cellular phones."

Once again, the Commission responded to those who expressed concern that new telephone technology would lead to other ways for "messengers" to place wagers from their out of state sponsors. The Regulation imposed enforcement of the prohibition on sportsbook personnel and hotel casino security staff. They had to enforce a Regulation that prohibited all communication through a cell phone in the sportsbook area. They had to stop all communication from people in the area even those who might be engaged in personal matters with family member. All conversations over a cell phone in a sportsbook "area" had to be stopped even if that speech were "free speech" protected by the Constitution.

The Regulation failed to define the "premises" of a sportsbook. Judgment about where to enforce the Regulation was left to the "enforcers". Since sportsbooks are not confined to specific areas in casinos there is no standard that would apply to all of them. The premises could extend as far as the eyes of the enforcers could see, if and when those enforcers had the time and or the desire to see.

Attempts to implement this Regulation caused more problems than it was worth. The Regulation was repealed on August 21, 2008. The fact the Regulation was rescinded proved that Commission members had been more responsive to arguments of the opponents of the industry rather than to those in the industry in Nevada who knew the Regulation would cause problems and solve none. The Commission succumbed to an argument that created appearances to accommodate the interests that were opposed to the industry not to help the people in the business. Commission members forgot "appearances can be deceiving" but not to people in the know.

Since the repeal of the Regulation, there have been no reported violations of the laws that prohibit interstate wagers because cell phones are now permitted on the premises of sportsbooks. Most sportsbooks posted a notice that cell phones are not permitted at the counters where transactions are made. The notice protects the posteriors of sportsbook owners in case someone tries to use a cell phone at the counter.

This adventure did not deter the Commission from other attempts to bend over to respond to those outside the industry. The Gaming Commission imposed another standard that went beyond the Regulations that were needed to create an order for the operations of the industry.

Regulation 22.121 assigned sportsbook personnel the responsibility to report suspicious wagers. Sportsbook employees were responsible to detect who and or what might be behind a wager.

Section 1 of Regulation 22.121 defines suspicious as "a wager which a sports pool licensee knows or in the judgment of it or its officers, employees and agents has reason to suspect is being attempted or was placed...." As stated in Subsection (a) "on any amateur, non-collegiate or collegiate sports or athletic event." Subsection (b) added "...on or behalf of a coach or participant in a collegiate sport or athletic event..." who according to Subsection (c) "has no business or apparent lawful purpose or is not the sort of wager which the particular patron would normally be expected to place, and the sports pool licensee knows of no reasonable explanation for the wager after examining the available facts including the background of the wager."

If this weren't more than a mouthful for any sportsbook to swallow the Commission added a Section 2 which describes in detail how the sportsbook is to report a "suspicious" wager. A report is to be filed with the Board (a) "if it involves or aggregates to more than $5,000 in funds or other assets... or (b) ... regardless of the amount if the licensee believes it is relevant to the possible violation of any law or regulation. Sections 3, 4, and 5 of the Regulation describe the procedures to be used to report the suspicious wager.

This Regulation failed to acknowledge the fact that sportsbook personnel are on alert for bettors and wagers that could be threats to their profits. They don't need a job description dictated by the Gaming Control Board. Why then would there be a need for a Regulation that is not necessary? Why would the Board attempt to specify who in particular might be a "suspicious" bettor? College coaches would not be at the top of any "suspicious" list for sportsbooks, but appearances can be deceiving.

No one in the sportsbook industry suspected that then Indiana University basketball coach Bob Knight intended to "throw" a game against Illinois. No one was suspicious after "sharps" bet whatever the sportsbooks would allow. No one was suspicious after followers also got down for whatever was the max.

Suspicions arose after the line had moved five points. On a Sunday morning with action levels at a peak, customers were able to drown the sportsbooks with "one way" action no one could explain. The customers themselves did raise suspicions.

There were no public reports of injuries that might have raised suspicion. Sportsbooks could not report what they did not know. All they could do was take the game off the board to protect themselves from further action.

After the reason behind the "steam play" became known no action was taken against the perpetrators because sportsbooks were the only entities punished by a lack of "integrity in this game." There were no howls of protest from the Gaming Commission, the

Gaming Control Board, or the so-called defenders of the "integrity of the game." Their silence was akin to a desert burial ground in Nevada where any utterance about the incident would have consequences for those who broke the code of silence.

The height of hypocrisy reached gold medal standards when no action was taken against the perpetrators of suspicious activity that profited the perpetrators. Beneficiaries of the "big fix" by Robert Montgomery Knight were paid without consequences. Sportsbooks had to swallow it all.

Other examples of incidents that could be defined as "suspicious" such as those by the so-called "computer group" were also considered part of the business by those in the industry. The fact that one of the leaders of the computer group was a prominent Las Vegas businessman freed those wagers from suspicion even though "inside info" behind some of those wagers might have fit the category.

The word "suspicious" had as many definitions as the reasons behind the language used by the Gaming Commission. The Regulators felt a need to respond to the outside opponents of the industry to cover their posteriors against anything that might later be deemed suspicious.

A Regulation that made sportsbooks responsible for the detection of those wagers was the answer for Regulators to free them from accountability to Senator McCain and others for anything that might have appeared out of the ordinary. Sportsbooks had to accept the burden of the responsibility for whatever those opposed to the industry might include in their arguments to prohibit the business.

The Gaming Commission expanded on their attempt to prohibit suspicious wagers through another Regulation that was designed to satisfy the interests of the federal government. Regulation 22.061 "Wagers in excess of $10,000" and Regulation 22.062 "Multiple Wagers" were added in 1999.

Sportsbooks became responsible for reports on those wagers and on the people who made them. Regulation 22.061 requires a sportsbook to obtain information on anyone who attempts to make a wager in excess of $10,000. That information includes an address, social security number, and an identification credential such as a driver's license or another acceptable alternative. This Regulation is comprised of six sections that stipulate how, not *why* wagers in excess of $10,000 must be treated as separate and apart from other wagers.

Regulation 22.062 Multiple Wagers supplements Regulation 22.061. Seven sections of this Regulation stipulate how a sportsbook is to handle attempts to "circumvent Regulation 22.061 through multiple wagers that "... use a series of wagers that are designed to accomplish indirectly that which could not be accomplished directly."

The complexity of this process is described in Section 2 which states, "Each book shall record in a wagering multiple transaction log all non-pari-mutuel wagers in excess of $5,000 or in smaller amounts that aggregate in excess of $5,000 when any single officer, employee, or agent of the book has actual knowledge of the wagers or would in the ordinary course of business have reason to know of the wagers between the book and a patron or a person who the book knows or has reason to know is the patron's confederate or agent."

Nevada Regulators did not stipulate that a law degree was a condition of employment in order to make certain employees could understand and implement this Regulation. Instead, employees are required to give a business card to customers who ask about the need to provide background information in order to make a wager.

That card stipulates "The U.S. Government and State of Nevada requires" (us) "to obtain your name, government-issued identification, taxpayer identification number (e.g., social security number), and other relevant information in order to complete certain transactions."

A second paragraph adds, "This requirement is part of the government's broader fight against money laundering and other financial crime, which allow criminals to conceal and profit from illegal activities. These activities include drug and human trafficking, terrorist financing and other types of organized crime."

There was no requirement for sportsbook employees to ask the bettor to raise a hand and take an oath to "tell the truth, the whole truth, and nothing but the truth" about the wager; however, sportsbook employees are required to answer a question on the report form as to whether that bettor may appear to be someone from North Korea, Somalia, Iran, or another country that is on the federal government's list of "rogue" nations. So far, sportsbook employees do not have to pass a test that requires them to distinguish North Koreans from South Koreans as a condition of employment, but they are required to attend sessions that train them for the implementation of these Regulations.

The Regulations reflect the extent to which the business in Nevada has become entwined in agendas of the federal government as well as other opponents of the legal industry. Regulations that govern the industry have exploded from approximately one typewritten page of ten sections, without subsections, that comprised Regulation 5.020 Race Horse books and sports pools which was passed in 1960. Regulation 22 Race Books and Sports Pools passed in 1985 and amended in 2009 is comprised of approximately sixteen typewritten pages with thirty sections of Regulations with as many as 22 subsections.

The attempts by opponents of the business forced Nevada Regulators into defensive positions some of which were indefensible such as cell phones and the prohibition on wagers on college teams in Nevada. On other matters, Regulators surrendered Nevada's sovereignty to the federal government and to opponents of the industry through Regulations that attempted to attribute motives behind wagers, to assume responsibility to identify those who make wagers, and to make certain that wagers on sports come only from the money that belongs to Nevada residents.

While the Regulators flip-flopped on Regulations designed to dictate how aspects of the business would have to be conducted, they were consistent with the Regulations that determined who the players would be on this home field. Who was the side of the coin that would determine whether the business could withstand the challenges from its opponents.

The Corporate Sportsbook Industry

The corporate influence behind the Regulations that govern the sportsbook industry reveals another layer behind evolution of the business in Nevada. Regulators had to eliminate the turf clubs in order for the business to become part of big business. Regulation had confined the business to turf clubs such as the Churchill Downs Race and Sportsbook on Las Vegas Boulevard near Harmon. Sportsbooks were prohibited in hotel casinos on the "Strip" and Downtown for all the reasons stated in the Regulation.

The "stringent controls" clause in the Regulation restricted turf clubs to horse and sports wagering. Turf clubs could not offer other forms of gambling such as craps or blackjack. Craps and blackjack players might have been vulnerable to a corruption transmitted by the presence of sports betting in a way similar to the way the "flu" is transmitted by association. No "intoxicating beverages" could be "dispensed" at the sportsbooks because, according to the Regulation, alcohol and sports betting in the same building did not mix. Fortunately, local law enforcement agencies in Nevada did not follow this lead to add a provision to DUI laws that included wagers on sports.

These Sections of the Regulations reflect beliefs about this industry that led to the segregation of the business within the state that accompanied the federal segregation of the business in America. The Regulation was a response to the evils about the industry promulgated during the hearings conducted by the Kefauver Commission. The ten percent tax imposed on the industry amounted to a poll tax to keep customers away from sportsbooks. The intent was similar to the one behind the poll taxes that kept African-Americans from voting booths.

For over two decades the ten percent tax helped to keep the business in its place. The first step away from that took place when Nevada Senator Howard Cannon used his political influence to attach an amendment to a tariff bill passed by the House of Representatives. The amendment to exempt the business from the ten percent tax was approved by a voice vote on the tariff bill in August 1974. Objections in the House of Representatives to all of the pork barrel amendments to the bill forced a compromise in Senator Cannon's amendment. Instead of a repeal of the Tax, it was reduced from ten percent to two percent.[37]

Even before Senator Cannon worked to help the sportsbook industry he had been involved in the removal of a $250 Tax on every slot machine imposed as a result of the Kefauver Hearings. In 1971, he

---

[37] Biography of Senator Howard Cannon by Michael Vernetti, pp 143-4

worked on behalf of Hotel Casinos to pass an amendment to a tax cut bill proposed by President Nixon that provided a rebate of $200 to casinos on the $250 Tax. Further rebates through 1983 eliminated that tax.[38]

The Nevada Gaming Control Board responded to the reduction in the tax with a Regulation that opened the door for casinos such as Little Caesar's and casino hotels such as the Stardust and the Castaways to make sportsbooks a part of their businesses. But Senator Cannon was not finished with what he had started. The 2% tax on sports was reduced to .025% in 1983. His bill to eliminate the tax was amended by the Senate to *reduce* rather than repeal the Tax. After passage of the bill, Senator Cannon said, "This is welcome news for a segment of Nevada's gaming industry which had been hit hard by the economic downturn and the pro football strike. It will lift an approximately $10 million dollar annual tax burden on establishments which often teeter on the brink of profitability or insolvency."[39]

This effort on behalf of the business also included a reduction in the occupational tax on sportsbook employees from $500 to $50. The Senator was able to weave his agenda through a Congress that was amenable to tax cuts that would help to end a recession. He helped to end what the Kefauver Commission began more than thirty years earlier. Reduction in the Taxes was a big bang for the industry in Nevada. Hotel casinos were forced to include sportsbooks in their business in order to keep customers who might go to another casino where the sports option was available.

Gary Austin, then owner of the Austin Edge Race and Sportsbook, also helped to change the structure of

---

[38] Ibid, page 144

[39] Las Vegas *Review Journal,* 10/2/1982, pp 1-2

the industry. He contributed to the demise of independent turf clubs after he used financial reserves for the business which included deposits by customers for telephone accounts to bet on the St. Louis Cardinals to win the 1985 World Series from the Kansas City Royals. His actions compromised the integrity of the business in Nevada. Closure of his business by the State of Nevada contributed to the closure of the turf clubs.

The Gaming Commission was forced to respond in a way that ensured customers that their deposits were safe. Regulation 22.040, Reserve requirements, stipulated through fourteen sections the way the solvency of a sportsbook would be maintained. That solvency would ensure the safety of money from bettors already wagered or deposited in accounts. The Regulation addressed the concerns about a repeat of what Gary Austin had done to his customers.

New Regulations also imposed requirements that forced sportsbooks to end certain methods of operations. The system of handwritten tickets was replaced by automated systems.[40] The cost of these new requirements added to the reserve requirements added to the consolidation of the industry within hotel casinos. Cost factors almost precluded even the possibility of the individual ownership of a sportsbook. The elimination of competition by Regulators kindled interest in the business from casino corporations.

Computerized wagering systems also impacted the behavior of those behind the counters of sportsbooks. Automated systems helped to close loopholes that had allowed "insiders" the opportunity for early retirement through this industry's version of "insider trading." No longer would a person behind the counter be able to write a ticket long after the event was no longer in doubt. No longer would a manager be able to tell a

---

[40] Regulation 22.145 Account Wagering Systems

clerk to write a ticket on the New Orleans Saints +7 ½ after New Orleans scored to take a lead of 21-10 late in the game.[41] Multiple Regulations addressed that loophole.

Casino auditors who might also be part of the "insider trading" schemes were also addressed in the new Regulations. Those auditors would no longer be able to ignore the lack of a time stamp on a ticket that would them "fix" the outcome of a transaction. Additional Regulations reinforced the integrity of the system. Managers and supervisors of sportsbooks had to register with the Gaming Control Board. Background checks on them included a ..."complete history of arrests, detentions or litigations... Background checks on them included a "...complete history of arrests, detentions or litigations..." Applicants also had to "...consent to a full licensing investigation..."[42]

In addition to Regulations that stipulated in detail how a sportsbook had to conduct business within a casino, the Gaming Control Board also addressed the need for the industry to take advantage of new technology that would open more doors for phone accounts.[43]

Gaming Regulators helped to create a business that had become corporate owned. Corporate ownership opened the door to the possibility of satellite sportsbooks. Regulators defined satellites in a way that would allow corporate-owned sportsbooks the ability to use a "hub" that would have control over sportsbook operations owned by the same corporation in other locations.[44]

---

[41] An eyewitness account of a wager dictated by a sportsbook manager to a writer who was in the process of writing a ticket for me on another game...

[42] Regulation 22.035 Registration of employees

[43] Regulation 22.165 Use of an operator of a call center

[44] For example, the sportsbook at the Red Rock Hotel and Casino is in control of operations at all other Station Casinos. Red Rock is the "hub."

Regulators also had the foresight of a handicapper who "nailed it" when they included Regulations that might raise questions about the integrity of the industry. The requirement in Regulation 22.150 to post House Rules may have saved the industry from a fatal wound caused by a game played between UNLV and Wisconsin in 2002.

Wisconsin led UNLV 27 to 7 before a power outage at a Nevada Power station near Sam Boyd Stadium where the game was played led to the sportsbook industry's nightmare of "lights out." Wisconsin had moved from -3 favorites to -7 at most sportsbooks because of the influx of money from Badger fans who had accompanied their team to Las Vegas.

House Rules at all sportsbooks stipulated that a game had to go at least 55 minutes in order to be official for sports wagering purposes. Since the game fell 2:41minutes short of that minimum, all bets had to be refunded. Threats to sportsbook personnel that accompanied refunds to bettors might have led to action but for the house rules to which they could direct the attention of customers who would not accept their words for the inability to collect.

Regulators covered themselves as well as the industry from charges of a lack of integrity in their game with the requirement to post House Rules. When Regulators focused on rules that imposed standards on the industry that would establish the integrity of our game, they were "on the money." Regulators became part of the problem when they succumbed to opponents of the industry with Regulations that were either unenforceable or an accommodation to opponents of the business.

The Bottom Line

The bottom line is the reason there are opening lines at Nevada sportsbooks. Even though that line is at the bottom compared to other casino games the profit is enough to justify the inclusion of sportsbooks in casinos. The tax revenue for Nevada from that profit is enough for the state to do whatever it might take to protect its monopoly from opponents of the business.

The worth of that bottom line has been calculated through a measurement that documents gaming revenue per square foot of casino floor space. This measurement that began in 1984 included 145 casinos. Even though all of the casinos in the comparison did not offer all of the games that were included in the study, the measurement of gaming revenue per square foot is an equalizer for all the differences.[45]

This method documents the amount of floor space used by four categories of casino games. The four categories are Pit games such as craps and blackjack, Coin-Operated Devices such as slot machines, Poker and Pan, and Race and Sports Books.

In 1984, Pit games occupied an average of 6,553 square feet within 135 casinos. Coin-Operated Devices averaged 10,826 square feet in 141 casinos. Poker and Pan measured 1,043 square feet in 72 casinos. Race and Sportsbooks were spread over an average of 3,692 square feet in 36 casinos.

The average revenue generated by Pit games was $1,479 per square foot. Coin-Operated Devices produced a profit of $1,003. Profit from Poker and Pan was $796. Race and Sports books averaged $314 of profit per square foot.

The result of this measurement was one reason sportsbooks inherited the moniker "the unwanted stepchild." The profit per square foot from race and sports was less than half of that produced by Poker

---

[45] UNLV Center for Gaming Research: Annual Comparison: Gaming Revenue Per Square Foot Statewide casinos with gaming revenue over $1,000,000.

and Pan, yet race and sports occupied more than three times the space of Poker and Pan.

Pit games were approximately five times more profitable than race and sports even though those games occupied less than half the space of race and sports. Coin-Operated Devices were approximately three times more profitable. They occupied three times the space of race and sports.

Measurements vary from year to year because of the "luck" factor. When players win big they can change the statistics. Measurements also vary because the floor space occupied by these games was redesigned for efficiency. Remission of the federal tax on sports bets also contributed to a change that showed improvement in profit per square foot by sportsbooks.

Statistics for 2007 reflect that impact. 270 casinos were included in the measurements as opposed to the 145 in 1984. Those statistics document the change in the gap between Poker and Pan and Race and Sports. Between 1984 and 2007, Poker and Pan increased from 1,043 to 1,931 in the average square feet they occupied. At the same time, Race and Sports decreased the average square feet they occupied from 3, 692 to 3,565.

The gap in profit per square foot for the two types of games also narrowed. Poker and Pan increased in profit per square foot from $796 to $1,095, but Race and Sports had increased from $314 to $651. What had been a difference of approximately three times the profit per square foot in favor of Poker and Pan in 1984 narrowed to approximately two times in 2007.

This trend was similar to what happened between Pit Games and Race and Sports. The space occupied by Pit games had increased from 6,553 square feet in 1984 to 7,803 in 2007 compared to the decrease for Race and Sports from 3,692 to 3,565.

Profit per square foot for Pit games increased from $1,479 in 1984 to $2,752 per square foot in 2007. Compared to the increase in profit for Race and Sports from $314 to $651 the gap between the two types of games had also narrowed. In 2007, Pit games were a little more than four times more profitable than Race and Sports per square foot instead of what had been a gap of approximately five times in 1984.

The amount of space for Coin-Operated Devices increased from 10,826 square feet in 1984 to 22,937 square feet in 2007, but the profit per square foot only increased from $1,003 to $1,355. The amount of space more than doubled, but profits only rose by approximately one third.

What had been a gap that was approximately three times greater in profit per square foot for Coin-Operated Devices had decreased to approximately two times the average in comparison to Race and Sports.

All of the measurements document the fact that Race and Sports became more profitable for casinos, but sportsbooks were responsible for most of that increase in profits for casinos. The "unwanted step child" became "wanted" in more ways than one.

Other statistics also document the way in which the business of sportsbooks had grown. There were 182 sportsbooks that were measured between October 1, 2008 and September 30, 2009. Those sportsbooks produced a total win amount of $128,272,000 for casinos. The win percentage was 5.13%. In 2011 the win amounted to $140,731.332, a 4.89% hold on the total amount of $2,878,579,031. The total amount won was nearly three times the amount of $42,658,617 documented in 1988. The total win percentage had increased almost two percent from the 3.22% that had been documented in 1988.[46]

---

[46] These are the only statistics the Gaming Control Board can provide for the year 1988. Gaming Control Board records only go back to 1988.

Amounts that are won and held vary from year to year because of "luck" and other factors such as strikes that curtailed the seasons for several professional sports. But the total amounts won and the win percentages have been consistent between the years 2000 and 2009 just as they have been for other casino games.

At times, sports wagering performed better than other casino games. Statistics for 2009 reveal that at one end of the win vs. hold comparison Keno had the highest percentage held at 27.32%—more than five times the 5.33% held by sports, but the $38,573,000 won by Keno was less than one-fifth of the $123,836,000 won by sports. Keno generated less business, but was more profitable than sports.

In the middle of that spectrum, race books held 16.60% of $68,711,000. The percentage held was more than three times the amount won by sports, but the total amount won was less than one-half of the money generated by sports. Race books won less money than sports, but held more of what was won.

At the other end of the spectrum, the win percentage for Twenty-One was 11.52%. This game generated the highest win total of $1,063,942,000—almost ten times the amount for sports. The 11.52% that was held was slightly more than double the amount for sports. Although Twenty-One was ten times more popular with gamblers, the percentage held by sports closed the gap between the two.

Sports held less than any other game except bingo. That game held 3.27%. The amount won by sports was less than the amounts won by Twenty-One, Craps, Roulette, and Baccarat. Sports won more than any of the other individual games except for 3-Card Poker. The win amount for that game was close to sports.[47]

---

[47] Yearly Gaming Reports between 1988 and 2009.

These statistics and studies document the fact that sports wagering is profitable. Even though the total amount won by the sportsbook industry is approximately one percent of the total win for the gaming industry, there is enough to satisfy corporations and the state.

Profits from this endeavor attracted attention. Success led to another challenge to Nevada's monopoly. A Nevada gaming regulator predicted that Nevada would face competition because "the most pent-up demand is for sports wagering." Some states will turn to race and sports books as a solution to "intense revenue pressures, more than we've ever seen before."[48]

But the worth of sportsbooks extends that bottom line. Sports bettors may stay after their wagers to play other casino games. Others may stay to watch the games and contribute to casino profits through expenditures on drinks and restaurants. Sportsbooks may also attract bettors who come to bet other games. And sportsbooks attract customers from out-of-state who prefer to transact sports legally.

Sportsbooks proved to be worth the fight initiated by casino corporations and Nevada politicians to eliminate the ten percent federal tax. The lines on the boards of the sportsbooks helped propel the business to a level of popularity that raised the bottom line closer to the top of the line for the state as well as the Nevada gaming corporations.

A Picture in Motion

The State of Nevada exerted States Rights to defend its business from opponents who attempted to

---

[48] Las Vegas Sun article 11/17/2009 by Richard Velotta and Brian Wargo "Threat Seen to Nevada's sports betting monopoly."

post a closed sign on the entrances to the sportsbooks. Nevada took the steps that were necessary to prove that the business could be regulated. The State enacted all of the measures that were necessary to insure the integrity of its game.

Oddsmakers would not dare address the odds on the success of those endeavors before they reviewed snapshots of the business from Las Vegas that added to the data bank for the business. Those snapshots had evolved from "only in Las Vegas to "what happens in Las Vegas remains in Las Vegas" to the end of the era for the "sports betting capital of the world. Those snapshots would share the experiences of "what happens in Las Vegas does not remain in Las Vegas."

CHAPTER THREE

LAS VEGAS

ONLY IN LAS VEGAS
What happens in Las Vegas stays in Las Vegas

If it could only happen in Las Vegas oddsmakers would make the sportsbook industry the favorite for where it happened in the onetime "sports betting capitol of the world". If it happened in the sportsbook industry the odds would favor "NO" that it would not stay in Las Vegas.

The Fix

The "Fix" by Indiana basketball coach Bob Knight would make a list of the attempts to compromise the integrity of the game. His success in compromising that integrity would merit him a position at the top of a list of people "who did it and got away with it." But what he did in Las Vegas did not remain in Las Vegas.

Only Coach Knight knows when he made the plans for this crime. Only Coach Knight knows who else knew about his plan and when they knew. Those who were "in the know" had time to take advantage of his "inside info" to make wagers on the "fix" in Las Vegas. Only the coach knew whether one of his motives was to "stick it" to the "City of Lights." Perhaps the pointspreads on his games from the "Sports Betting Capital of the World" had rubbed him the wrong way.

The inability of his starters and subs to perform the way they had been coached led the coach to think the unthinkable. He decided to "punish" the top seven players on the team for their inability to be what he wanted them to be both on and off the basketball court.

After the game, the coach provided one reason for his action. "I think there comes a time that somebody needs to be jolted a little. And if jolting them doesn't get them playing to what their potential is then they've got to think about dropping out of it or play somewhere else."[49]

He added to that explanation another reason that applied to one of the starters. "I felt [he] could sit out an entire game, watch kids who I know are going to play awfully hard...and play a lot harder than we had all year."[50]

The coach had not described those feelings about the players in public prior to the game. His plans to punish those players remained private. But the way his plan was "leaked" to those who could use the inside info led to a day in infamy in which a "leak" led to a tidal wave that engulfed the sportsbook industry.

Employees behind the counters of the sportsbooks began to feel it as early as 9 a.m. Pacific Time when bettors "stormed the bastions."[51] A national television audience found out what was about to happen from CBS announcers around 1 p.m. Pacific Time.

Las Vegas sportsbooks had opened Indiana a -2 ½ point favorite over Illinois in a game to be played in Champaign. By the time the game was taken off the boards by Las Vegas sportsbooks, Illinois had become a -2 ½ point favorite. Action was one way only.

---

[49] *Los Angeles Times*, 1/21/1985 SD_B 1

[50] *New York Times*, 1/29/1985, p. A 24

[51] Thanks to the late Jerry Porterfied for the term. Jerry managed sportsbooks at the Showboat, the El Rancho and the Lady Luck Hotel and Casino.

"Sharps" did not buy back on the move in order to "middle" the game. Why they refused to buy back could have been a question for a criminal investigation of the incident.

Those in the know who initiated the move on Illinois did not tell the sportsbooks to take the game off the board in order to protect them from the hurt that could come from additional wagers on the game. Usually those who receive special favors from a sportsbook (such as a larger betting limit or a "special" line) will tell a manager the reason behind the wager in order to keep them in the good graces of that sportsbook. This gesture of courtesy ensures the customer future access to that sportsbook. They could be banned from a sportsbook if they do not extend this courtesy. Perhaps these people did not care because it was a one-time-only for them. This time there was no warning from anyone who got down on the game. That allowed followers who hang around the books to get down.

Sports information services, oddsmakers, and handicappers in the business were in the dark. They could not help the sportsbooks. Managers of the "books" protected themselves the only way they could. The game was taken off the boards between one and two hours before game time.

Research by people in the business led to unconfirmed rumors that the two top subs for Indiana had been left behind in Bloomington. Mike Giomi, the top rebounder and Winston Morgan, the best defensive player were rumored to have not accompanied the team. That information alone would not have led to this move on the game.

People in the business in Las Vegas and the national television audience found out from the CBS announcers what the coach was about to do. Billy Packer and Al McGuire told them about the two substitutes that were left behind in Bloomington and what was about to happen to the starters who made the trip to Champaign.

They shocked the sports world with the announcement that Coach Knight decided to bench his starters with one exception. The center, Uwe Blab, would start because the numbers dictated that one starter had to play. He, along with the four freshmen—Sloan, Hillman, Eyl, and Brooks were announced as starters. These freshmen had not played much up to that point.

What had been Indiana's starting five became their starting one. Those who had started all year for Indiana were sentenced to time on the bench. Steve Alford, Todd Meier, Stew Robinson, and Dan Dakich would not play one minute of the game. Even after Brooks fouled out, the coach replaced him with Pelkowski, another freshman who had not played much.

Indiana met few requirements for team effort in the first half. Indiana had led the nation in field goal percentage. In this game, they shot 28% in the first half—almost 25% below their average. Two free throws added to five field goals set an Assembly Hall record for fewest points in a half. Nine turnovers helped to contribute to this record for a first half that ended with Illinois ahead 24 to 12. Illinois shot 30% for the half. One of three free throws added to their total of 24, a season low that kept the game close rather than the blowout it should have been.

A halftime "pep talk" from the coach may have helped Indiana in the second half. Their shooting percentage improved to 43% from the field. This "pep" talk did not extend to the free throw line where they made 3 of 15 attempts. Despite the improvement,

Illinois kept the lead between 7 and 17 points. They won 52-41.[52]

Las Vegas sportsbooks paid from the bowels of their bottom line for this "fix." So did illegal bookmakers around America. Fans who attended the game also paid for a product that was mislabeled. CBS should have demanded a refund on a product for which they paid top dollar but delivered at a wholesale price to the audience.

The Las Vegas press ignored the impact of the game on the local sportsbook industry. The *Las Vegas Sun* limited their coverage to a wire service comment that "senior center Uwe Blab led the Hoosiers with 13 points.[53]

The *Las Vegas Review Journal* extended their coverage to "Indiana coach Bobby Knight, who chose to ignore most of his regulars using only senior center, Uwe Blab, and six freshmen for the entire game."

The media and sports fans outside Las Vegas expressed anger. One writer for the Indiana *Daily Student*, the school newspaper, wrote an article that described the outrage among students towards Coach Knight for "throwing" the basketball game.[54]

Sports fans called a Bloomington radio station to express their outrage at the coach. "The station has been getting quite a few calls..." It's been a 'what the hell's going on' type thing," said Joe Smith, sports director of radio station WBWB. "It's frustrating. They just can't understand it," he added.[55]

Similar sentiments were expressed to the sports department of the *Indianapolis Star*. "...what Bobby Knight did today is a disgrace." "He (Coach Knight)

---

[52] *Las Vegas Sun* January 28, 1985, p. 3D and the *New York Times* January 28, 1985.

[53] Ibid

[54] *Indiana Daily Student* January 31, 1985. Opinion by Steve Sanders.

[55] *Los Angeles Times* January 29, 1985 SD_B5

doesn't represent the true ideals of Indiana University" were among those conveyed to the newspaper.[56]

Coach Knight added to his previous comments about the decision when he said, "If my primary purpose around here at Indiana is to go out and win basketball games I can probably do that, maybe as well as anybody can. I'd just cheat get some money from a lot of people around Indianapolis who would like to run the operation that way and get the best basketball players I can and then we'd beat everybody all the time."[57]

"The people" expressed their outrage, but "the people" at the NCAA did not express those sentiments. They decided to take another path to deal with the damage that had been done to the integrity of their game. They chose silence in order to ignore the fact that wagers were made on Illinois because the intentions of the coach had been leaked. The NCAA gambled the facts might "disappear" if they kept quiet.

Silence contradicted their approach to other transgressions of the standards set by them for violations of the integrity of the game. Those transgressions had consequences for the perpetrators. Other violations of the integrity of college basketball games, such as those at CCNY in the late 1940s and early 1950s and at Boston College during the 1978-79 season were handled by law enforcement as violations of law. In those cases, law enforcement helped enforce the NCAA sanctions.

Perhaps the NCAA thought it best to keep their sounds of silence on the transgression by "The General" until the time was right in 2003. Rich Neuheisel, then coach at the University of Washington, was fired for his participation in an NCAA Basketball Tournament pool. After someone "snitched" on him,

---

[56] Ibid
[57] Los Angeles *Times*, January 29, 1985 SD_B

the NCAA and the University were forced to remove him as the coach. He had violated the prohibition of wagers on sports that was a condition of employment.

Professional sports leagues, however, had taken other paths to enforce the integrity of their games. Coaches or managers of professional teams would have been prohibited from the action Coach Knight had taken. No professional coach or manager could have benched a player of the caliber of a "Steve Alford" let alone an entire team without a public declaration before the game was played. Public injury reports and suspensions are a part of the integrity of professional sports.

The NFL took additional measures to help enforce the integrity of their games. At one time, the security division of the NFL would make calls throughout the week to Las Vegas sportsbooks to inquire whether there might be more than money behind point spread moves.[58] They had to make calls elsewhere to find out if owners of NFL franchises who bet on their teams might be behind the moves.

In addition, the NFL took direct action against players whose behaviors might have endangered the integrity of the games. Paul Hornung and Alex Karras were suspended from the NFL in 1963 because they wagered on football and because of their associations with gamblers.

Major League Baseball took another path to enforce the integrity of their games when Pete Rose was forced to "retire" from baseball because of his wagers on games. The League had made it clear after the "Black Sox" scandal that there would be consequences for players who bet on their games.

The NBA added their twist on integrity. They League forced referee Tim Donaghy to resign because

---

[58] When Sonny Reizner was the Director of the Castaways sportsbook he would check with his staff to make sure his response to NFL inquiries were accurate.

of his transgressions that included wagers on professional basketball games and "inside information" he sold to bookmakers and bettors. Apparently the NBA was unaware that long before those incidents another employee of the League had sold "inside info."[59]

When Sonny Reizner was the Director of the Castaways sportsbook he would check with his staff to make sure his response to NFL inquiries were accurate. I was in a meeting with the manager of a sportsbook when a trainer for one of the NBA franchises interrupted in order to thank the manager for the room and meals that were given in exchange for injury information that was not public. That "inside info" helped the manager adjust his betting line.

Even the NHL had taken action to protect the integrity of its game when the League suspended Rick Tocchet after he pleaded guilty to his part in a syndicate that featured sports transactions. He was sentenced to a two-year suspension from the League.

The nuances in the way the integrity of the game is expressed and enforced leaves the door open for the Professional Leagues and the NCAA to use the caveat to serve their interests. The varieties of transgressions that range from participation in an NCAA Tournament pool to an attempt to "throw" a World Series is indicative of an umbrella that has been opened to fit the purposes.

That umbrella opened the door for Bob Knight to add his two cents to the definition twenty-five years after his lack of integrity. He said, "We've gotten into this situation where integrity is really lacking and that's why I'm glad I'm not coaching. You see, we've got a coach at Kentucky who put two schools on probation and he's still coaching."[60]

---

[59] Ibid
[60] *Chicago Sun Times*, 12/18/2009

His comments were also met with silence from the NCAA. A response would have triggered the issue of whether punishment was in order. Punishment is necessary to back the integrity of the game with more than words. People in the business must be reassured by the leagues that not even one baseball, football and basketball game can follow the script for the "wrestling match" that was refereed by Coach Knight.

Why did the NCAA and law enforcement decide that the unspoken word would prevail in his case? Did they reach this conclusion because there was no evidence of a motive to benefit financially from the decision? Or was it because even a verbal rebuke would have opened a can of worms that would not suit their taste?

Even without "evidence" of a link behind the coach's decision and what happened in Las Vegas, common sense would have led to the conclusion there were consequences for sportsbooks in Las Vegas because of that decision. One of those consequences led to a result similar to the one in the Black Sox scandal, except in this case it was the coach, *not* the players who "fixed" a game.

Silence also may have stemmed from the fact that NCAA rules did not require the Coach to make his decision public before the game was played. That would make them an accessory to the crime perpetrated on the sportsbook industry. If the Coach had made his decision public, there would have been no question about the integrity of that game. That game would have been off the boards.

Even though the NCAA chose to keep silent the door was still open for those who suffered the consequences of the decision. They could have made it a public issue. They could have pursued action that was necessary to secure justice for the business. However, the silence from the NCAA was matched by those in Nevada who were in a position to protest the violation of the integrity of their game, even if that protest came after the fact. Silence from the Nevada Gaming Commission, the Gaming Control Board, and the corporations that own the sportsbooks reinforced the belief that the unwanted "stepchild" might not be worthy of the protection afforded to other casino games.

Nevada Regulators had taken action against those who violated the integrity of other casino games such as slots and card games, but an attack on the integrity of the sportsbook business went unacknowledged even though Nevada Regulations made sportsbooks responsible for the integrity of their game. Sportsbooks were required to be on the lookout for coaches who might try to bet, but what about those who bet on a game because they knew a coach would try to "throw" a game? And even after that game had been "thrown" there were no "House Rules" to announce that sportsbooks had the authority to withhold payments made on those "suspected" games. The online bookmaker Betfair had to set that precedent when they withheld payments for winning tickets on tennis matches whose outcomes they believed were fixed.[61]

Nevada Regulators remain silent on this issue. Perhaps that silence is due to the fact that more than two decades after the "fix" the DNA evidence remains and perhaps rewards from the NCAA after the fact merit the continued silence. The NCAA sanctioned the Las Vegas Bowl which is estimated to have generated $14 million for Las Vegas in 2009. All of those Bowl games are estimated to have generated over $150 million for the city since 1992.[62]

More than twenty years after the "fix" the NCAA granted another payback to the city in the form of

[61] *The Guardian*, August 3, 2007, Matt Scott "Top seed Davidenko pulls out in third set in Poland. Drift in pre-match odds prompts investigation."
[62] KOLO TV.com, December 22, 2009, "Las Vegas Bowl Brings Money."

approval for Conference Basketball Tournaments. The West Coast Conference held their playoffs at the Orleans Hotel and Casino in 2008. Even though odds on those games could not be posted at the Orleans sportsbook per NCAA insistence, odds were posted on the board at the Gold Coast Hotel and Casino several blocks away. Both hotels are owned by the Boyd Corporation.

Evidently, Las Vegas corporations are open to one foot in the door rather than none, even if the foot is through the back door where integrity is enclosed. If that back door had not remained closed during that time, Coach Knight could have been sentenced to the Nevada Black Book beside Richard "the fixer" Perry and then the Encore Hotel and Casino would not have been the beneficiary of the Coach's presence during the 2009 NCAA Tournament.

The Encore agreed to a network show in which Knight and Billy Packer would sit outside the sportsbook in order to give viewers a "feel" for the atmosphere of the Tournament in Las Vegas. This "feel" excluded one that would have been enhanced by the participation of the employees of the sportsbook, handicappers, and oddsmakers. This con job would be similar to an attempt by TV networks to sell their viewers the line that the effects of Viagra could be felt through their commercials rather than through the pills.

Las Vegas would not have even been in a position to accept these IOUs if the attack on the sportsbook industry from Arizona had not been confronted by the people in the business in Las Vegas. What could have happened to Las Vegas would have ended what had happened only in Las Vegas.

Pain from McCain

Political warfare erupted over turf that transcended borders when a politician from Arizona challenged the legitimacy of a business restricted by law to Nevada. The proximity of Arizona to Nevada was coincidental to his challenge. The economic benefit to Arizona was essential to the challenge.

Although this attack appeared to be from one state against another, the target of Arizona Senator John McCain was Las Vegas, the (then) sports-betting capital of the world. He explained the reason behind the attack in these terms. "Not only does the Las Vegas betting clearinghouse send a confusing message about the propriety and legality of amateur sports gambling, the publication throughout the country of Las Vegas-generated pointspreads fuels illegal gambling in the judgment of the NGISC[63] and steals victories from young athletes who manage to beat their opponents, but not the spread."[64]

In spite of the fact that the sports-betting industry in Las Vegas did not have an impact on any legal business in Arizona, Senator John McCain led an attack that could have ended the business in Las Vegas. An end to wagers on college sports could have brought an end to the sportsbook industry in Las Vegas.

This attack began after Senator McCain became Chairman of the Commerce Committee in 1997. Revocation of provisions of the Professional and Amateur Sports Protection Act of 1992 (PASPA), also known as the "Bradley Bill," became part of McCain's agenda. The "Bradley Bill" had granted Nevada an exemption from the federal restriction on sports

---

[63] National Gambling Impact Study Commission
[64] *Los Angeles Times*, March 14, 2007, Dispatches from Las Vegas by Richard Abowitz, "McCain Offers NCAA Gaming instead of Gambling."

transactions. Nevada had been granted the legal right to continue its business.

Opponents of the business used scandals at Northwestern University and Arizona State University to revive their battle against the legal business in Nevada. Two Arizona State players were indicted and later convicted on charges of conspiracy to commit sports bribery. They admitted to payoffs for their efforts to determine the pointspread outcome of four games during the 1993-4 season.

In addition, Four Northwestern University players were indicted for their attempts to fix three games during the 1994-5 season. A former football player was also indicted for "booking" the wagers.

Opponents of the business lobbied for implementation of the recommendation from the "NGISC" that was completed in 1997. That Commission had recommended a ban on all wagers on college sports.

Senator McCain used this recommendation as a way to carry the ball for those who opposed the business. He proposed the Amateur Sports Integrity Act of 2001 (ASIA) as the answer to this recommendation. This Act would "prohibit government from sponsoring or authorizing gambling schemes based on amateur games or performances by high school, college, or Olympic athletes."[65]

Senator McCain proposed this legislation in spite of the relationship he had with the corporate casinos in Nevada who owned the sportsbooks that accepted wagers on the college sports he proposed to ban. Benefits from the Senator's relationship with the Las Vegas-based casino corporations came in the form of gratuities while he gambled in Las Vegas, as well as from the lobbyists for the industry in Washington who contributed to his political ambitions that included campaigns for the Presidency.

[65] Summary, S 2340 Amateur Sports Integrity Act of May 1, 2000.

"Only six members of Congress have received more money from the gambling industry than Mr. McCain and five hail from the casino hubs of Nevada and New Jersey according to data from the Center for Responsive Politics dating back to 1989."[66] Senator McCain said in response, "Literally every business in America falls under the Commerce Committee."

The business behind ASIA was the wealth that had been generated for the NCAA through their college football and basketball enterprises. The Senator chose to ignore the business of sports to justify his legislation. Instead, he framed the justification in terms of morality. According to the Senator, "Sports wagering threatens the integrity of sports, it puts student athletes in a vulnerable position, it can serve as a gateway behavior for adolescent gamblers and it can devastate individuals and careers."[67]

While those words attempt to justify the Legislation, they do not reveal who and what was behind them. They avoid a reference to the interests that made ASIA a priority for Congress. Those interests had not retreated from their effort to end the business in Nevada even after PASPA had been enacted. The odds rose in their favor when they were able to reach into the pocket book of the Committee Chairman. The benefits they could offer to Senator McCain would compete with whatever Las Vegas casino corporations could offer.

The NCAA Bowl Championship Series was among those benefits. Arizona had not played host to a college football championship game until 1999 when the NCAA awarded the BCS Championship Game to the state. This game was played at Sun Devils Stadium in

---

[66] *New York Times,* September 28, 2008 article by Jo Becker and Don Van Natta Jr. "For McCain and Team, a Host of Ties to Gambling" pp. 2-3

[67] It's Past Time to Ban Amateur Sports Gambling by Senator John McCain, Press Office Release August 1, 2001

Tempe. Arizona State was host to a second BCS Championship Game played at the same stadium in 2002. In 2006 the game was moved to the University of Phoenix Stadium in Glendale.

The first BCS Championship game generated an estimated $131 million dollars for the economy of Arizona. That was three times more than the amount from the previous the year. Senator McCain responded to this gratuity in 2001 through his leadership on behalf of ASIA through the Senate Commerce Committee which he then chaired.[68] Even though ASIA became stalled in Congress by Nevada politicians, the NCAA continued to play ball with the Senator.

The second BCS championship game brought an estimated $228 million dollars to Arizona's economy, almost double the amount from the previous game in 1999.[69] The third BCS championship game played in 2006 brought an estimated $401.7 million dollars to the Arizona economy more than double the amount from the previous year's Fiesta Bowl.[70]

Glendale was selected as the site for the 2011 BCS Championship game. Fiesta Bowl President John Junkers said, "We hope this (future BCS champion-ships) will be a larger economic impact."

Add to the BCS Championship games the impact of the Tostitos Fiesta Bowl also played every year in Arizona and the revenues from the NCAA basketball tournaments that were awarded to Tucson and the US Airways Center in Phoenix. Arizona had the clout even Las Vegas corporations could not match.

But the late J. Terrance Lanni, then Chairman of the Board and Chief Executive Officer at MGM Grand in Las Vegas, expressed surprise that Senator McCain would turn his back on one of the businesses of the

---

[68] Press Release, April 26, 2007 from a study by W.P. Carey Sports Business Program at Arizona State University.
[69] Ibid
[70] Ibid

Nevada gaming industry. "I can't think of any other issue," he said.[71]

In spite of that stab in the back, Mr. Lanni hosted a fundraiser for Senator McCain in May 2007 that raised $400,000 for his presidential campaign. For Mr. Lanni and others in Nevada, "let bygones be bygones" became the political operative.[72]

Sig Rogich, a Nevada businessman and political activist who helped raise $2 million for Senator McCain said, "Beyond his support for gaming, Nevada supports John McCain because he's one of us—a Westerner at heart."[73] Evidently Mr. Rogich experienced a loss in his sense of direction when he made the comment. He forgot the sportsbook industry was legally confined to his western state.

In contrast to the passivity of Terrence Lanni to the Senator's stab in the back, members of the sportsbook industry in Las Vegas responded in another way. They made attempts to reach the Senator to express their views about the legislation.

Vic Salerno, President of the American Wagering Corporation, made preparations to host a fundraiser for Republican House candidate Jon Porter that Senator McCain was scheduled to attend. The Senator cancelled after he found out that the meeting would include as many as twenty members of the sportsbook industry who would be there to express their views on ASIA.[74]. The Senator cancelled the meeting "because of the appearance that it was a *quid pro quo*." He said he did not want to create an appearance "that people had to pay to come to talk to me."

---

[71] *New York Times* September 28, 2008 article by Jo Becker and Don Van Matta, Jr. "For McCain and Team, a host of Ties to Gambling" p.3
[72] Ibid
[73] Ibid, p.2
[74] *Las Vegas Review Journal*, August 9, 2000 article by Dave Berns "McCain snubs sportsbooks" pp. 1-4; *Las Vegas Review Journal*, August 10, 2000 article by Jan Moller "Porter defends GOP visits used to generate money" pp. 1-2

Las Vegas bookmakers learned a lesson about the price behind freedom of speech. Their $100-a-head fundraiser was not enough to compete with the bottom lines of the interests behind the legislation. The Senator did not want to be in a position to respond to what was behind his form of "double-dipping." He could take money from interest groups on either side of the issue and at the same time take away the freedom of people at the heart of the issue.

If the Amateur Sports Integrity Act had passed, the professional sports leagues would have likely followed suit with legislation to ban wagers on their teams. The NFL had sent a letter to Senator McCain. They said, "We write to urge in the strongest possible terms that the bill (Amateur Sports Integrity Act) be expanded to prohibit gambling not only on amateur teams, but on professional teams as well.[75]

Senator McCain encountered resistance from Nevada politicians who acted on behalf of Nevada lobbyists for the casino industry. Nevada politicians happened to be among the six others who received more money from corporate gaming interests than Senator McCain.

Senators Harry Reid and John Ensign had to use political clout and their abilities with parliamentary procedures to protect their interests. In May 2001, Senator Ensign, a member of the Senate Commerce Committee, added an amendment to the Bill that would have called for a national study of illegal gambling as a substitute for Senator McCain's proposed ban on wagers on amateur sports. Senator Reid, the Democratic whip of the Senate, was able to convince enough members of the Committee to vote for the amendment. That vote ended in a 10 to 10 tie, a defeat for Senator Ensign's amendment. But this tie

---

[75] *Las Vegas Review Journal,* February 3, 2000 article by Steve Tetreault "NFL, NBA, want betting ban" p.1A

was akin to a political version of a "backdoor cover" for the sportsbook industry.[76] Senator Reid was able to use the tie vote to raise doubt about the bill itself. The legislation never came before the Senate where a majority would have likely voted in favor of the Amateur Sports Integrity Act. The political version of "house rules" prevailed over a final outcome that might have ended the sportsbook industry in Nevada.

Three years after this initial attempt to pass the legislation the Amateur Sports Integrity Act was no closer to passage. As a result, the NCAA decided to change priorities after Myles Brand succeeded Cedric Dempsey as President. Mr. Brand said, "...the Senator needs to take the lead."[77] "...at this point I can't really say it's imminent, and until then, I think we've got to work on other aspects."[78]

Senator McCain responded, "I don't want to bring up something that we can't win." He later admitted that Congress would not pass the bill until there was another gambling scandal. He predicted, "...there will be another scandal."[79]

After ASIA was defeated, Senator McCain exposed his lack of conviction about integrity when he invited visitors to his website to use their skills to compete with him in the selection of winners for the men's 2007 NCAA basketball championship. He had picked North Carolina to win the Tournament. Winners of the contest were awarded a "McCain Fleece" jacket, a McCain jacket, or a McCain pin.

---

[76] A term used to describe a late score that determines the point spread winner in a game in which the outcome had already been determined.

[77] *Las Vegas Review Journal*, March 5, 2003 article by Tony Batt "NCAA won't lead bet ban push" p.1D

[78] *Las Vegas Review Journal*, February 3, 2004 article by Tony Batt "Betting ban not discussed at meeting on college sports reform, but still has support" p.1D

[79] *Las Vegas Review Journal*, March 3, 2004 article by Tony Batt "McCain says sports betting ban bill unlikely this year" p. 1D

"This is not betting or gambling in any way, shape or form," said a spokesman for the "Fleecer."[80] Evidently this type of participation in the selection of winners limits the stimulation to what might be similar to the stimulation for those who watch commercials for Cialis. Both the makers of Cialis and Senator McCain know that everyone else knows "one thing can lead to another."

If the Senator decides to resurrect ASIA he might want to reformulate the justification for the legislation from integrity to freedom. He might want to launch the effort from Las Vegas where he could promise to liberate sports bettors and bookmakers from their segregation.

"An end to legal sports betting in Las Vegas will mean an end to segregation for you bettors and bookmakers. You will be free to leave Las Vegas and Nevada and enjoy the same freedoms everyone else in America has," he could pontificate as long as his face could contain the smirk that would fight for control. Even if he were able to keep a straight face he would have to duck the people in the business who would ask him, "How can taking away our freedom to practice our profession make us freer than we were before?"

People in the business should also force the Senator to explain to why the NCAA decided to hand the ball off to his counterpart from Arizona in order to continue the fight. Myles Brand, President of the NCAA, decided to abandon ASIA in favor of the initiative by Senator Jon Kyl of Arizona. Evidently, the Unlawful Internet Gambling Act of 2006 (UIGA) had the potential to reap greater dividends for the NCAA from their investments in Arizona.

---

[80] *Las Vegas Review Journal*, March 15, 2007 article by Tony Batt "McCain joins in on contest fun" p.1A

UIGA changed the focus of the battleground from Las Vegas to offshores. The sovereignty of America replaced the integrity of the game as the justification for the NCAA to oppose the expansion of the business beyond Nevada.

Another Road to the Final Four

After the failure of the ASIA, economics reshaped the relationship between Las Vegas and the NCAA. An economic system had developed that would be difficult to fit into economic theories. Most economists do not have the "inside info" behind the big picture of our business. The economic terrain is contoured by the legal segregation of the sports betting industry.

Legal segregation had created a situation that allows Nevada corporate casinos to use their monopoly on sportsbooks to exploit a product that is owned by the NCAA. Sportsbooks profit from the use of property owned by the NCAA. Casino corporations do not pay the NCAA for the use of their Tournament. The "Big Dance" has patent protection rights, but that does not preclude the exploitation of the product by Las Vegas corporate casinos.

After ASIA was rejected, the NCAA was confined to a self-imposed corner. They could not negotiate an agreement with the corporate-owned sportsbook industry that would enable them to collect revenue from the use of their product. NCAA policies that contribute to the segregation of our business to Nevada led to the folly of self-exploitation. The NCAA exploits itself through their efforts to keep the sportsbook industry segregated.

This economic system has evolved to where the two monopolies find their interests are suited by the preservation of the status quo. Profits from the Tournament are enough for the non-profit NCAA to keep them from another challenge to the legitimacy of

93

the system in Nevada. Profits from the use of the Tournament product by Nevada casino corporations are enough to keep them from a challenge to the legal segregation of their sportsbooks to Nevada.

Profits from the men's basketball tournament comprise approximately 80 percent of the NCAA operating budget. Those profits exploded from a time when eight teams competed for the national championship to a time when 65 teams compete in what has also become a symbol of business. The NCAA patented the Tournament with the names "Big Dance" and "Final Four."[81]

Expansion of and competition for the television coverage of the Tournament are responsible for most of the profit. In 1963 the NCAA championship game between Loyola University of Chicago and the University of Cincinnati was televised in Chicago, on delayed tape, on a local network, late Saturday evening. The game was not important enough to be televised live to the Chicago audience.

Ten years later, NBC paid the NCAA $1,165, 755 for the rights to the Tournament. In 1983, NBC paid $9.9 million for those rights. Because of a conflict with "The Johnny Carson Show," NBC could not televise games that would be played on Thursday and Friday evenings.

CBS was able to exploit this situation. They agreed to pay the NCAA $16 million per year for the rights to televise the Tournament for the next three years. Payment for those rights increased to $143 million per year from 1991 to 1995. The last contract that began in 2004 and ends in 2013 pays $545 million per year.[82]

[81] October 10, 2005 "Once an afterthought, the Dance is now big business" by Darren Rovell, ESPN.com pp.1-3

[82] April 22, 2010 "NCAA Agrees to $10.8 Billion Deal to Broadcast Its Men's Basketball Tournament" by Brad Wolverton, THE CHRONICLE of Higher Education, pp. 1-2

The opportunity for additional revenue led the NCAA to consider expansion of the Tournament to 96 teams. CBS did not find that expansion in its interests. They renegotiated a contract with the NCAA that expands the coverage to Turner Broadcasting. This $10.8 billion contract is for 14 years. Profits from these television contracts lined the pockets of those who manage the NCAA. Walter Byers, the first "President" of the NCAA, earned $78,450 in 1983. Annuities, pensions, and deferred compensation might have raised the benefits to close to $200,000. A no interest mortgage loan in the amount of $118,000 added to those benefits.[83]

NCAA President Cedric Dempsey earned $650,000 in 1997. That amount was almost double what he was paid at the start of his eight-year contract. His successor, Myles Brand, earned close to $1 million dollars in 2009.

Nevertheless, Mr. Brand found room in his conscience to criticize basketball coaches for increases in their salaries. "You have to ask some very hard questions, whether this is really in tune with the academic values, whether we've reached a point already that these high salaries and packages for coaches has really extended beyond what's expected with the academic community," he said.[84]

Those salaries spiked from the time when John Wooden earned $25,000 during his last year at UCLA in 1974-5. Ten years later, Jerry Tarkanian, coach of UNLV, was able to double that salary to $53,000 per year. In 1991, Tarkanian's salary increased to approximately $204,000 per year. Business deals that

---

[83] October 6, 1986 "In the kingdom of the solitary man" by Jack McCallum, *Sports Illustrated*, p.5

[84] April 2, 2009 "Brand: '"Hard questions' need to be asked about rising salaries" by Steve Weiberg, *USA TODAY*, p.1

accompanied the position raised his income to approximately $600,000 per year.[85]

John Calipari signed an eight-year contract for $31.65 million in 2010 to coach the University of Kentucky basketball team. He will earn approximately $3.3 million during the first year.

This growth in revenue from the Tournament also had a "spillover" benefit for the adversary of the NCAA. The victim became the victimizer. Where else in America does an industry reap profits from another business without compensation for that product? Exploitation of the NCAA by Las Vegas corporations is one consequence of legal segregation. The NCAA "reaped what it had sown," especially in Las Vegas.

The NCAA no longer promotes legislation that would eliminate the business in Las Vegas. Abandonment of that option expanded the opportunities for Las Vegas casino corporations to do whatever the NCAA could not stop them from doing.

The NCAA used patent rights to resist the exploitation of their product. The NCAA prohibited Las Vegas casinos from the use of advertisements for Tournament parties that use the terms "March Madness" and "Final Four."

Casino corporations circumvented that restriction with the use of terms such as "college basketball tournament party" for their promotions. So far, there have been no reported cancellations to these parties by visitors to Las Vegas or by locals because they could not attend "March Madness" or "Final Four" festivities.

Neither patent rights nor segregation has generated one penny of revenue for the NCAA from the use of their Tournament product in Las Vegas; however, Las Vegas casino corporations have been able to use this product to help pay their bills. Bettors

---

[85] February 3, 1991 "'Tark the Shark' biggest fish in high-paying pond" by A.D. Hopkins, *Las Vegas Review Journal*, p.1A

pay them the "juice" for transactions on Tournament games. "Juice," along with losing tickets, is revenue for casino corporations. Part of that revenue becomes tax revenue for the State of Nevada.

Casino corporations have already paid for all the necessities to show Tournament games. Those games neither add to the cost for space nor the television service. The additional cost for employees during the Tournament amounts to chump change. Casinos also pay nothing for a Tournament that benefits their bottom line from other casino games that are played by visitors who come to Las Vegas to wager on the Tournament. "College basketball fans interested in wagering on their favorite teams wagered on more than just sports," said Frank Streshley, chief of the Nevada Gaming Control Board Tax and License Division.[86]

Micah Roberts, then Director of Race and Sports for Station Casinos added that the first weekend of the NCAA Tournament was one of the busiest weekends for wagers in Las Vegas. He said, "Sports bettors also like to play blackjack, poker and slots."[87]

Casino revenues for March 2005 support his observation. Those revenues "shattered all previous monthly win totals during the third month of 2005." Casinos won $1.031 billion. This amount surpassed the $930.3 million won in March 2004. The amount also surpassed the total amount won by the casino industry during the entire year of 1974.[88]

Although there are no official records, an estimated $25 million was wagered statewide on the Tournament in 1992. Ninety percent of that amount came from Clark County, which includes Las Vegas. In

---

[86] *Las Vegas Review Journal*, May 10, 2006 article by Howard Stutz, "Gaming win tops $1 billion" p.2

[87] *Las Vegas Review Journal*, March 6, 2006 article by Howard Stutz, "GAMING MILESTONE: Casinos' win tops $1 billion. Industry enjoys 'absolute blockbuster' March results" p.2

[88] Ibid p.1

1994, the Tournament handle was estimated to have grown to $60 million. That amount exceeded the amount bet on the Super Bowl by $4 million.[89]

Wagers on the Tournament rose to an estimated $85 million in 2004.[90] The next year casinos won $16.2 million from a total amount of $170.9 million wagered on basketball. That was a 16.7 increase from the previous year.[91]

Revenue reports for 2008 add another perspective to the impact of the Tournament. Statewide wagers on basketball rose from $116.7 million in February to $238.9 million in March. The "March Madness" tournament contributed to that increase of 105% from February to March.[92]

"Combined, the first two weekends of March Madness are bigger than the Super Bowl," said Brian Stedeford, Senior Director of Gaming Operations for the Hard Rock Hotel and Casino.[93]

During those 17 years, estimated wagers on the Tournament rose from $25 million statewide to 238.9 million. And, as if the casino profits from those wagers weren't enough, Las Vegas was able to bilk more from the NCAA. Las Vegas "double dipped" when the City became host for "Little Dances."

Las Vegas danced between the raindrops of an amendment to NCAA bylaws that read, "...a certified event shall not be conducted in a venue where sports wagering on inter-collegiate athletics is permitted on property sponsored by an establishment that permits

---

[89] Estimate from Frank Streschley, Chief Statistician and Tax Analyst for the Nevada Gaming Control Board.

[90] *Las Vegas Review Journal* April 3, 1994 article by Stephen Nover, "Books experience March Madness" p.11E

[91] Las Vegas Review Journal March 6, 2006 article by Howard Stutz, "Casinos' win tops $1 billion. Industry enjoys 'absolute blockbuster' March results p.1

[92] *Las Vegas Review Journal* March 18, 2009 article by Benjamin Spillman "Smaller maddening crowd expected" p. A1

[93] Ibid, p.2

sports wagering on intercollegiate athletics or branded with signage for such an establishment."[94]

Despite this restriction on the "Big Dance" one Las Vegas corporation was able to find a way to host the "Little Dances" that helped to pave the road to the "Final Four." The West Coast Athletic Conference (WCAC) signed a contract with the Boyd Corporation to play their 2009 Tournament games at the Arena which is in the confines of the Orleans Hotel and Casino. That tournament set a WCAC record for attendance for all of the games, as well as for a single game. Those results prompted the WCAC to sign a three-year deal with the Boyd Corporation.

The financial success of that tournament prompted the Western Athletic Conference (WAC) to move their tournament back to Las Vegas. They would also play their Tournament games at the Arena in 2011. The Mountain West Tournament returned to Las Vegas in 2007 after a hiatus of several years. Those games are played at the Thomas and Mack Center.

The fact that Conference Tournament games are played not only in the City that allows wagers on those games, but at the Orleans where wagers on those games can be made at the sportsbook should have been a cause for concern for the NCAA given their history of objections to the business. The fact that they have not raised objections may be indicative of a wait-and-see attitude that might pave the way for the NCAA to lift the prohibition against Las Vegas as a regional site for the "Big Dance."

If the WCAC and WAC Tournaments are played without controversy, the odds for Las Vegas to become a regional site for the "Big Dance" will rise from unlikely to possible. Empty seats for games at other regional sites will raise those odds to likely.

---

[94] *Las Vegas Review Journal* article October 9, 2001 article by Tony Batt "COLLEGE SPORTS BETTING Tourney rules vote set" p. 1D

Segregation may enable Las Vegas to develop its patent right on another version of the "road to the Final Four."

Dancing with the NBA

Unlike the NCAA, the National Basketball Association (NBA) used the power given to them by Nevada to prohibit wagers on their games that would be played in Las Vegas. People in the business in Las Vegas had to deny their integrity as well as the integrity of their game in order for the games to be played on their home turf.

The plight of the Utah Jazz was tip-off time for this conflict. In 1983, Utah decided to move eleven home games from Salt Lake City to Las Vegas. The team was close to a day-to-day situation for economic survival.

Owners of the franchise gambled on a "quick fix" for cash. They believed that revenue was more likely to come from fans who would attend those games at the Thomas and Mack Center in Las Vegas. They proved to be right for game one. The Michael Jordan-led Chicago Bulls championship team brought 13,186 fans to the Thomas and Mack, the largest crowd in Utah Jazz history.

Before those eleven games could be played, Jazz owners and NBA officials had to address their problem with possible wagers on those games. They demanded that sportsbook operators keep those games off the board.

Vic Salerno, CEO of Leroy's Sports, represented the independent sportsbook owners at a meeting with NBA officials. He resented the attempt by then Deputy Commissioner David Stern to dictate the terms of the way the sports-betting business would be conducted in Las Vegas. "We were legitimate businessmen, doing something that was legal and regulated, and they were trying to make us out to be the bad guys," Mr. Salerno said. He added, "To the best of my recollection, it (the negotiation) was pretty heated. The NBA wanted all the (Jazz) games off the board and there was no way we were going to stand for that."[95]

After the negotiations failed, the NBA petitioned the Nevada Gaming Control Board to impose their demand on the industry. The Board voted 3-2 to allow sportsbooks to accept wagers on the eleven games the Jazz would play in Las Vegas. As part of the politics of this vote, sportsbook operators later provided cover for the Board. They reversed their position. They agreed to keep those games off the board as a "gesture" to the city.[96]

Jazz Executive Vice President David Cheketts welcomed their decision. "It was the League's concern that anyone coming to those games should just cheer about what's happening out on the floor," he said. There was no picture that accompanied this quote with his tongue in cheek. Mr. Cheketts added, "The League didn't want a situation where Darrell Griffith hits a three-point shot at the buzzer to win a game for the Jazz and people boo him because they have money on the other team." Mr. Checketts failed to think before he spoke. That shot would not have made a difference in the pointspread outcome of a game in which the Bulls were favored by more than two points.

David Stern added his less than two cents' worth when he said, "When a team wins a game it shouldn't be booed because they didn't cover the spread." Apparently the future Commissioner of the NBA had the ability to distinguish boos from people who had wagered on the game from those of fans who had not. Perhaps he added that ability to his resume to enhance his chances to become Commissioner.

---

[95] *Las Vegas Review Journal* February 18, 2007 article by Steve Capp "History made, missed..." p.4
[96] Ibid, pp. 3-4

Utah Jazz coach Frank Layden had the courage to challenge those comments. He said the prohibition, "...was silly. But I think people in the sports-betting industry felt, and rightly so, that they were picked on..."[97]

The Gaming Commission would never again allow independent sportsbook operators to have the voice they had in this matter. New Gaming Regulations eliminated independent sportsbooks in favor of those owned by casino corporations.

In addition, in July 1985, Gaming Regulators adopted Regulation 22.120 (d). This Regulation would prohibit "wagers on any event...played in Nevada involving a professional team....(after) the team's governing body files with the commission a written request that wagers on the event or series of events be prohibited and the commission approves the request,..." These so-called members of the "home team" opened the door for visitors such as the NBA to have home court advantage in Las Vegas.

Since that Regulation was approved the NBA has requested and been granted every appeal to prohibit wagers on NBA pre-season games that would be played in Las Vegas. An additional appeal was granted for game four of the first round playoff game between Portland and the Lakers in 1992 that was moved to Las Vegas because of the riots in Los Angeles. This appeal process was the only option left for the NBA to prohibit wagers on their games after the defeat of ASIA. The League had hoped Senator McCain would add a ban to wagers on professional sports as well.

Despite that failure, the NBA was able to add another dimension to their version of home field advantage. Commissioner Stern appealed to the Gaming Commission for a prohibition on wagers on

---

[97] Ibid, p. 4

the 2007 All-Star game that was scheduled to be played in Las Vegas.

The appeal was made even though an NBA All-Star game would rank near the bottom of the barrel of interest for sports bettors, along with NBA preseason games. That did not faze the Commissioner. For him, Las Vegas was "...a test case—for both neutral sites as well as Las Vegas as such a site.[98]

He agreed to play that game in Las Vegas after Joe and George Maloof lobbied him to do so. The Maloofs are owners of the Sacramento Kings franchise and at the time were owners of the Palms Hotel and Casino.

There was speculation that this game might be a test run for Las Vegas to prove the city could be the site for an NBA franchise. "Sooner, rather than later, there's going to be an NBA team in Las Vegas," said Joe Maloof.[99]

Las Vegas Mayor Oscar Goodman supported the effort, but the reason behind his support extended beyond the All-Star game. He said, "Hopefully I can change his mind (about Las Vegas as site for the NBA) before his meeting with Stern during All-Star week."[100]

Some members of the sports-betting community supported the move to prohibit betting on the All-Star game. "We're talking about one basketball game (All-Star Game) right now and it's really an exhibition," said Chuck Esposito, then Assistant Vice President for Race and Sports Operations at Caesar's Palace.

Nevada Gaming Commission Chairman Peter Bernhard agreed. "The amount of wagering on NBA All-Star games is relatively little compared to the

---

[98] *New York Times* February 11, 2007 article by Liz Robbins "Las Vegas Has Got the Game, but it wants a team" p.3
[99] Ibid
[100] Ibid

benefit for the state of being able to host this kind of event," he said.[101]

The comment by Chuck Esposito about business on the All-Star game was tempered when he added that if all NBA games were taken off the board that "would have much more of an impact on the industry."[102]

Transactions on basketball account for about 23 percent of the money bet at Las Vegas sportsbooks. Less than half the amount is generated by the NBA. That amount is fourth behind the amounts wagered on the NFL and NCAA football and basketball.

Speculation about the possibility that the NBA might come to Las Vegas ended after the All-Star game. There were negative perceptions from both sides of the endeavor that brought the game to Las Vegas. Besides the reported increase in crime on the Strip, revenues for the casinos also hit bottom. "He (David Stern) can keep the All-Star game and not bring it back here as far as we're concerned," said Terry Lanni, MGM Chief Executive Officer.[103]

Commissioner Stern responded with a statement that said the NBA would not return to Las Vegas unless a new 'state-of-the-art' stadium was built.[104]

There was one consolation for the sportsbook industry. People in the business could not be blamed for the failures that accompanied a game they did not want in the first place and would not miss in the future.

Another power of the NBA to control the business was relinquished after the demise of the All-Star Game

---

[101] *Los Angeles Times,* June 24, 2005 "Betting Ban Approved in Bid for 2007 All-Star Game" p.1

[102] *New York Times,* February 11, 2007 article by Liz Robbins "Las Vegas Has Got the game, but it wants a team" p.2

[103] Bloomberg.com "MGM's Lanni says NBA All-Star Weekend Was Bad for Las Vegas" by Mason Levinson, Danny King and Josh Fineman

[104] Ibid

as one of its tools. The NBA had been able to enforce a prohibition on wagers on all NBA games at Las Vegas casinos where the owners of those casinos also owned NBA franchises.

The NBA exerted this power after the Maloof family purchased the Sacramento Kings and ARCO Arena, the team's home court on July 1, 1999. As part of the deal, the Maloofs agreed to take all NBA games off the board at their Fiesta Hotel in North Las Vegas. This ban continued at the Palms Hotel and Casino in 2001 after the Maloofs sold the Fiesta.

These owners lost revenue that could have been made from wagers on NBA games other than those that involved the Kings. They paid the price for their failure to confront the argument that their ownership of a franchise could affect the integrity of the game unless wagers on them were prohibited.

In 2008, the NBA Board of Governors lifted that ban at the Palms except for games played by the Sacramento Kings. The Board had to reconsider the prohibition on all NBA wagers after they granted Harrah's Corporation the right to accept those wagers after CEO Gary Loveman became a minority owner of the Boston Celtics. The ban at Harrah's was limited to wagers on the Celtics which included the Celtics' championship series with the Lakers in 2008.

This change is indicative of a change in the attitude of the Commissioner about their need to re-address the perceptions of the integrity of the game. He began with the change in the perception that Casino franchise owners have the power to influence the outcome of all games. Now that perception is limited to games that are played by the owners of the team.

There is more evidence that the "writing on the wall" about the perceptions of integrity may force the Commissioner to go even further to make an accommodation with the new economic climate of the time for the NBA. He did not blame Las Vegas for the actions of NBA referee Tim Donaghy. All of his bets were made with illegal bookmakers. NBA security measures to prevent that possibility did not work. The League had to accept responsibility for the failure to prevent what happened.

The fact that this incident did not impact fan interest in the game coincides with a flip-flop by the Commissioner about gambling and the integrity of the game. "Considering the fact that so many state governments...don't consider (gambling) immoral, I don't think anyone (else) should," he said.[105]

He elaborated on his position on morality when he said that nationally legalized gambling on the NBA was possible and "may be a huge opportunity." He added, "The betting issues are actually going to become more intense as states in the U.S. and governments in the world decide that the answers to all of their monetary shortfalls are the tax that is gambling."[106]

When asked if it might be in the interest of the NBA to support legalized sports betting he said, 'It has been a matter of league policy to answer that question 'No.' But I think that league policy was formulated at a time when gambling was far less widespread...even legally."[107]

Even the Commissioner has had to acknowledge the bottom line that dictates business is business. The integrity of his game can be redefined in order to fit the circumstances of the need for additional revenue for the League.

---

[105] "Stern open to legalized betting, rule changes" by Ian Thomsen, Sports Illustrated.com, December 11, 2009 p.1
[106] Ibid
[107] Ibid

From the Diamond to the Ice and into the Ring

Major League Baseball (MLB) was the beneficiary of perks from Nevada that the NBA might have envied. The NBA had grounds to protest this discrimination.

In 1996, the Oakland A's were forced to move six of their home games to Cashman Field in Las Vegas because of renovations to the Oakland Coliseum. Baseball Commissioner Bud Selig had not submitted a written request to the Nevada Gaming Control Board to prohibit wagers on those games. No request was submitted even after Gaming Control Chairman Bill Bible waived the 30-day requirement. He kept the door open for a request to prohibit wagers on those games until game time.[108]

Mr. Selig chose to ignore this gratuity. That left Chairman Bible with the obligation to require sportsbooks to keep those games off the board. He relied on a Gaming Regulation that prohibited wagers on certain games played by professional teams in Las Vegas. Even though the A's were hosts for only six days of the season, the Chairman decided the rule would be applied. He said, "People had kind of forgotten about it (Regulation 22.120 (d).) I was unaware of its existence. The issue had not come up in the context of baseball. It came up in basketball, but never baseball."[109]

People in the sportsbook industry decided to put the bottom line above principle. They accepted the decision because as Bob Gregorka, then Director of Race and Sports at the Sands said, "Personally, it

---

[108] *Las Vegas Sun*, "To bet or not to bet" article by Tim Graham, March 25, 1996, p.1

[109] *LasVegas Sun* March 27, 1996 "Athletics hot, betting's not" article by Steve Capp, p.1

doesn't mean that much. It's not like we're making a lot of money off of baseball."[110]

To his credit, Mr. Gregorka did not use the decision by the Nevada Gaming Board to justify his lack of integrity. In July 1985, when then Commissioner Peter Ueberroth requested that the Nevada Gaming Control Board prohibit wagers on any professional teams located in Nevada, the Board responded with an order that all bets on Nevada teams would be prohibited "until such time as the commission orders otherwise."

The issue reemerged in 2009 when sportsbooks began to take wagers on the Reno Aces, an AAA Pacific Coast League team. Russell Sayre, a member of the Board, had to remind the industry about the prohibition. He left the decision to them whether to appeal the ruling. No one in the industry pursued his suggestion. That petition would not have been worth the time or effort.[111]

In contrast to this hypocrisy with MLB, there was no need for the sportsbook industry to respond to a petition from the National Hockey League about wagers on minor league hockey teams in Las Vegas. Odds on games played by the Las Vegas Thunder of the International Hockey League were posted at the Imperial Palace sportsbook between 1993 and 1999. Odds were also posted at the Orleans sportsbook in 2007 on playoff games for the Las Vegas Wranglers. The Wranglers were part of the East Coast Hockey League (ECHL).

ECHL Commissioner Brian McKenna said the League did not have the authority to stop the wagering on those games. "We don't have any jurisdiction or prohibition on anybody outside our league. It's not

---

[110] Ibid, p.2
[111] *Las Vegas Sun* June 12, 2009 "Regulator reminds sportsbooks they can't take bets on Aces, 51s" article by Richard Velotta, p.1

something we condone, but we also recognize that we're not an entity that's going to be able to control that," he said.[112]

The NHL had not submitted a formal request to the Gaming Control Board to prohibit wagers on their minor league leagues as MLB had done. Perhaps the NHL did not raise the issue because they did not believe that wagering on those games would affect their integrity.

However, there was one issue on which the NHL and the NBA received the same treatment from the Gaming Control Board. When ITT Corporation became the owner of Caesar's Palace, wagers on NHL and NBA games were prohibited. ITT owned the New York Rangers as well as the New York Knicks and Madison Square Garden. The prohibition on wagers on those teams ended when Hilton Hotels bought Caesar's Palace.

NHL Commissioner Gary Bettman had taken a position similar to that of the other professional leagues on wagers on an NHL team that could be based in Las Vegas. He said, "At minimum we'd be looking to have a team treated the same way that the local college teams are treated."[113] At that time wagers on UNLV and UNR were prohibited.

Others disagreed with Mr. Bettman's position after this incident. "It's the wrong time for the league to relocate to Las Vegas. I think it's a very sensitive issue to move a team to a city where betting on the team is legal," said *New York Post* hockey columnist, Larry Brooks.[114] Those who supported his position failed to mention the exposé of the involvement of Phoenix

---

[112] *Las Vegas Review Journal* April 26, 2007 "Book it: Hockey interests bettors" article by Matt Youmans, p.1

[113] *Las Vegas Review Journal* September 29, 1999 "NHL, NBA officials won't write off LV" article by Tony Batt, p. 2

[114] *Las Vegas Review Journal* April 26, 2007 "Book it: Hockey interests bettors" article by Matt Youmans, p.1

Coyotes coach Rick Tocchet and Janet Jones, the wife of Wayne Gretzky in a NEW JERSEY, *not* a LAS VEGAS-based scandal that involved sports trans-actions.

Mr. Brooks might have also been unaware that according to Jay Kornegay, then Imperial Palace Sportsbook Director, NHL wagers amounted to less than two percent of the sportsbook's wagers.[115] The NHL did not have "juice" on this issue. Wagers on hockey were not important enough for them to make the concessions that were made to the other professional leagues.

Even if a hockey franchise were to be relocated to Las Vegas, then MGM Mirage Sportsbook Director Robert Walker said, "I want to put all games on the board. The bottom line sets a bad precedent once you start taking things off the board. How bad do we really want an NHL team?"[116]

"Or any team," he should have said to the Leagues who live by the argument that the business compromises the integrity of their games. The experience of the business with boxing provides the evidence to refute those claims.

No sport could be more vulnerable to compromises of integrity than contests in the ring. Yet there has never been a need for the Las Vegas sportsbook industry to use that concern to prohibit wagers on matches held in or out of Las Vegas. Sportsbooks do not need approval from the governing bodies that sanction the bouts nor from the Nevada Gaming Control Board in order to post them on their boards.

Even the suggestion of a prohibition on wagers for a boxing match would be a knockout blow for the integrity of that game. Wagers on boxing have always

---

[115] *Las Vegas Review Journal* September 29, 1999 "NHL, NBA officials won't write off LV" article by Tony Batt, p.2
[116] Ibid

been part of the integrity of this game. A match between James Corbett and Robert Fitzsimmons for the heavyweight championship fought in Carson City Nevada in 1897 reportedly generated a side bet between the two for $10,000. The purse was $15,000. There was no thought of a prohibition on a side bet between the participants.

Boxing is the gambler's sport. Boxing has its roots in betting and intrigue and mystery and payoffs and dives—it's a gamblers sport," said John Romero, a former judge at championship fights in Las Vegas.[117]

None of the entities that govern the sport would disagree. Neither would the sportsbooks who would be hurt the most by a "fix." The risk is part of a deal that generates the revenue a championship fight can generate for promoters of the fight, the city of Las Vegas, and the casinos.

Boxing matches in Las Vegas generated approximately $4.2 million in revenue for Nevada in 2007. In 2008, the sport produced $4.1 million. Matches that featured Floyd Mayweather, Jr. against Oscar De La Hoya and Ricky Hatton and another match between Manny Pacquaio and Oscar De La Hoya would not have been held in Las Vegas if wagers on them had been prohibited.

The incorporation of the business as an essential component of the integrity of this game by the Nevada Gaming Control Board contradicts the policies and actions they apply to team sports. This governing body also turns its head to the fact that the outcome of the match is determined by judges and kept secret until the match is over.

The Nevada Gaming Control Board does not allow sportsbooks to take wagers on any other sport or event that is decided by votes. Wagering is not allowed on

---

[117] *New York Times* October 12, 1981 "Las Vegas Is Betting on Its Sports Future" article by Joe Jares, p. C11

political contests or on events such as the Academy Awards or on sports such as figure-skating.

Boxing also extends the assumption of integrity of the game beyond the borders of America. There are no restrictions in Las Vegas on wagers for matches held anywhere in the world. The sportsbook industry, as well as the Nevada Athletic Commission, assume the standards of integrity that apply in Las Vegas apply everywhere else in the world.

While boxing has paved the way to refute the argument that sports transactions impugns the integrity of the game, auto racing has also helped to dispel the myth. The connection between integrity and gambling was as close as it could be in the situation that involved Brendan Gaughan, the son of Michael Gaughan, then owner of the Orleans Hotel and Casino. Brendan admitted he had bet on himself to win NASCAR races in 1994. Even though there was no suggestion that those wagers violated the integrity of their game, Penske later banned him and other drivers on the Team from wagers on car drivers or teams.

NASCAR does not have a policy that would prohibit those types of wagers. Reasons behind the ban from Penske may have been for public appearances rather than the possibility that drivers might try to fix races. That possibility is almost beyond a mathematical calculation. Also, the possible payoff for a fixer would not be worth the potential cost. Sportsbook limits for wagers on those races would make the payoff worth less than the risk.

The fact that NASCAR is more important to Las Vegas than to the sportsbook industry has given this sport slack the Nevada Gaming Control Board would not allow for sports. Revenues from one weekend in 2009 brought $189 million to the economy of the city. Wagers on the event were not worth the effort to calculate.

The City returns the favors from auto racing and boxing when the sportsbooks add their juice of integrity to those games. These events have been held in Las Vegas with no allegations that wagers on them influenced their outcomes. This is additional evidence to challenge the argument from the professional sports leagues that wagers on their games compromises their integrity.

"After further review..."

"We write to urge in the strongest possible terms that the bill (Amateur Sports Integrity Act) be expanded to prohibit gambling not only on amateur sports but on professional sports as well," said then National Football League (NFL) Executive Vice President Jeffrey Pash. The support was prompted by more than the need to protect the integrity of their games.

The NFL is aware of the amount of money generated by their product in Las Vegas and the State of Nevada. Wagers on the NFL in Nevada account for more than half the total revenue generated by the sportsbook industry. The statewide handle of $94.5 million on the Super Bowl alone in 2006 set a record for the industry. In 2012, $93.9 million was wagered on the Big Game. The amount wagered on that game during the last ten years is close to $900 million.[118] Since the inception of the Super Bowl, that amount would reach into the billions. The total amount wagered in Nevada on all NFL games during the last half century might reach a trillion dollars.

The NFL has not been compensated from the revenue generated by the sportsbook industry. While the League complains about the violation of its patent

---

[118] *Las Vegas Review Journal* "SPORTS BETTING: Guess where big bettors spend their money"? article by Matt Youmans September 22, 2005, p.1

rights, there is no complaint from the League about other forms of compensation that come from the interest in wagering on their games. That compensation could also reach into the trillions.

The conflict between the NFL and Las Vegas has scripts that are different from those of the NBA and MLB. There are no NFL minor league football teams in Las Vegas. No pre-season games are played in the City. The NFL cannot appeal its perception of the misuse of their product to the Gaming Control Board; but the League was able to throw a jab in the direction of Las Vegas when then Commissioner Paul Tagliabue decided to allow Mexico City to host a regular season game between the Arizona Cardinals and the San Francisco 49ers in 2004. After a turnout of 103,467, he suggested a regular season game at that site might become an annual tradition. He could accept the fact that wagering on the NFL is legal in Mexico City.

Perhaps he found a way to work out a deal with the Mexican government that would require bets to be made in Spanish and with pesos instead of dollars in order to keep a semblance of integrity to that game or else he knew there was no need for him to be concerned about the integrity.

The capacity of Estadio Azteca in Mexico City would compensate the NFL for the use of their patent right. That bottom line makes a difference in the standards that apply to sportsbooks in Mexico City and to those in Las Vegas.

Six years after that game, NFL Commissioner Roger Goodell was asked about the possibility that Las Vegas could be home for a franchise. He suggested that the need to keep his League separate from sports-betting would make it unlikely for Las Vegas to have a franchise. The game played in Mexico City must have slipped his mind.[119]

The NFL does not have the offensive firepower of the other Leagues. They have been limited to the prohibition of the use of their patent right in Las Vegas. Sportsbooks cannot use the term "Super Bowl" to identify the match-up on the boards. Casinos cannot use the name in their advertisements for parties on game day. They have to use names such as "Big Game" or "NFL Championship" game or other terms that do not infringe on the patent right to the name "Super Bowl."

This does not mean that use of the name "Super Bowl" is prohibited within the area of a sportsbook. Those who are licensed to sell promotional items for the game use that name even though their items for sale may be located within feet of where wagers are made on the game. Those who sell Super Bowl paraphernalia pay casino corporations for the use of that space. That enables casino corporations to milk both ends of the situation. They can take wagers on a game whose name they can't use while at the same time sell space to those who can use the name to sell their paraphernalia.

The NFL has also exercised the power of patent rights through the control over advertisements during playoff games and the Super Bowl. The League had prohibited advertisements for Las Vegas in 2004. An advertising agency circumvented that restriction. Instead of advertisements on the national networks, commercials for Las Vegas were shown during the games on local stations for those networks in cities such as Chicago, New York, and Los Angeles.

"Those ads are a violation of our policies. It shouldn't have happened in the first place and we

---

[119] *Las Vegas Review Journal* "Only sure bet: NFL hypocrisy" column by Ed Graney, January 28, 2010.

certainly don't want it to happen again," said Greg Aiello, an NFL spokesman.[120]

After the downturn in the economy the NFL was no longer in the driver's seat on the issue. The pool of advertisers for those games had shrunk. When advertisers such as Fed Ex, Pepsi, and GM could no longer afford to buy time, advertisers such as the City of Las Vegas resurfaced as an option.

The NFL rescinded the prohibition against advertisements for Las Vegas as long as they did not allude to gambling on the Strip. The commercials could show Red Rock Canyon, Mount Charleston, Decatur Boulevard, a traffic jam on Interstate 15, and maybe even a traffic jam on Las Vegas Boulevard as long as the neon from the Casinos did not suggest a visitor could gamble in Las Vegas.

The prohibition on advertisements that include any reference to gambling extended the definition of integrity beyond sports-betting. The NFL must be concerned that keno, slot, blackjack, and poker players might also watch their games. If these venues are close to a sportsbook, they might be included as threats to the integrity of their games.

There appears to be no limit to the "Hail Marys" the NFL will throw at the city in order win the battle over the integrity of their game.

What Happened Here?[121]

These tales from Las Vegas have their patent rights because the business is illegal outside Nevada. They could happen only in Las Vegas. Unfortunately, they were too heavy for the gossip columns in Sin

---

[120] *Las Vegas Review Journal* "NFL vows to close Las Vegas advertising loophole" article by Chris Jones, February 4, 2004, p.1

[121] Thanks to Dr. Hans J. Morgenthau for his insistence on the need to document what people say and do in order to get at the truth.

City...and they were too "deep" for the neon on Glitter Gulch, but they fit the words from "Hall of Famer" Sam Brown that, "Life's a con game."[122]

The stories document the axiom those who have the power to define have the power. They can define integrity so that it suits the interests of their organizations. What happened in Las Vegas refutes them. Those stories redefine the way the conflict with Las Vegas has been portrayed by the corporate sports monopolies. The "Fix," the Amateur Sports Integrity Act, the Final Four, Dancing with the NBA, and "After further review..." "...tell it like it is."[123]

If the NCAA had its way, the Association would have abolished the legal business in Las Vegas. The organization argued that sports transactions compromise the integrity of its games, yet "The Fix" documented that people who run the NCAA lacked the integrity to set standards that would have precluded all coaches from "throwing" games." After "The Fix," they lacked the integrity to reprimand the coach and apologize to their fans. Perhaps they thought it would not matter to the people who had paid for a product the NCAA did not deliver.

People in the business in Las Vegas swallowed what happened to them without a challenge to the system. Politics made it easier for people in the business to "Shut up, rather than put up." What happened here stayed here.

Politics determined why it stayed here. People in the business in Nevada chose the politics of the sounds of silence to "telling the world what had happened in Las Vegas." Instead of a challenge to the NCAA for its compromise of the integrity of our game,

---

[122] I made "investments" for Sam during his 90th decade of life. He made them from a hospice in Las Vegas to a phone room at a Las Vegas sportsbook.
[123] Thank you, Howard.

Nevada let it slide. They compromised the patent right of the business by turning a cheek.

Their silence had consequences. It led to further action by the NCAA to end the business. After the "kick below the belt," the NCAA enlisted the political support of Senator McCain who had been the beneficiary of gratuities provided by Las Vegas casino corporations for his play at their craps tables.

He returned the favors from the casino corporations through his sponsorship of the Amateur Sports Integrity Act. ASIA could have led to the end of casino sportsbooks. The Legislation would have also helped the NCAA dodge the need to require coaches to report injuries and suspensions. If there was no legal business, who would care about those reports?

The failure to enact Asia had consequences for the NCAA. Casino corporations were able to exploit the victory with control over their product in Las Vegas. The sportsbook industry returned the low blow from "The Fix." While Las Vegas casinos were prohibited from using the terminology "Road to the Final Four" and "Big Dance," the city carved its own road to business from those patent rights.

Then Las Vegas became the City of choice for Conference Tournaments. Tournament games were played in casino arenas with sportsbooks around the corner. They silenced what was left of the argument by the NCAA that the business compromised the integrity of the games. Only in Las Vegas could people wager on a game at a sportsbook owned by a casino that also owned the auditorium where they would watch the game. This tale stamped the imprimatur of the integrity of the business on the integrity of the game.

However, the tale of dancing with the Stars of the NBA also failed to make the neon that lights the Strip. Lack of integrity impaired the performances of both sides of this conflict.

Compromises by the Nevada Gaming Control Board with the integrity of its game allowed the Commissioner of the NBA to impose his prohibition of transactions into Las Vegas sportsbooks. The Commissioner left the politicians in Nevada with the ultimatum take it or we will leave it. Las Vegas politicians chose to have the NBA games played in the city rather than defend the patent right of its product.

Politicians tried to have their cake and eat it too. Cave into the NBA demands to prohibit transactions on games played in Las Vegas with the hope that the city might secure a franchise. People outside the business coerced people who owned the business to bend over backwards to meet demands that led to nothing except the exposure of their lack of integrity.

Owners of casinos who also owned NBA franchises added to the tales of hypocrisy. They sacrificed the integrity of the business at their sportsbooks with their acceptance of the prohibition of wagers on their teams. Their desire to purchase a team prevailed over the integrity of business at their casino. Owners sold out to the argument that appearances defined by the NBA dictated that their sportsbooks could not accept transactions on the teams they owned.

A change in the economic climate for the NBA has backed the Commissioner into a position where he has had to face the reality that legal transactions on NBA are here to stay. He has been forced to acknowledge that legal business might be extended beyond Nevada. Mr. Stern might then have to do what he failed to do in Las Vegas. The NBA might have to make a deal with the business to use their product in exchange for residuals.

Changes in the economic climate will not likely lead to compromises by the NFL to its opposition to the business. The business in Las Vegas might not be able to add enough to the bottom line of the NFL that would warrant any compromise by the monopoly whose interests are protected by Congress.

At one time people in the business in Las Vegas might have had a chance to work out a deal. They failed to exploit the help they provided to the League. At a time when Las Vegas was the "sports betting capital of the world," NFL Security would call the sportsbooks for reassurances about the integrity of their games. Sportsbooks provided them with information about movement on the pointspreads.

Las Vegas kept that happening here. When the NFL no longer needed Las Vegas for that information, they joined with the other sports leagues in their attempt to prohibit the industry through the Professional and Amateur Sports Protection Act, the Amateur Sports Integrity Act, and legislation that would prohibit sports transactions via the Internet.

The NFL also attempted to keep what happens here with restrictions on advertisements for the city on commercials for the Big Game. That offensive was sacked by the economy. Lack of sponsors opened the door to tidbits of information about Las Vegas that could be leaked by the commercials. If that is all the business can extract from the League in an economic depression, there is little hope for a "deal" between the exploiters of each other's products.

These tales from the city shed light on the dilemma for the people in the profession. Compromises made by "owners" of their profession with those who have tried to prohibit the profession led to legal segregation of people in the business.

While Las Vegas has shed its neon on this picture, there is more to the picture than meets the eye. What happened in Las Vegas could only happen in America.

CHAPTER FOUR

SANCTUARIES

Location, location, location...
Homes beyond THE HOME

There are pockets of legal freedom for people in the business beyond the borders of Nevada. There are bastions of freedom for the legal business beyond the borders of America.

The "Grandfathers"

While the business industry in Nevada could serve as a model for other states, no other State can implement that system. While Nevada has established its constitutional right to regulate the business, other states have been denied that right by the federal government. Those states do not have the last word on this matter.

The Professional and Amateur Sports Protection Act (PASPA), also known as the "Bradley Bill,"[124] has the last word. Since 1992, PASPA has been the final word to dictate what states can do about the legalization of the business. This legislation confers that power on the federal government. A "grandfather" clause in PASPA grants the right to implement the business to Nevada, Delaware, Montana, and Oregon. Those states had legal systems in place before the

---

[124] Former Senator Bill Bradley (D) New Jersey sponsored the legislation hence the moniker.

federal legislation was enacted. The other forty-six states are prohibited from the legalization of the business within their states.

States that were "grandfathered" are restricted to the implementation of the systems that were in place before PASPA was enacted. Since no state had a system in place similar to the business in Nevada, they cannot replicate the sportsbook industry as it is in Nevada.

Delaware, Montana, and Oregon cannot establish a system in which sports transactions can be made on single events. That legal wager can only be made at Nevada sportsbooks. "Straight" bets[125] are prohibited because these "grandfathers" had not included them in their systems before PASPA was enacted.

Delaware had implemented a sports pool in 1975. This lottery system known as "Scoreboard" was restricted to transactions on the National Football League. This lottery offered customers the option to make transactions "Football Bonus," "Touchdown," and "Touchdown II. Transactions could be made at the 150 lottery outlets throughout the state.

"Football Bonus" divided fourteen NFL games into two pools of seven games. Players had to pick winners of all seven games in either or both pools in order to win. If a customer picked seven winners in both pools that player would win the "All Game Bonus." Wagers on those games ranged from one to ten dollars.

"Touchdown" transactions could be made on fourteen NFL games with three ranges of point spreads. Players could pick three, four, or five games, but also had to select the margin of victory on those games.

"Touchdown II" was introduced in mid-season to replace "Touchdown." One pointspread for twelve NFL

---

[125] Wagers on single games are also known as straight bets. It is the transaction that defines the industry.

games was published on Wednesday. Customers could play a minimum of four to a maximum of twelve games against that spread. Payouts ranged from $10 to $1,200. Consolation prizes were awarded to those who picked winners of nine out of ten, ten out of eleven, or eleven out of twelve games.

Unlike the payouts for parlays that are posted at Nevada sportsbooks, the lottery payouts were based on how much was in the pool after the state took its share of the money. Payouts to the winners were made from the amount of money that was left. That amount was apportioned according to the number of winners for the various games. This was a pari-mutuel system in the context of the state lottery.

Team names were listed by city alone. Names such as "the Bears" did not accompany the name Chicago. Delaware avoided a conflict with the NFL over patent rights to the nicknames of their teams. This endeavor that began in September was cancelled in December because pointspreads for two games in "Touchdown II" were as much as nine and half points "off" the Las Vegas line. There was no explanation for the discrepancy. Transactions that had amounted to $25,000 for the previous two weeks had risen into hundreds of thousands of dollars that week because of the "wrong" lines for these games. Those wagers were refunded.

Even though the sports lottery was cancelled, the NFL filed a lawsuit the next year to contest the legality of the system. The NFL argued that betting on sports is a game of skill, not the game of chance that was permitted by the Delaware Constitution. The NFL anointed itself as the power to define games of skill and chance. Lawyers for the League argued that the Constitution prohibited wagers on games of skill such as sports. According to the NFL, sports betting could not be part of the lottery because the Constitution allowed wagers only on games of chance.

In 1977, a Federal Appeals Court ruled in favor of the Delaware sports lottery. With qualifications, the Court concluded that parlay wagers were endeavors of chance, not skill. The system in Delaware was declared legal even though the sports lottery was no longer offered as an option to bettors.

The issue remained dormant until 2007 when another economic recession prompted Delaware to explore additional sources of revenue. Sports transactions resurfaced as one of the options. This time the state incorporated the experience from the experiment that failed in 1975 to rectify errors that were part of that system. Lottery officials decided to use a system of parlay wagers based on stated odds. Instead of payouts from a pari-mutuel pool, customers would win payouts that were advertised, as they are in Las Vegas. Those in charge knew that a lottery system based on pari-mutuel payoffs could not stimulate the level of interest that was necessary to generate the revenue needed to help the state.

In addition to parlay wagers based on stated odds, the state added straight wagers as another option for customers. All of those wagers would be made at three race tracks in Delaware instead of with lottery agents. Opposition by race track owners to the competition they expected from sports transactions ended after surrounding states with race tracks added the option of slot machines for those who wagered on horses. That option was prohibited in Delaware. In order to remain competitive, Delaware race track owners accepted sports wagers as an option on their premises.

Opponents of sports transactions formed an alliance to fight this system. They filed a lawsuit that argued football was a game that required speed, skill, and strength. According to them, football was not the game of chance that was authorized by the Constitution of Delaware. This argument was rejected by the Delaware Supreme Court. The Court decided that the sports lottery was a game of chance. Wagers on football were protected by the state constitution. "...the Delaware Constitution authorizes not only games of pure chance, but also games in which chance is the dominant factor."[126]

The Supreme Court incorporated the conclusion of a Federal judge in the litigation that took place in 1977. That judge had said that lotteries were not restricted to games of pure chance. "An element of calculation or even certainty" could be involved as long as chance was the dominant factor.[127] However, the justices added that although parlay bets were constitutional, they did not have the evidence to "opine on the constitutionality of single game bets.[128] Despite the fact that the Court took a pass on the issue of straight bets, Delaware Governor Markell said, "With this guidance in hand we are moving forward with implementing a successful sports lottery in Delaware."

Opponents of sports transactions decided to take advantage of the door left open by the Court to file a lawsuit against the state in Federal District Court. They argued that the state plan "would irreparably harm professional and amateur sports by fostering suspicion and skepticism that individual plays and final scores of games may have been influenced by factors other than honest athletic competition."[129]

The plaintiffs added that because single game bets were not offered by the state in 1976, PASPA would prohibit that option. The intentions of the opponents went beyond those specifics. "The intention was all along that we wanted to stop further spread of legalized gambling on our games," said Brian

---

[126] *Delaware State News* May 29, 2009, "High Court Ok makes way for sports lottery..." article by Leah Burcat, p.1
[127] Ibid
[128] Ibid
[129] *Delaware State News* July 25, 2009 "Pro leagues, NCAA sue Del. Over betting..." article by Leah Burcat, p.1

McCarthy, Vice President of Communications for the NFL.[130]

One day after a federal judge denied an appeal to stop the State from its plan to offer wagers on single games until the lawsuit from the plaintiffs had been decided, the NCAA pursued another course of action. They announced that no playoff games would be permitted in states that allowed bets on single games.[131]

That announcement did not deter the State, but prior to the start of the 2009 NFL season the U.S. Court of Appeals did halt one aspect of the endeavor. The Court ruled that the Delaware sports lottery would have to be restricted to parlay bets of at least three games. Transactions on single games would be prohibited. "Because single game wagering was not "conducted" by Delaware between 1976 and 1990, such betting is beyond the scope of the exception in (the federal law) and thus prohibited under the statute's plain language," said Judge Thomas Hardiman.

The judgment restricted Delaware to parlay wagers. The verdict allowed the state to proceed with parlays that had stated payouts. Those transactions could be made at the three race tracks in Delaware instead of with lottery agents.

Delaware implemented an endeavor that began in 1976. This outcome was different from the fight between Nevada and the opponents of sports transactions. That conflict ended with a TKO victory for the State. The contest in Delaware ended in a TKO victory for the opponents after the U.S Supreme Court decided to let stand the decision by the Appeals Court

---

[130] Ibid, p.2

[131] *Delaware State News* August 7, 2009 "NCAA bans playoff games in Delaware," p.1

that expansion of the business to straight wagers would violate the restriction of PASPA.

That decision would not have an impact on the contest between Montana and the coalition opposed to sports transactions. The Montana Constitution authorized the legislature to control the manner in which people could gamble. The legislature passed the Sports Pool Act in 1973. Title 23, Chapter 5, of the Montana Code describes the games that are authorized and the rules for them.

Article 23-5-806 of the Code prohibits "...betting or wagering on the outcome of an individual sports event." Other Articles authorize sports pools, fantasy sports leagues, Calcutta pools,[132] and sports tabs.[133]

None of the professional sports leagues contested this system. It bore little resemblance to the systems in Nevada or Delaware. They decided a court fight over these games was not worth the effort.

The NCAA was the only opponent of the business to contest the system. They decided to extend the prohibition on playoff games to Montana. They would treat Montana the same as Delaware. Universities in Montana would not be able to host playoff games as they had in the past.

The NCAA rescinded this decision after Montana argued that state law prohibited wagers on single games and restricted sports betting to fantasy leagues. The NCAA said in response, "No predetermined or non-predetermined session of an NCAA championship may be conducted in a state with legal wagering that is based upon single-game betting...in which the NCAA conducts a championship."[134]

---

[132] A bet in which an auction is held before a sporting event. Bettors can bid against each other for the right to bet on a particular player such as a golfer.

[133] A game card with numbers that match the final score for a winning team.

[134] *Associated Press* August 7, 2009 "NCAA clarifies sports betting policy. Montana schools OK to host playoff games.

Delaware and Montana were spared from the blow delivered to Nevada. Montana politicians expressed gratitude. "I applaud the NCAA for coming to a common sense conclusion that preserves Montana's right to host playoff and tournament games..." said Montana Attorney General Steve Bullock. He added, "Along with the NCAA, we remain committed to protecting the integrity of college sports."[135]

His statement about the integrity of the game is affirmation for the adage "the more things change, the more they remain the same." Oregon added another twist to the adage. Unlike Montana, the system in Oregon met with opposition from all the usual opponents. The corporate sports monopolies united in their opposition to Sports Action, a game that was included in the State Lottery in 1989.

Sports Action offered sports bettors the option to wager from $2 to $20 on a minimum of three teams. Three team parlays paid $10 for a $2 wager. Four team parlays paid $20 for $2. Parlays of five teams or more were paid from a pari-mutuel pool in which 60% of the total amount available would be shared by the winners.

Wagers on Sports Action were limited to NFL games. Lottery officials added the game to the lottery despite the threat of a lawsuit from the League. "We didn't come out here to threaten anyone, but there are some very viable legal issues here that we're going to evaluate," said James Noel, NFL Assistant Counsel to the Lottery Commission before they approved the game.[136]

He voiced a theme heard before. The Lottery game was "a genuine threat to the integrity of our sport." He added the twist that "...the entire nation is watching.

---

[135] Ibid

[136] *New York Times* July 18, 1989 article by Frank Litsky "Oregon Lottery Unit Creates Weekly N.F.L. Betting Plan," p.1

Lottery officials in other states have publicly stated that if Oregon does this successfully, they will try it too."[137]

The NFL only had those words to oppose the Lottery. Oregon had learned from the experience with Delaware how to avoid patent rights and trademark conflicts with the League. The Lottery did not use NFL nicknames.

In addition, the Oregon Constitution had granted the legislature the right to establish lottery games. This deterred the NFL from a lawsuit similar to the one they had lost in Delaware. A state's right would likely prevail in Oregon as it had in Delaware.

Sports Action generated $7.2 million in sales during the first year. $2.6 million of that amount was profit that the state distributed to academic institutions. Encouraged by those results, the state decided to add NBA games the following year. The Portland Trailblazers would be excluded from the Lottery as a courtesy gesture to the franchise.

Nevertheless, the NBA responded with a lawsuit to prevent the use of their league product. NBA officials argued that Sports Action would violate federal anti-gambling statutes and the Oregon Constitution. They added that pointspread wagers were an exploitation of property rights and an infringement on the trademark of the NBA and its teams.

The lawsuit was dropped after Oregon made a decision to discontinue wagers on NBA games. Ticket sales that had dropped to $35,000 during one week led to the decision. As part of the settlement, Lottery officials agreed to end wagers on NBA games for at least five years.

In the midst of this controversy with the NBA, the state survived another challenge to Sports Action from the federal government. Since Sports Action had been

---

[137] Ibid

implemented in 1989, PASPA which was passed in 1992 "grandfathered" this game as an exception to the prohibition on sports transactions; however, PASPA did have an impact on what appeared to be an agreement between Oregon and the Grand Ronde Indian tribe to allow sports transactions at their Spirit Mountain Casino. After PASPA was passed, State officials decided the State did not have the authority to authorize the business at Indian casinos. That left the Grand Ronde tribe with the option to contest the PASPA legislation. Grand Ronde decided a fight with the federal government over the legality of sports transactions at their casino was not worth the effort.

In spite of the fact that Sports Action game generated almost $25 million in revenue for the State, the legislature decided to end the game at the end of the 2006-7 NFL season. While the revenue from Sports Action had been sufficient to continue the game for almost twenty years, a coalition of state administrators and legislators decided enough was enough.

In their estimation, the potential benefits from a performance of the Big Dance at the Rose Garden in Portland would outweigh the revenue generated by Sports Action. Just in case those revenues did not compensate for the loss of revenue from Sports Action, legislators added one percent of the total lottery proceeds to replace the revenue from Sports Action. That money enlisted the added support of the universities who were the beneficiaries of the revenue from Sports Action.

Sports Action became expendable despite the fact that the game had proven its worth to the State. The conflict over Sports Action is a tale that could have been a topic for round table discussions on both news and sports networks. Those round tables could shed light on the big picture of the business in America. These round tables might not be suitable for networks that televise professional and amateur sports.

A promo for the show that features people in the business who either participated in Sports Action or had opinions about it would help explain why.

"I don't bet on anything else," said Darin Frazier, a construction inspector who went to Tom's Pizza every week to play Sports Action. "I don't play poker or slots. I like football."[138]

"Because of Sports Action, people will be able to go to their local Safeway and buy a quart of milk, a loaf of bread and the Seattle Seahawks minus two and a half," James Noel, an assistant counsel for the NFL responded.[139]

"There were days I walked in here in my slippers and pajamas just to get my bets in," said John Hardy an electrical contractor who bet at Tom's in North Portland.[140]

"Getting rid of Sports Action was worth it. Okay, maybe not to the chain smokers who hang out in the neighborhood lounge, filling out their tickets. But to the rest of us, and for this region, and for the teams and local businesses, the NCAA Tournament was a big win," said John Canzano, an editorial contributor to *The Oregonian* newspaper.[141]

"...even...small action Sports Action fans are disappointed to lose a weekly pleasure available statewide "just to promote one week of tourism" in Portland," said Dale Scharette, Manager of the state's top Sports Action retailer.[142]

"That argument misses a few points, not the least of which is the pernicious influence of sports betting

---

[138] *The Oregonion* January 28, 2007 article by Rachel Bachman "Fans rue Sports Action's passing," p.1

[139] *New York Times* July 18, 1989 article by Frank Litsky "Oregon Lottery Unit Creates Weekly Betting Plan," p.1

[140] *The Oregonion* January 28, 2007 article by Rachel Bachman "Fans rue Sports Action's passing," p.1

[141] *The Oregonion* March 22, 2009 editorial "That was great--let's do it again."

[142] *The Oregonion* January 28, 2007 article by Rachel Bachman "Fans rue Sports Action's passing," p.2

on college athletics," said an editor of *The Oregonian*.[143]

"The whole idea that we need to be protected from ourselves is ridiculous," said Jim Maas, a supporter of Sports Action.[144]

"Over the years, the most serious scandals involving college basketball have revolved around point shaving. Oregon allows the kind of sports betting that enables this kind of cheating," said an editor of *The Oregonian*.[145]

"But isn't Sports Action limited to the NFL?" the moderator could have asked.

"March Madness would mean far more to Oregon than preserving a couple of marginal lottery games," said the editor.[146]

Drew Mahalic, Chief Executive Officer of the Oregon Sports Authority added, "The East Bank Saloon in southeast Portland had a boost in sales during the Tournament. That's pretty typical of the kind of business that the basketball tournament brings to the hotels, the restaurants, the retail stores." He projected benefits to reach $10 million.[147]

But Tom Cody, owner of Tom's Pizza, estimated he would lose 20 percent of his Sunday business, especially the few dozen guys who come in early and eat breakfast while mulling over their bets.[148]

Robert Whelan, an economist with ECON Northwest consulting firm added, "Most of that $10 million would go the national headquarters of Marriott,

[143] *The Oregonion* March 19 2009 editorial "Welcome back to Oregon, March Madness, p.1

[144] *The Oregonion* October 23, 2007, Letters to the Editor "Bring back sports betting."

[145] *The Oregonion* May 16, 2005 Editorial "Bidding on March Madness..."

[146] Ibid

[147] *The Oregonion* January 28, 2007 article by Mike Tokito "March madness coming back," p.1

[148] *The Oregonion* September 22, 2009 article by Rachel Bachman "Fans rue Sports Action's passing," p.3

Hilton, and other hotel chains. Talking about doing away with Sports Action, he said, "It was stupid. I don't think it's going to be a net positive."[149]

"It was a game that really did a disservice in its philosophy of gambling on sports to raise money for sports. Its demise is a benefit just because Oregon is now eligible for the NCAA tournament, but I think it's healthier, really, for the whole state," said Drew Mahalic.[150]

"It didn't bring in huge numbers, but it was a loyal player base," Lottery spokeswoman Mary Loftin said about Sports Action. "It was a very different environment and community that Sports Action created."[151]

Paul Roshak might have the last word. Dressed in a Chicago Bears jersey with the name Brian Urlacher on the back, he rued the end of Sports Action. He reminisced about the followers he attracted after he won $1,000 the previous week.

A dozen followers mimicked his parlay the next week, a bet that hinged on the Steelers covering a four-and-half-point spread. The Steelers were ahead by three points late in the game. A turnover by the Bengals' quarterback led to a safety. The Steelers won by five points. The mistake by the quarterback "turned the bettors into leaping, screaming thousandaries," he said.[152]

The moderator might have added that bettors such as Paul Roshak would have to make illegal wagers in order to continue to make sports transactions. They no longer had the option to do what they did legally. That right granted to them by the

---

[149] *The Oregonion February 26,* 2009 article by John Hunt "Betting on March Madness Payoff," pp.1-2

[150] Ibid, p.2

[151] Ibid

[152] *The Oregonion* January 28, 2007 article by Rachel Bachman "Fans rue Sports Action's passing," p.2

state could be rescinded without their input because business is business.

At the conclusion of the promo, viewers might have been enticed to speculate about how a right that was granted by the Oregon Constitution to "the People, a/k/a sports bettors" could be taken away by a coalition of interests that included the NFL, NBA, NCAA, the Oregon Sports Authority, the Oregon Legislature and the Governor, and other economic organizations.

"What are the odds that 'the constitutional rights of the people' could beat that coalition?" the viewers might have speculated. Whatever those odds might be, they would be similar to those for people who want to make sports transactions in states that weren't grandfathered.

The Other 46, Canada and Mexico

PASPA rescinded the right of the other states to decide whether to legalize the business. PASPA could not control the big picture of the economic environment for these states. An economic recession opened the door to possibilities for the legalization of the business. The recession created a climate in which proponents of the business had the chance to make their case.

Eighteen years after PASPA was enacted, Iowa Senate President Jack Kibble sponsored legislation that would legalize betting on professional sports. He argued that Iowa could generate millions in revenue from the legalization of sports betting.[153] There was support for his legislation from Senator Bill Dotzier. He said, "The people that do sports betting, they're doing

---

[153] *USA Today* February 4, 2010 article by Jennifer Jacobs, "Iowa lawmakers back bill for pro sports gambling" from the *Des Moines Register,* p.1

it now on the Internet and there's a lot of it going on underground. I think this is a way of controlling it."[154]

Senator Jerry Behn opposed the legislation. He said, "Gambling in general is...a tax on the people who can afford it the least..."[155]

Lisa Pierce, Director of Central Iowa Gambling Treatment Program Inc. supported him. She said, "The more access we have to the different forms (of gambling) the worse the problem."[156]

The Senate State Government Committee voted 10-5 to approve legislation that would authorize gaming regulators to allow sports bets at racetracks and riverboat casinos. Even if they are able to pass the legislation, supporters admit that its implementation would be contingent on the repeal of PASPA.

Proposals to support the legalization of the business were also made in New Jersey. State legislators initiated efforts to reestablish the right to the business that had been "grandfathered" by PASPA. That legislation had established a deadline for the state to meet in order to implement its legal system. After that deadline passed without action by the legislature, New Jersey joined the other 45. All forms of sports transactions became illegal by federal law.

A decline in revenue from casinos due to the economic recession rekindled interest in the legalization of the business. In 2008, State Senator Raymond Lesniak urged then Governor Jon Corzine to file a lawsuit to overturn the federal prohibition. "If he chooses not to take up this cause, I will file suit myself on behalf of plaintiffs with standing to challenge the federal law," the Senator said.[157] He introduced Senate Resolution No.19. This Resolution authorized the

---

[154] Ibid
[155] Ibid
[156] Ibid
[157] *The Star-Ledger,* May 19, 2008 "NJ lawmaker seeks repeal of U.S. ban on sports betting" article by Carly Rothman, p.1

President of the Senate (Senator Lesniak) to take whatever legal steps are necessary to overturn the restriction of PASPA.

A Senate Committee held hearings on a proposal for a public referendum on the legalization of sports transactions. The Referendum would become part of the November 2010 elections. A vote in favor would amend the New Jersey Constitution. The business would become legal at the eleven casinos in Atlantic City, at race tracks, and over the Internet.

The NFL opposed the proposal. A spokesman for the League argued that gambling on the NFL games could undermine their integrity."[158]

Senator Lesniak said in response, "Gaming and the NFL—perfect together."[159]

The Bill to authorize the 2010 November referendum cleared a Senate committee. It awaits action by the Legislature.

A politician in the State of Washington also voiced his support for the legalization of the business. A bill was introduced by State Representative Marko Lilas that would allow bettors to pick squares on board games for events such as the Super Bowl. A player would win if the numbers on the squares matched a final score.

This legislation would also allow bettors to enter bracket pools for the NCAA Tournament and to wager on fantasy leagues. The maximum payout would be $100. Payouts of more than $100 would be illegal.

"We're just trying to let the little guy do the office pool and let people like me bet on Georgetown without fear of breaking the law," Representative Lilas said. He added, "I think that when our laws don't recognize reality, it makes our legal process a joke to the citizens. This bill fixes this single little problem and

---

[158] *New York Post* April 13, 2010 "Bettor Believe It" article by Wayne Parry, p.1
[159] Ibid

sets some simple limits on it,"[160] His proposal is on the agenda of the Senate Committee.

The status of legal sports betting in the other states can be summarized:

Legal sports transactions in New York are restricted to fantasy pools and wagers with pari-mutuel payoffs.

Kentucky abandoned SuperSports, a lottery game that would have allowed wagers on the NFL. Even though the Kentucky Supreme Court lifted an injunction that would allow the game to become part of the lottery, the Governor declared the proposal a bad idea after the horse racing industry expressed opposition.

California Governor Arnold Schwarzenegger signed a bill that would reduce penalties for participation in sports pools on events such as March Madness and the Super Bowl. What had been either a felony or a misdemeanor was reduced to a maximum penalty of $250. Sports pools with payoffs more than $2,500 and online pools were excluded from the Bill. This legislation was passed after a grandmother in her 70s was arrested because she ran a $50 pool at an Elks Lodge.

The Attorney General of Florida declared that Section 849.14 of the State gambling law prohibits the operation and participation in a fantasy sports league whereby contestants pay an entry fee. "I am of the opinion that the operation of a fantasy sports league...would violate...[that statute]."

The proposal to include sports transactions as part of the Illinois lottery met with opposition from the professional sports teams based in the state. That opposition helped to shelve the lottery proposal as well

---

[160] *Herald Net* February 1, 2010 "Legalize low-stakes sports betting..." article by Jerry Cornfield, p.1

as the consideration of the addition of sports transactions as an option at riverboat casinos.

The other states will have to wait in order to reclaim their state's right to make the decision on whether or not to legalize the business. They would be the beneficiaries of the efforts undertaken by the states in the forefront of the battle to return that right to the states.

Canada and Mexico

The professional sports leagues cannot use their leverage in PASPA to control sports transaction on their games in other nations. Borders impose an additional restriction on the NCAA. This monopoly is unable to use leverage they have in America to grant sites for football playoff games and basketball tournament games to states that prohibit wagers on their games.

However, there is no need for these leagues to exercise their power in Canada. The Canadian Parliament enacted legislation that prohibits wagers on single games. "Straight" bets are illegal.

Part VII of the Canadian Criminal Code prohibits a "bet." A bet is defined as one "that is placed on any contingency or event that is to take place in or out of Canada and without restricting the generality of the foregoing, includes a bet that is placed on any contingency relating to a horse race, fight, match, or sporting event that is to take place in or out of Canada."

Consequences of the economic recession generated opposition to this restriction. Revenues dropped for the Province of Ontario from casinos in Niagara Falls and Windsor. Sports transactions became part of a plan by legislators to offset the revenues that had been lost.

Sportsbooks in those casinos cannot offer the option of straight bets. Transactions are limited to the government lottery game, Action Sports. This game offers the option to pick three or more games on a parlay ticket. In order to expand sports transactions beyond parlay wagers, the Canadian Criminal Code would have to be amended.

A member of the Canadian Parliament (MP) addressed that possibility. Mr. Joe Cromartin proposed an amendment to the Criminal Code that would allow straight bets because, according to him, "...[sports betting] would do is generate traffic into the casino for the particular type of betting and then you also pick up additional business." He said that sports betting would give the casinos "a major competitive advantage "since it (sports betting) is not allowed in Michigan or New York."[161]

MP Tim Hudad supported him. He said, "...a properly regulated, trusted and professional sportsbook would help reduce the growing illegal sports betting taking place in Ontario by Ontario residents on off shore and unregulated internet sites."[162] This proposal would extend the option of sports transactions to racetracks in Canada such as the track at Woodbine in Ontario.

While there was support for the proposal at the provincial and national levels of Canadian government in 2008, no action has been taken. Two years after Mr. Cromartin raised the issue his proposal had not extended beyond the level of a matter for discussion at the International Masters of Gaming Law, a Canadian Summit.

Lack of progress defies the groundwork that had led to his legislation. Two Canadian Provinces had

---

[161] thestar.com July 3, 2008 "Casinos eye sports betting" Robert Benzie and Richard Brennan pp. 2-3
[162] Ibid

resolved a dispute with the NBA that might have been a deterrent to the proposal from Mr. Cromartin.

Before the Vancouver Grizzlies and the Toronto Raptors could begin play in the 1995-6 season, the Provinces of British Columbia and Ontario were asked to comply with a demand from NBA Commissioner David Stern that the NBA be kept off the lottery game Sports Action.

There was opposition from the public to a demand by this foreign corporation. The NBA ignored the fact that part of the $1.56 million wagered on the NBA in 1993 was dedicated to health care services in British Columbia.

Opposition to the request by Commissioner Stern led to an agreement between owners of the Grizzlies and the Prime Minister of British Columbia. Owners of the Grizzlies agreed to contribute $500,000 to the Province, half of which was allocated to health care and the other half to a hospice for children. In return, the NBA would not appear on Sports Action in British Columbia.

The Province of Ontario reached a similar accord with the NBA. Owners of the Toronto Raptors agreed to pay millions of dollars each year to a charitable fund and to the lottery corporation to compensate the Province for the loss of revenue that would accompany the absence of the NBA from the lottery.

The NBA exercised clout with wagers on their games Canada's pastime could not match. None of the NHL teams receive a portion of the profit from wagers on their teams through Sports Action. A complaint about this lack of compensation for the League was backed with documentation to show that the Provinces lost more than $100 million in revenue during the NHL lockout in 2004-5. Despite this fact, the Provinces rejected the request to share profits with the League.

Resolution of these conflicts with the NBA and NHL should have paved the way for the consideration of the proposal to legalize sports betting; however, the NFL had the clout to delay a vote. The League decided to "test the waters" for expansion into Canada with regular season games.

MP Cromartin said he would be pleased if the legalization of sports betting in Canada would keep the NFL out of Canada. "I'm on the side that's opposed to having the NFL in Canada. I think it would be the death knell of the Canadian Football League (CFL) and I'm strongly in favor of keeping the NFL out. The eight teams we've got across the country have a more substantial value, economically and culturally, than one or two or three NFL teams would have."[163]

Despite that opposition, regular season home games for the Buffalo Bills and other NFL teams have been played in Toronto a short distance from Windsor—the area Mr. Cromartin represents. Even though additional games are scheduled for Toronto, the NFL has not raised objections to the inclusion of those games on the Sports Select lottery game. The issue would become part of the negotiations on whether to move an NFL franchise into Canada. The inclusion of the Toronto Blue Jays on Sports Select has not led to action by MLB that would keep baseball off the lottery game.

Conflicts between U.S. corporate sports mono-polies and those who are interested in the business in Canada have not crossed the border into Mexico. Unlike the U.S and Canada, Mexico legalized sports-books. The sports leagues would have to negotiate prohibitions on wagers with the Federal Government of Mexico.

None of the Leagues have teams based in Mexico. Although regular and preseason NFL, NBA, and MLB games have been played there, single games have not

---

[163] The globe and mail.com July 30, 2008 "Canada hopes betting bill keeps NFL out."

been worth a fight similar to the one that took place in Nevada. Objections from the Leagues to wagers on those games would confront two legal options for that have been made available by the federal government.

Pro-Touch is one option. This is a lottery game operated by the federal government. Transactions are made at Pronosticos lottery windows throughout Mexico. A $1 investment entitles the customer to a chance to win a $150,000 jackpot. This jackpot grows if no one is able to predict the outcome of fourteen NFL games.

Another option became available in 1989 when the national government granted permission to the Caliente Group to offer the option of sports transactions at their race wagering sites. The sports-books offer the option of a straight wager on all U.S. amateur and professional sports leagues.

Wagers cannot be made from the U.S. by phone or via the Internet; however, sportsbooks are located where commuters from Arizona, California, and Texas would find options that are similar to those offered in Nevada.

None of the sports leagues have asked the U.S. government to employ border patrol guards to document American illegal sports-bettors who return from Mexico after they make wagers. Those illegals were able to cross the border to wager on the regular season NFL game between the Arizona Cardinals and the San Francisco 49ers played in 1996 in Mexico City. They were also able to cross the border to wager on the regular season NBA game between the Houston Rockets and the Dallas Mavericks played in Mexico City in 1997.

Nevada could only wish to have had this freedom from harassment by the corporate sports monopolies. On this issue there is greater "freedom" in Mexico than there is in America. Location, location, location...

Across the Atlantic

Even the approximation of the industry in England would be "a dream come true" for the profession in America. But even that dream world for people in the profession in England turned into a nightmare when the tentacles of corporate imperialism were extended from America across the Atlantic.

After the NFL decided to play regular season games at Wembley Stadium in London, the League exercised clout that had never been exercised by Soccer Leagues who also play their games at the Stadium. Supposedly, soccer is the most important business for the sportsbooks in England, yet the NFL was able to exercise its imperial power over England on wagers on NFL games that would be played at Wembley Stadium in London. The NFL requested that the forty to fifty outlets for wagers within the stadium be closed on the days that NFL games were played there.

Organizers who had brought the Miami Dolphins-New York Giants game to Wembley in 2007 agreed to close those bet shops within Wembley for that game, as well as for the other NFL games that would follow. Those who attended the game and also wanted to wager on it had to make their transactions at Betfred shops around the Stadium not inside. Members of the profession had never before been prohibited from doing business inside Wembley on Premier Soccer League games that were played there.

Prior to the game between the Dolphins and Giants, NFL spokesman Gary Aiello expressed the position of the League. "We requested and were granted a restriction on gambling at the Stadium.

There will be no onsite betting facility. Those will not be operating the day of the game."[164]

The League did not request that wagers on this game be prohibited at the other betting shops in England. "We did not think that was necessary or appropriate. Those are legal operations," Mr. Aiello said.[165]

When asked about a comparison of this demand with the demands made on the Las Vegas sportsbooks, Mr. Aiello said, "This has nothing to do with Las Vegas. We can't control where there's legalized gambling. There's legal gambling in other places near where we play games."[166] No reporter followed up with a question that would clarify what he meant about control, legalized gambling, and other places close to where they play games.

Several years later, State Senator Raymond Lesniak of New Jersey challenged Mr. Aiello. Senator Lesniak said, "When Manchester United plays at Wembley Stadium, London in the Premier League, the second most successful League in the world, fans can place a bet on either team right at the stadium. When the 49ers take on the Broncos at Wembley Stadium on October 31st of this year (2010), the fans will not be able to place a bet at the stadium because the National Football League, to protect the integrity of its sport, will not allow the betting windows to open..."

The profession in England was exposed to a sample of the power behind the illogic of the opponents of the business in America with one exception: The NFL did not use the argument of the integrity of their game in England as the reason for the request to prohibit transactions at Wembley.

---

[164] *Las Vegas Review Journal* October 10, 2007 article by Matt Youmans "League Stance Softened with London gambling," p.1
[165] Ibid
[166] Associated Press article 10/24/2007 "Betting on the NFL in London, a sure thing"

That argument would have even been beyond the limits for the British comedy group "Beyond the Fringe," a group that had no limits for satire. They would have had a field day with the NFL request in a context in which wagering on soccer and tennis in England remains legal despite the attempts that have been made to bribe players to fix the outcome of games and matches.

The independent bookmaker, Betfair, is the example people in the business could use to show the NFL how to protect the integrity of their games. Two months before the Dolphins and Giants appeared at Wembley Stadium, Betfair took action to address the appearance of a lack of integrity in a tennis match. Betfair refused to pay the winners for wagers they had made on the Nikolay Davydenko vs. Martin Vassallo Arguello tennis match. This match was played at the Polish Open in August 2007. Suspicions were aroused by a pattern of wagers that appeared out of the ordinary. Customers had wagered on Arguello prior to and during the second set, even though he had lost the first set to Davydenko 6-2 and was ranked 87th among the players on the tour. The wagers were in amounts that tipped the betting odds in favor of Arguello. Davydenko had been a prohibitive favorite.

Betfair decided to review the match after Davydenko withdrew in the third set. Wagers had been made through the Betfair in-play system. The system allows players to make transactions while the game is in progress. Betfair became suspicious because more than $7 million was bet on the Davydenko-Arguello match. Wagers on other second round contests averaged $3 million.

A spokesperson said, "Betfair has suspended settlement of the match-odds market on this afternoon's second-round match of the Association of Tennis Professionals (ATP) Orange Prokom Open in Poland between Martin Arguello and Nikolay

Davydenko pending consultation with relevant regulatory authorities." Betfair added, "We are committed to ensuring our sport remains corruption free and have strict rules in place governing this area. We have an integrity and fraud team of more than 40 people."[167]

Bet shops in England are part of a system that is designed to ensure the integrity of the tennis matches on their boards. This system protects the interests of everyone involved. The data analysis that alerted people in the system to patterns of wagers that were suspicious was also used by the Association of Tennis Professionals (ATP) to help them investigate the incident.

Davydenko was cleared of throwing that match after the ATP was unable to review phone records that were withheld and afterwards destroyed. Phone records were necessary to add documentation to the suspicious betting patterns. The suspicious betting pattern included nine Betfair accounts based in Russia that would have won $1.5 million if Davydenko lost. Two additional Betfair account holders would have won close to $6 million. Betfair said the incident "led us to share betting data with the ATP under the rules of the Memorandum of Understanding we have with them." They added that a "joint investigative body with the ITF (International Tennis Federation) and the WTA (World Tennis Association) to deal with issues of this kind should act as a blueprint for all other sports."[168]

After the investigation into this incident, there were ranked players who admitted they had been asked to throw a match. They said they had heard other players had been approached to do the same.

---

[167] *New York Times*, September 12, 2008 article by Joe Drape "Inquiry into Betting Clears Davydenko"

[168] TennisBetSite, August 3, 2007 article from *The Guardian* by Matt Scott "Betfair fixed match," pp. 1-2

The investigation into this tennis match led to the formation of the Tennis Integrity Unit. The Unit was created by tennis organizations to help insure the WTA and ATP Tours, the International Tennis Federation, and the Grand Slam Committee that the games they promote are honest.

These organizations adopted an Anti-Corruption Code that was used by the Tennis Integrity Unit to investigate a tennis match between Caroline Wozniacki and Anne Kremer during the Luxembourg Open in 2009. Wozniacki had withdrawn from that tournament after she had won the first set and was leading in the second 4-1. She said, "I did not think I could play the second round on Thursday, so I chose the sporting option to let her (Kremer) proceed. She is playing at home."[169]

Wozniacki had been a 1-100 favorite to win the match. Her intentions to withdraw were heard in the Polish language on a microphone worn by her father. Viewers who overheard the conversation on a live broadcast of the match on the Internet took the odds against her and wagered on her opponent who was 40 to 1.

The Women's Tennis Association suggested that the Anti-Corruption Unit be included in the investigation of the situation. They said the involvement of the Anti-Corruption Unit was warranted because wagers were made on Kremer after the information about Wozniacki's intention to withdraw was transmitted to bettors.[170]

Betfair did not express concern about the incident because they did not consider the circumstances suspicious. Experiences with other attempts to fix

---

[169] *Daily Telegraph*, October 21, 2009 article by Paul Kelso "Caroline Wozniacki investigated by WTA over withdrawal from match," p.1
[170] Ibid

matches led them to this decision. Wozniacki was not charged with fixing the match.

The Integrity Unit acted on another matter when they fined Ekaterina Bychkova $5,000 and suspended her for 30 days after she failed to report attempts that had been made to obtain inside information on matches.

Sportsbooks were also included in the system that was designed to protect the integrity of soccer matches. In 2006 World Cup organizers used data analysis that was provided by sportsbooks to investigate suspicions that were raised about the integrity of soccer matches. The Federation de Football Association (FIFA) used information that derived from the internet wagering system to assist in their investigation of matches that had been played in Brazil, Italy, and Germany.

An agreement to use the information provided by sportsbooks is part of the FIFA Early Warning System. The word "early" was added to the Warning System in order to emphasize the fact that the Unit would be able to detect problems that might arise while tournaments were in progress. Data from Internet wagering on games in progress would serve as their alert mechanism.

This Early Warning System was used to investigate on a match that appeared suspicious. The sportsbook reported "heavy wagering" on a team that had been behind 2-0 at halftime. That team won the match 5-2.

The sportsbook that reported the suspicious activity remained anonymous. Urs Scherer, Chief Executive of the Early Warning System, said that this secrecy was important, otherwise the system would be rendered "impractical and ineffective" if those bettors who were involved in the fix would know in advance to avoid bookmakers who might report their suspicious activity.[171]

This incident led to the addition of another policy that would be included in the Early Warning System. The assignment of referees would be delayed until two days before kickoff. All referees would be required to stay at the same hotel. These measures were added to one that requires referees, players, coaches, and their families to sign a declaration that they would not bet on World Cup matches.

The System would allow FIFA to take action before rather than after the fact. "We are ready to react within hours. We can take action like changing a referee," said Heinz Taennier, Chief Attorney for FIFA.[172]

These measures were taken in response to the conviction of a German referee for his role in fixing matches. This need for additional measures became evident after the Supreme Court in Brazil annulled the outcome of eleven soccer matches after a referee admitted he took bribes in exchange for his help to determine the outcome of games. Suspicious activities in twelve other countries added to the need for the expansion of the role of the Early Warning System.

A statement from UEFA said, "UEFA has been actively involved in the investigation and has given assistance via detailed information through its Betting Fraud Detection System. This system monitors all UEFA competitions and second division matches for suspicious betting patterns."[173]

This effort was focused on the integrity of the World Cup Tournament that was held in South Africa in June 2010. There was concern that World Cup revenues that had amounted to $620 million from

---

[171] Bloomberg.com May 25, 2006 "World Cup Betting Companies to Flag Possible Match-Fixing," p. 1

[172] Ibid

[173] ESPN Soccernet November 20, 2009 "Police allege Champions League fix attempts" from Reuters Nevada. They are illegal in all of the other states.

sponsorship of the 2002 Tournament might be jeopardized along with viewership of the event that had reached 29 million. This peril might entice U.S. sports leagues to say, "We told you so. Sports and gambling do not mix."

The European sports leagues could retort, "We have a better way to deal with sports and gambling." Instead of a replication of the system in the U.S that attempts to prohibit the business, European sports leagues accept the fact that the business is part of the game. They accept the fact that sports and wagering are inseparable.

Architects of the European system could add Taiwan as an example to support their argument. Attempts to fix baseball games led to a loss of viewers and a 45% decline in attendance over a period of five years. The prohibition of legal wagers led to even more attempts to fix them. Prohibition did not work. Their game is in jeopardy because of the prohibition.

European sports leagues employ legal sportsbooks to help them detect suspicious wagering patterns. They incorporate the information only those in the business could provide. That information helps their investigative authorities take measures to deter and uncover attempts to compromise the integrity of their games.

"Let that be our lesson to you," they could lecture America. Our system incorporates the profession of sports transactions in order to help ensure the integrity of our games. We have proven there is an alternative to prohibition. That alternative establishes the legitimacy of the profession.

Borders, borders, borders...

These stories shed light on the plight of the legal business outside Nevada. Only those states that were grandfathered by PASPA have a legal right to the business. The business as it is defined by single game transactions is illegal everywhere in America except Nevada. Parlay transactions are legal in several of the grandfathered states besides Nevada. They are illegal in all of the other states.

Parlay transactions are also legal in several provinces in Canada. Straight bets are illegal everywhere else in Canada. In Mexico, all types of transactions are legal just as they are in England and Nevada.

If this scenario were applied to the practice of medicine in America, doctors in one state would be able to use all the tools of their trade. Doctors in other states would be prohibited from using basic tools of their trade such as stethoscopes and sphygmomanometers. And people who are carpenters, lawyers, or teachers are not subject to legal prohibitions that restrict their practices to boundaries defined by federal legislation.

The practice of the profession in Nevada, Mexico, and England is evidence there is more to the prohibition on the business than meets the eye. The European system is evidence there is more to this prohibition than the need to protect the integrity of the game. The European system proves that the business can be used to establish the integrity of the game.

What could happen only in America has roots that lie behind the need to protect the integrity of the game; yet the integrity of the game is the justification for the Professional and Amateur Sports Protection Act.

CHAPTER FIVE

SEA OF TROUBLES

"The second worst form of tragedy is one that is imposed on the victims by others."[174]

Prohibition

America's attempts to amend the "Commandments" could have created a tone in the laughter from their Author that might have generated a fear that "the end is near."

Instead the response to the attempts to play "god" were delivered in the form of a wrath that condemns those who don't learn from the sins of the past to suffer the consequences.

If the anticipation of unintended consequences accompanied the attempts at prohibitions perhaps the proponents might give second thoughts to their effort. All of the attempts at prohibition in America have had unintended consequences for those who attempt to enforce prohibition as well as for those who are their targets. The costs of the effort to enforce a prohibition have ranged from the need to repeal the effort to reaffirmation of the pursuit the effort whatever the cost.

In the most notable case of unintended consequences, the Constitution was amended to empower federal and state governments to enforce a prohibition against alcohol. The Volstead Act did not

---

[174] Aristotle's Poetics

project the costs of enforcement. No one measured the cost of what it would take to enforce a law "the people" would reject. They found the way to buy and sell alcohol. They forced those who were in charge of enforcement to take measures to close those avenues.

Those measures raised the cost of enforcement beyond the value of the prohibition. Despite the authority that accompanied a constitutional amendment, "the people" fought for their right to decide whether or not to consume alcohol. They took measures to circumvent the prohibition that included the participation of those who were authorized to enforce the enforcement. They could not resist the gratuities that were offered to them if they turned their heads the other way. The Amendment was repealed because it could not defeat the will of the people. Even though the prohibitionists were proven to be right about the potential dangers from the consumption of alcohol, the people decided to retain the right to make that decision.

That lesson about consequences that may stem from prohibition was ignored by the coalition behind the attempt to ban the use of marijuana. Prohibition of the sale and use of marijuana has led to a conflict between the federal and state governments. The federal government has had jurisdiction over the sale, possession, and use of marijuana, but state and local governments have resisted that authority. They argue that benefits would accrue to them from the sale of the product that they could regulate.

The cost of prohibition has been inflated by the need to extend enforcement measures into other nations. Prohibition in America has led to the "big business" of production and trafficking of marijuana in other nations. The federal government decided it was necessary to send the U.S. military to those nations to help them enforce the prohibition on a product that is in demand in America.

Despite the extension of the enforcement of prohibition to other nations, "the people" have found ways to get the product. Marijuana has been approved for medical purposes. Legal exceptions for the medical use of marijuana are used by state and local governments to justify their right to regulate the product. Despite federal efforts to close the doors on marijuana throughout the world, a back door for the production, sale, and use of the product has been opened in America.

Prohibitionists failed to anticipate the unintended consequences that would stem from enforcement. Implementation of the prohibition on marijuana has raised the cost of enforcement beyond what could have been anticipated. The full cost of this amendment to the "Commandments" has yet to be billed.

Costs and benefits of the enforcement might have been at least considered if the prohibitionists had observed the benefits that accompanied the regulation of the world's oldest profession. Despite the hypocrisy that has accompanied the attempts to deal with prostitution there is proof from one state that regulation does work.

Except for all of the counties in Nevada outside Clark and Washoe Counties, prostitution is prohibited in America. Although there are federal laws that address prostitution, the decision as to whether brothels can be a legal business enterprise has been left to the states to decide.

The stigma attached to the business is almost more than even the State of Nevada can bear. Although brothels are legal, the state refuses to use tax revenues from the business the way other tax revenues are incorporated into the budget. Revenue from brothels cannot be used for state programs. Those tax dollars are regarded as tainted. As a result, they cannot be used for education, law enforcement, or other programs that can benefit residents. Instead, the revenue is designated as general revenue that is to be used for other purposes; however, without the legal regulation of brothels, even those dollars would be lost.

Regulation generates revenue for the counties and the state from patrons who visit the brothels; however, benefits that could also accrue to Reno and Las Vegas from regulation are prohibited because Washoe and Clark Counties do not have the legal right accorded to the other counties.

The profession is both regulated and prohibited within Nevada. Revenues derived from regulation are restricted from general use by the state. The attempt to address the profession has proven that government can legitimize hypocrisy when integrity is excluded from the agenda.

Consequences that have stemmed from the attempts at prohibition have ranged from repeal to the need for international involvement, to costs that challenge the benefits, to a disregard for integrity, but none of the consequences resulted in segregation until the focus of prohibition turned to sports transactions. Attempts to prohibit the business outside Nevada established a class by itself for the profession.

If left unchallenged, that consequence alone could lead to a redefinition of freedom in America. In order to avoid the need for that redefinition, an examination of the whys and wherefores that led to segregation might lead to the rectification of a situation that would return America to the definition of the nation that is described in the Constitution.

The Professional and Amateur Sports Protection Act

Interest was kindled in the business of sports transactions by the economic recession that lasted from 1987 to 1993. The need for additional revenues propelled New York, California, New Jersey, Texas, and Connecticut, among other states, to consider the legalization of the business. Potential tax revenues enticed those states to consider options that ranged from a sports lottery to the system similar to the business in Nevada.

This expression of interest kindled a response from a coalition of interests united by their opposition to wagers on sporting events. Their fear that legalization of the business might spread beyond Nevada led them to propose legislation that would prohibit the possibility. They proposed the Professional and Amateur Sports Protection Act (PASPA). The legislation established legal authority for the federal government to prohibit the spread of the business beyond Nevada and other states that had "grandfathered" versions of sports wagers in the form of lotteries.

Former Senator Bill Bradley (D-NJ) allowed one of his copyrights to be used to support this legislation. Senator Bradley had been christened with the moniker "Dollar Bill" after he signed a contract for the New York Knicks in 1967 for the then record amount of $100,000. That record amount was due in part to the business that had helped the NBA survive the era before television. But neither "Dollar Bill" nor the other beneficiaries of that support acknowledged this contribution to their financial success. Instead "Dollar Bill" responded with legislation that was intended to prohibit the business.

Senator Bradley was neither a member of the Senate Judiciary Committee nor was he a lawyer, yet he was at the forefront of the initiative by the Senate Judiciary Subcommittee on Patents, Copyrights and Trademarks. "Dollar Bill's" other copyright "Bradley Bill" became synonymous with the name "PROHIBITING STATE-SANCTIONED SPORTS GAMBLING." That name for the legislation had already been abbreviated with the initials PASPA for the Professional and Amateur Sports Protection Act.

The moniker "Bradley Bill" helped the coalition opposed to the business establish a connection designed for public consumption between sports legislation and the Subcommittee on Patent Rights, Copyrights and Trademarks, but the name "Bradley Bill" alone could not explain the need to make sports legislation the agenda of that Subcommittee of the U.S. Senate.

State governments had exercised jurisdiction over the regulation of gambling. The coalition that opposed the legalization of gambling on moral grounds had focused their efforts to outlaw gambling on state governments. That level of government had the authority to regulate or prohibit gambling.

The effort was redirected to the federal level of government after the professional and amateur sports leagues assumed the leadership in the coalition opposed to wagers on sports. They redirected the effort to the federal government because as Senator Dennis DeConcini (D-AZ), Chairman of the Subcommittee said, "The interstate nature of sports clearly demonstrates the appropriateness of the Congress addressing this issue. Sports are inherently interstate. Teams cross lines, players move from the state, the games are broadcast over interstate transmissions."[175]

Since there was no Senate or House Subcommittees on the "moral opposition to sports betting," the coalition was forced to make the prohibition a business matter. Senator DeConcini helped to redirect the effort with his assertion that wagers on sports was an interstate business. That definition enabled his Subcommittee to assume jurisdiction over sports

---

[175] PROHIBITING STATE-SANCTIONED SPORTS GAMBLING: Hearings before the Subcommittee on Patents, Copyrights and Trademarks p.2, (hereinafter referred to as PASPA)

transactions as a matter of patent rights, copyrights, and trademarks. The Senator's deftness with definitions could have qualified him for work at Webster's or Merriam's. His skills also helped repay a debt to the NFL for its support in the decision to relocate the St. Louis Cardinals NFL franchise to Arizona. Senator DeConcini initiated his campaign to prohibit sports transactions at the time the Cardinals expressed their intention to move from St. Louis. He began what Arizona politicians would continue in support of the campaign to prohibit the business.[176]

Senator DeConcini welcomed the leadership of Senator Bradley. "I want to thank my friend from New Jersey, Senator Bradley, for his strong support of this legislation. He has personal background and understanding of it," said Senator DeConcini. Senator DeConcini might have reconsidered the accolades after questions from Senator Grassley exposed Senator Bradley, a Rhodes Scholar, for his lack of knowledge about the subject matter of the legislation. The Rhodes Scholar would have lost to a fifth grader in a contest about who knew more. Unlike the Rhodes Scholar, the fifth grader would have done the homework.

Senator Bradley exposed himself when Senator Grassley asked about his statements that suggested state-sanctioned sports lotteries would be more detrimental to sports than the betting system in place in Nevada. Senator Grassley asked, "What is the difference between—from your standpoint, backing this legislation, pushing for it, banning state-sponsored lotteries as opposed to where logos are used by bookmakers and casino gambling like what might go on in Las Vegas?"[177]

Senator Bradley did not answer the question. Instead he discussed the potential impact of sports

---

[176] Ibid
[177] Ibid

betting on young people. He argued that sports-betting is detrimental to the impact great athletes (such as Michael Jordan) can have on young people. "I think that (importance) would be diminished if the States sponsored sports gambling."[178]

"But if private-sector gambling uses logos and has sports-related gambling, that doesn't detract from it but state-sponsored lotteries do?" Senator Grassley asked. He persisted with his point about two types of state-sanctioned sports betting that were addressed by PASPA.[179]

Senator Bradley responded, "I think the imprimatur of the state is a much stronger expression of what our community believes is appropriate than any individual or private action."[180]

"I hope you are aware—that there are sports team logos used in gambling casinos and in other private sector gambling," said Senator Grassley.[181]

"I'm not sure what you're talking about," said Senator Bradley.[182]

"You can go to casinos and bet on teams in those casinos based on the outcomes of games, just as you can win in a state-sponsored lottery," said Senator Grassley.[183]

"Let me assure you that when you have a sports lottery available at your corner pharmacy, it's a lot different than if you go into some casino somewhere. I'm not aware of these games you're referring to, but I think there's a difference because one does not deal with sports—the other does," Senator Bradley responded.[184]

---

[178] Ibid
[179] Ibid
[180] Ibid
[181] Ibid
[182] Ibid
[183] Ibid
[184] Ibid

"They both deal with sports...you're asking the Congress to speak out on this subject, they would be speaking out on the use of sports-related logos and betting on teams whether it's in a state lottery or wherever the betting might go on. Gambling is gambling, isn't it?" Senator Grassley asked.

Senator Bradley responded, "I think the commissioners who follow and the representatives of the gambling industry can give you a better answer to that question than I am able to give you."[185]

"If gambling of this nature is bad, it's bad, whether it's state-sponsored or whether it's private-sector-sponsored," said Senator Grassley. He lectured Senator Bradley for his failure to respond.

The Rhodes Scholar also exposed his lack of knowledge about two parts to PASPA. One part addressed state lotteries (S473). The other part addressed sports gambling under state law (S474). Senator Bradley was not able to address Senator Grassley's point that there were two types of sports betting addressed by the legislation.

Even though Senator Grassley did not mention it, Nevada law and regulations dictate how the business operates within the state. Nevada sanctions the business just as other states sanction sports lotteries. Senator Grassley could have said to Senator Bradley, "Sports-betting is sports-betting, isn't it?" instead of "Gambling is gambling, isn't it"?

Dollar Bill's statement, "I am not aware of these games...but I think there's a difference because one does not deal with sports, the other does..." exposed his ignorance about the subject matter of the legislation as well as the business of sports transactions. The Rhodes Scholar copped out of his ignorance with a response to Senator Grassley that he

---

[185] Ibid

would leave it to the Commissioners of the sports leagues to explain what he did not know.

Despite the fact that the Senator from New Jersey could not explain the legislation or the business that would be prohibited by it, proponents of the legislation relied on him to find the way to circumvent the Constitution in order to pass the legislation. They banked on his academic background in American history as well as the legislative experiences from his membership on the Senate Finance Committee to help find the way. Those skills led him to a reinterpretation of the Constitution. He decided that the Commerce Clause of the Constitution could be used as the spin to justify federal jurisdiction over a state's right to decide whether to sanction the business.

The Commerce Clause had been used to justify other types of legislation that conflicted with the constitutional requirement to treat states equally. In support of his tactic, Senator Bradley said, "The Supreme Court has explicitly held that there is no requirement of uniformity when Congress is exercising its power pursuant to the Commerce Clause." He added there was "no legitimate constitutional basis" for objections to PASPA because of the discrimination among the states.[186]

This argument, as well as the historical precedents, was not as "self-evident" as he had proclaimed. There were no precedents in the Commerce Clause for the legal segregation of a profession to one state or restrictions on the way the business could operate in three other states.

Uniformity in the application of laws through the Commerce Clause has been a matter for debate among constitutional scholars.[187] Equal treatment is also a

---

[186] Virginia Law Review article by Thomas Colby April 2005 Volume 91: 249, p. 260

[187] "Revitalizing the Forgotten Uniformity Constraint on the Commerce Power" article by Thomas Colby Virginia Law Review 249, 2005

matter for "the people" to discuss. They know that laws reflect the political and economic interests behind them. They know that legislation serves the interest of the proponents. If equal treatment extends to others, it is coincidental.

Even the debate among legal scholars over PASPA admits that "powerful lobbies can purchase an unfair advantage (or bring about a disadvantage) for a single state or group of states." Sponsors of PASPA candidly admitted that they "agreed to "grandfathering" because (they) had no choice."[188]

Opponents of the legislation who testified at the Hearing added, "It is unwarranted and inappropriate for the Federal Government to tell the states what they can and cannot do to raise the needed revenue. For this reason alone the Executive Committee of the National Conference of State Legislatures (NCSL) voted unanimously to pass the attached resolution in opposition to S. 474."[189]

Proponents of the legislation did not respond to that political argument; instead, they relied on economics as their justification. They argued that sports lotteries did not generate the amount of revenue that would be critical to state budgets. Senator DeConcini said, "I sympathize with the plight of states' financial officers. However, I do not believe that the answers to budgetary problems should be to increase the number of lottery players or sports bettors."[190]

NBA Commissioner David Stern added, "Games run by the state, such as sports lotteries, simply cannot compete with bookies who offer larger returns, credit, anonymity, and 'tax free' winnings. And experience has shown that state-run gambling almost

---

[188] Ibid, p. 322
[189] Ibid, p. 231
[190] PASPA, p. 3

never realizes the revenues predicted by its proponents."[191]

Senator Bradley added his two cents on another matter where he lacked the expertise. "Certainly Oregon's dreams of balancing the budget through sports gambling were as ephemeral as the lottery player's dream of winning the big one."[192]

Defenders of the legislation argued that their calculations of the "small amount" of money that would be generated by sports transactions justified the prohibition. According to them, states would not miss that small amount of revenue they called insignificant. Senators DeConcini and Bradley, Commissioner David Stern, and others were able to prognosticate the amount of money that would be deemed significant for state budgets. If they were that good at forecasts, they should have applied their skills at sportsbooks in Nevada.

Representative Wanda Fuller, Assistant Minority Leader of the Kansas House of Representatives, disagreed with their calculations. She added the political aspect of the calculations the proponents had not mentioned. She said, "(PASPA) poses a serious threat to a fundamental tenet of state sovereignty and our ability to raise revenues to finance state services."

Her comment refocused the debate from economics to politics. Whether the amount of money that was raised by sports-betting was enough to be beneficial to the states was a matter for the states to decide. Representative Fuller argued that the right to raise that money, whatever the amount, was the issue—not the amount of money that might be raised by the lotteries.[193]

---

[191] Ibid pp. 99-100
[192] Ibid p. 10
[193] Ibid p. 49

Proponents of PASPA attempted to grease the skids for politics to stifle Rep. Fuller's argument. Politics would determine whether the legislation go forward. Economics was for public consumption. Proponents of the legislation offered four states an exception to PASPA through a "grandfather clause." They would be grandfathered in order to make it possible to pass the legislation. Without the votes from representatives of those states, the legislation might have been defeated.

Grandfathers were offered "monopolies" for the versions of sports transaction they had already implemented. They were guaranteed the freedom to continue those games in exchange for the votes that were necessary to pass the legislation.

None of the representatives of the business in Nevada testified against PASPA. The monopolists did not want to give up their privilege. The values of democracy and free enterprise are relative to who benefits.

PASPA (S.473) "A Bill To Amend The Lanham Trademark Act Of 1946 To Protect The Service Marks of Professional and Amateur Sports Organizations From Misappropriation By State Lotteries" preserved the monopoly trademarks of Professional and Amateur Sports Organizations. Monopolies would be guaranteed through the prohibition of sports transactions beyond states that had already implemented their versions of the games.

Sponsors of the legislation admitted they "agreed to 'grandfathering'" because [they] had no choice." They did not have enough votes to pass the bill without the appeasement of lobbies through an exemption for states that had already legalized sports betting or had already created sports lotteries.[194]

---

[194] Virginia Law Review article by Thomas Colby April 2005, vol. 91:249, p. 232

Opponents of the legislation responded, "It is important to reiterate that the authors of S. 474 have seen fit to exempt Nevada, Oregon, and Delaware from the legislation. They justify this exemption by referring to it as the 'most feasible political approach,'" said James Hooker, President of the Sports Lottery Corporation.

He added, "Grandfathering three states out of political necessity and foreclosing any opportunity for the others to raise such needed revenue via a sports pool lottery is hypocritical and self-serving. Why shouldn't your state have the opportunity to decide the issue?"[195]

The political tactics behind the gerrymander of the "grandfathers" circumvented the need to address another aspect of equal treatment that had not been raised by the opposition. Proponents of PASPA ignored the time factor in their prohibition. Their arguments were not challenged despite the fact that PASPA established a time for when the activity would become legal. The grandfather clause created a period of time that would establish when an activity that was legal would become illegal. This clause would come back to haunt the state. New Jersey politicians failed to meet the deadline that had been granted by PASPA to implement a system. After that deadline passed, New Jersey was prohibited from the implementation of the system that would include straight wagers.

States that had legalized sports transactions before PASPA would not be forced to repent for their sin. Their original sins were forgiven by the "almighties." Forgiveness for their original sin of sports transactions was a state of "limbo" that allowed them to continue an activity that would become criminal in the other states.

---

[195] PASPA, pp. 231-232

Systems that were in place before PASPA was enacted would remain legal despite all the arguments that were used to justify the prohibition against further expansion of the business. All of the arguments against sports transactions became moot for the "grandfathers." All of the statutes that prohibit monopolies were moot. All of the evils that could stem from sports transactions were moot for the residents of grandfathered states, including the potential to corrupt young people.

The potential impact of sports transactions on young people had been one of the justifications for PASPA. "Teenage gambling-related problems are increasing. Of the approximately eight million compulsive gamblers in America, one million of them are under twenty. Teenagers gamble on sports lotteries and card games...sports gambling creates a motivation for corrupting the youth of our Nation...we don't want them to start betting on sports events through state-sponsored lottery games," said Senator DeConcini.[196]

His argument did not express concern for teenagers in those states that would be grandfathered by his legislation. Nor did he address the fact that those states had addressed the concern about young people with a minimum age requirement that prohibited legal wagers on sports by those young people.

Nevertheless Senator Bradley added, "There are eight million gambling addicts in this country, Mr. Chairman, and one million of them are teenagers. When young people see the state involved in gambling on sports, can there be any doubt that even more young people will think that that's what sports are all about?"[197]

---

[196] Ibid, p.2
[197] Ibid, p.10

No one questioned statistics that could not document the number of teenagers in the grandfathered states who had become addicted because they circumvented the age restriction established by state governments. Silence from his opposition allowed the Senator to exclude that documentation—or else the silence stemmed from the fact that the opponents knew the argument was for public consumption not the truth in numbers.

Then NFL Commissioner Paul Tagliabue supported Senator Bradley's concerns about youth and sports-betting. He said, "Legalized sports gambling sends a terrible message to youth..." and "... worst of all, legalized sports gambling would promote gambling among young people."[198]

If sports handicappers had been invited to testify at their "lynching," they would have told him, "Don't tell us, show us." They would have asked for data from Nevada that would support his prediction about the impact of the legalization of the business on young people. Without the data to back the prediction, his opinions would not merit respect. The contradiction in the statement itself that the age restriction for legalized gambling "would" promote gambling among young people precluded the need to respond with respect.

Nevertheless, a lobbyist persisted with the argument. "Gambling among young people has been increasing at an alarming rate in recent years. I believe the spread of state lotteries in the past 20 years has contributed significantly to the problem," said Valerie Lorenz, Director National Center For Pathological Gambling. She added, "For states to establish sports lotteries or to legalize other forms of sports gambling

---

[198] Ibid, pp. 25-26

would be to take a bad situation already existing in this country and make it even worse."[199]

Senator Grassley (R-IA) asked her, "...every state law prohibits the sale of lottery tickets to minors and the same would be true for state-sponsored sports pool lotteries. What evidence do you have that teenagers would play state-sponsored sports pool lottery games?"[200]

Arthur Hamilton, Minority Leader of the Arizona House of Representatives confronted her with "(I) submit to you that state legislatures are equally-well qualified to help protect our children and to preserve the honesty of sports competition."[201]

Valerie Lorenz ignored those concerns. She said that despite state laws that prohibit sales of drugs, alcohol, and cigarettes to minors, they find ways to get what they want. The same would be true of sports lotteries." She added, "The main point, however, is not that our young people will necessarily participate in sports lotteries as teenagers, although many will try to do so, but that sports lotteries will encourage and teach them how to gamble on sports legally or illegally, since legalized gambling often leads to illegal gambling."[202]

Her response had more spin than a curve ball delivered by Steve Carlton. She could not provide an estimate of the number of teenagers who might try to participate in sports lotteries because there are no statistics for an opinion that served her business interest in pathological gambling. If only a few might be affected there would have been little need for her to testify. Numbers were ignored in order to justify an appearance that also became an advertisement for her

---

[199] Ibid, p. 75
[200] Ibid, p. 87
[201] Ibid, p. 233
[202] Ibid, p. 75

business—the National Center for Pathological Gambling INC.

The INC. after the name of her organization elicited a response from Richard Vave, a professor of rhetoric and communication. He argued that the use of the term compulsive. "...has become a perennial doctor's spot used to excuse irresponsible gamblers and increase the status and coffers of the gambling doctors who purport to treat it."[203]

He questioned why the term "pathological" is applied to gambling. The medical evidence did not warrant a comparison between gambling and other forms of so-called pathological behaviors. The word "pathological" has been applied to gambling in order to open the doors of doctors and other professionals for more "treatment" and the use of the word "teenage" would open the door to even more "patients."[204]

Besides the linguistic twist, the testimony of Valerie Lorenz also failed to offer an explanation of how sports lotteries could "teach" teenagers how to gamble. She either did not know or else would not acknowledge that the profession of sports transactions is different from other types of so-called gambling. Lotteries do not "teach" young people or anyone else how to gamble on sports.

Her argument implied that prohibition alone could not keep young people from gambling should have raised questions from the panel. They failed to ask about additional measures that might have to be taken to deny teenagers access to the illegal ways to do what they want to do. They allowed her to ignore the need to argue for the censorship that would be necessary to keep sports information from young people.

---

[203] *Wall Street Journal* article by Richard Vave, July 7, 1991 'Compulsive' Gambling Is a Phony Excuse.
[204] Ibid

The failure to propose other measures that would protect teenagers would suggest that prohibition is all that can be done, even though the argument admits that alone cannot keep young people from doing what they want to do. The failure to propose additional measures exposed a dilemma for the opposition. Alternatives were ignored because the argument about the need to protect young people was rhetoric designed for public consumption.

Senator Bradley added his two cents to the endeavor at public relations. He extended the concern about the impact of sports transactions on young people with the question, "Do we want young people to play the game because they love the game for the purity of the experience or do we want them to exacerbate that confusion by continually raising the question, is it a player's game and the fan's game or is it the gambler's game.?" Instead of "...personal achievement, sportsmanship, and respect for the winner...sports-betting would turn athletes into roulette chips."[205]

Former Chicago Bears linebacker Mike Singletary also testified on the danger of sports betting to young people. He said, "There is no greater threat to the role of athletics in the development of our youth than state legalized sports gambling—either in the form of state sports lotteries or in casino-style sports gambling."[206]

Athletes attempted to expand on the reputations they earned on playing fields to a subject that did not require athletic skills. They were used by proponents of the legislation to legitimize another version of the argument about the need to protect young people from sports transactions. Their arguments suggest that legal wagering on sports would have an impact on the way young people would perceive the games they play

---

[205] Ibid, p.10
[206] Ibid, p. 69

and how others would perceive the motives behind why young people chose to play those games.

The arguments concluded that somehow, someway young people would have to justify to themselves their participation in games on which people could make wagers because those transactions would discredit them as well the games. The legalization of sports wagers would somehow lead to a self-perception that they were roulette chips. People might perceive them as roulette chips in games they loved to play, according to Senator Bradley, "for the purity of the experience."

Mssrs. Bradley and Singletary argued PASPA would prevent those misperceptions that would result from legal sports wagering. If there were no legal wagers on sports, athletes would not be able to perceive themselves as roulette chips, but Senator Bradley ignored the fact that roulette chips are a means to make a wager. The placement of roulette chips by the bettor cannot determine the outcome of the game. His analogy had more spin than a roulette wheel.

The argument also ignored the fact that the legislation as it was grandfathered would not eliminate the business in Nevada, nor would it eliminate illegal wagering elsewhere. Young people would know that options to wager on their games would be available even if they did not know about PASPA. Young people would hear the words "favorite" and "underdog" used on their teams. Problems with self-perception and the perceptions of others would not be eliminated by PASPA.

"Way Beyond the Fringes"

If the Senate included a Representative from the State of the Unrepresented that Senator might have said, "...the argument about integrity ignores the fact that legal wagers help to establish the integrity of the games. What if all sportsbooks agreed to suspend wagers on amateur and professional team sports? What if they decided to treat those sports the same way they treat professional wrestling? What would be the impact of that decision on television ratings and the acceptance of those sports by the public?"

The reluctance to respond by members of the Senate panel could have led to another comment from the Senator, "...suspicions about the integrity of those games would make headlines beyond those on ESPN. A prohibition of wagering would raise concerns that the outcomes were pre-determined just as they are with professional wrestling. The professional and amateur sports leagues would be forced to convince the public that their games are legitimate. They would have to respond to a decision to end the free ride of integrity provided by the sportsbooks. An end to the legitimacy of their games established by sports transactions would mandate an explanation about why that profession chose to end their sponsorship of the integrity of the game."

Once again the reluctance of the panel to respond could have led the Senator to continue to use time which had never been allocated to the unrepresented. "...the perception of legitimacy provided by sportsbooks impacts the perception of the games young people may want to play. Unlike professional wrestlers, that perception is legitimized by the opportunities to make and accept wagers on those games. Unlike professional wrestling, self-perception is enhanced by the fact that wagers can be made on a game whose outcome has not been determined. That outcome is a gamble for people in the business as well as for athletes."

Silence would have allowed the Senator to continue. "...the distinction between legitimacy and fixed outcomes because of the ability to wager extends beyond pro wrestling to elections and other events that are determined by votes. Nevada prohibits wagers on elections and other events such as the Academy Awards. According to the gambling regulations in Nevada, there is more integrity to transaction on sports than there would be on elections for political offices. The legitimacy of the wager on sports is one reason why the image of those who participate in sports is one that those who run for our political offices would relish."

"What do you think about what I've said?" the Senator from the State of the Unrepresented could have asked NFL Commissioner Tagliabue. The Commissioner responded with an answer that would have led the audience to believe he had not heard one word of the Senator's comments. "Gambling threatens the integrity of and public confidence in team sports. Sports lotteries inevitably foster a climate of suspicion about controversial plays and intensify cynicism with respect to player performance, coaching decisions, officiating results and game results," said Mr. Tagliabue.[207]

Senator Orrin Hatch (R-UT) supported him. "There is no question that there is already widespread gambling, both legal and illegal. Extension of state approval to gambling on sporting events poses a special threat to the character of those games."[208]

The Senator could have responded, "Mssrs. Tagliabue and Hatch ignore the fact that the profession must police the games so they will not be hurt by a lack of integrity. You blame the sportsbooks for questions that would be raised about performances on the field, even if legal wagers were prohibited. Those questions might be different, but there would be controversies about performance. They would add not

---

[207] Ibid, p. 25
[208] Ibic, p. 16

be able to blame illegal wagers instead of their own players for a lack of integrity in their performances."

Once again their inability to respond would have allowed the Senator to continue. "You ignore the fact that integrity comes from the sportsbooks as well as the players for the sports leagues. They need each other to establish integrity and capitalize on the benefits in their respective ways. One complements the other. They are as inseparable as oxygen and carbon dioxide. One cannot exist without the other."

A voice with an English accent resonated within the room. "They try to ignore the situation that exists in Europe that refutes their arguments. Soccer and Tennis Leagues in Europe enlist the support of the sportsbooks to do what the sports leagues in America could do if the leagues enlisted the same kind of cooperation."

Security was not able to muzzle another outburst from that voice. "Instead, they choose prohibition. They forget American history, the prohibition on alcohol. You cannot prohibit what Americans want to do. There is no way to prevent or eliminate wagering on sports. Grandfathering is not regulation."

"Amen," the Senator responded. "Even though prohibition is impossible, the sports leagues and their supporters argue that prohibition is the solution to the controversies that would arise anyway from mistakes that happen on the field. Integrity of a performance, a decision, or an outcome is part of the game whether or not people wager on it."

That observation did not keep NBA Commissioner David Stern from changing his position. He said, "Gambling threatens the integrity of public confidence in sports. Gambling, particularly sports gambling, inevitably carries with it the suspicion of 'fixing'."[209] He added, "When a fan has bet money on a team, every

---

[209] Ibid, p. 51

missed shot, turnover and coaching misjudgment will inevitably give rise to speculation, suspicion of game-fixing and point-shaving."[210]

"Then you admit fans also bet on games?" said the Senator. "The fact that someone bets does not preclude them from also being a fan of the game. And there is no way to prove a fan who does not bet would not also question every aspect of a game that a bettor would. Just because a wager might intensify the scrutiny from bettors is no reason to prohibit it."

"For bettors as well as fans, someone wins, someone loses," a member of the profession shouted from behind doors to the room that was closed to them. "Losers who think they lost because game was fixed are offset by those who win because they think the game was legit. Fans do the same thing."

The Senator asked, "To change the focus of this hearing, I would like to know if this legislation has been presented as an amendment to the Lanham Trademark Act of 1946? How is it possible a law designed to protect trademarks in commercial activity can be used to protect young people and the integrity of the game?"

The Senator read, "The Lanham Trademark Act of 1946 is an Act to provide for the registration and protection of trademarks used in commerce to carry out the provisions of certain intentional conventions and for other purposes. PASPA would amend The Lanham Trademark Act with the addition of Section 40 (S. 473) MISAPPROPRIATION OF SERVICE MARKS OF PROFESSIONAL SPORTS ORGANIZATIONS BY STATE LOTTERIES."

NBA Commissioner David Stern responded, "Conducting a sports lottery or permitting sports gambling involves the use of professional sports leagues' games, scores, statistics, and team logos in

---

[210] Ibid

order to take advantage of a particular league's popularity and such use violates, misappropriates and infringes upon numerous league property rights. The NBA—like other sports leagues—owns the rights to its games and the manner of their exploitation. The NBA does not want these rights used in connection with gambling or in any other way that would tarnish or damage the game of professional basketball."[211]

"But what about all of this testimony about young people and the integrity of the game?" the Senator asked. The Senator would have asked the other panelists to question statements in S. 474 "A Bill to prohibit sports gambling under state law (PASPA)."

The Senator said, "This Bill was proposed because those who wrote the legislation had concluded even before the testimony that...and I quote "sports gambling conducted pursuant to state law threatens the integrity and character of, and public confidence in, professional and amateur sports, instills inappropriate values in the nation's youth, misappropriates the goodwill and popularity of professional and amateur sports organizations, and DILUTES AND TARNISHES THE SERVICE MARKS OF SUCH ORGANI-ZATIONS."[212]

"In other words, the undocumented conclusions that were emphasized about the harm of sports transactions to young people and to the integrity of the game are there for public relations. The real reason for S. 474 is in the words "Dilutes and Tarnishes the Service Marks," said the Senator.

The Senator added, "PASPA is also justified because it protects the trademarks of professional sports leagues from further infringement by states, whether through lotteries or by a system similar to the profession in Nevada. And, prohibition of sports

---

[211] Ibid, p. 51
[212] Capitalization added by author.

transactions beyond the states that are grandfathered would ensure protection against that trademark infringement."

Instead of a discussion of that justification for both sections of the legislation, Senator Hatch shifted the focus to show how the legislation would work. "Under S. 473 (and S. 474) any lottery or gambling scheme that is based on the games of a professional or amateur sports team would be deemed as exploiting the service mark of such a team. The Bill would protect the service marks of these teams regardless of whether states use the service mark directly or refer indirectly to the teams by their geographical location or in any other manner."[213]

"Does that mean the name 'Chicago' is the exclusive right of the sports leagues? Does that mean Nevada sportsbooks cannot use the name 'Chicago,'?" the Senator was asked.

Senator Grassley responded. "This Bill does not target Nevada's sportsbooks: it doesn't target Nevada's casinos, many of which use professional teams' names and logos. It does not target private, legal or illegal gambling in any way. Curiously, this legislation targets state-sponsored-lotteries—only."[214]

"S. 474 prohibits the expansion of the type of sports transactions in Nevada to any other state. If you can stop the expansion of the system in Nevada to other states, you prevent the use of those trademarks in other states. Those states cannot use the name 'Chicago' in sports lotteries because they cannot legalize sportsbooks," said the Senator from the State of the Unrepresented.

Senator DeConcini asked Commissioner Stern. "Knowing that the NBA logos are used in casinos and other gambling institutions, why is it the NBA has

---

[213] Ibid, p.16
[214] Ibid, p. 19

never attempted to enforce the rights you may have as owners of those logos?"[215]

David Stern said, "The only legalized sports betting of which I am aware in a casino-type setting is in Las Vegas, which long pre-dates the existence of the NBA. Congress has, in effect, acted to keep that from spreading through lotteries related to sports-betting through existing federal legislation. As far as the grandfathering of Las Vegas, it's geographically and legally isolated, and realistically, we don't think we can move against it."[216]

"Does that mean your property rights are violated by the use of placards with the names of your teams on the boards of the sportsbooks? Do your property rights extend to the written words that designate the city and the nickname of a team?" asked the Senator from the State of the Unrepresented.

Silence prompted Senator DeConcini to ask MLB Commissioner Fay Vincent a question about property rights. "Perhaps you have had to address it in the League. If your logos are being used in Las Vegas without permission, does that trouble you and why haven't you done anything about it?"[217]

Mr. Vincent responded, "It does trouble me and we haven't done anything about it because I think...what happens is that people take the hats or some other small item on which the logo has been placed, they carry it into the casino...in our view that's a very difficult item for us to enforce. The casino is not a licensee of ours and never would be...and our ability to enforce that kind of migration of items that carry the logo is difficult."[218]

The Senator from the State of the Unrepresented said, "Mr. Vincent either chose to avoid the question

[215] Ibid, p. 62
[216] Ibid
[217] Ibid, p. 63
[218] Ibid

about the use of baseball logos by sportsbooks to conduct their business or he did not know how to respond. He chose to comment about logos on clothing worn by customers in Las Vegas sportsbooks instead of logos that were on the boards of the sportsbooks for betting purposes. His answer avoided the observation made by Commissioner Stern about trademarks used by Nevada sportsbooks that pre-dated the NBA."

The sports monopolies have not addressed their dilemma of whether to pursue an attempt to preclude the use of nicknames from sportsbooks in Las Vegas or to ignore that infringement of their trademarks. League officials know that even if they were able to win a legal decision that would prohibit the use of nicknames such as "the Bears," that decision would not extend to the use of the name of a city such as Chicago.

While trademarks used on clothing and other items are protected by contracts that stipulate the use, sale, and profit to the Leagues, there are no agreements of that type with the sportsbooks in Nevada. None of the leagues profit from the use of their products in Nevada or in the other states that had legal sports lotteries. There are no monetary residuals to the sports leagues from any bets that are made at the sportsbooks in Nevada or from the sale of state lottery tickets.

The sports leagues choose to protect their trademark through the prohibition of the extension of the use of their product beyond the grandfathers. Prohibition against further expansion of sports betting was the best they can do to protect their trademarks at this time. Sports monopolies choose to address the issue of trademarks and patent rights through the prohibition of further expansion of the industry rather than through an agreement that would compensate them for the use of their product."

Senator Grassley said to Commissioner Vincent, "I have listened to why you didn't think you could take action against places where team names and logos are used...that it's not a part of sports period and that you ought to then be willing to take on any foe, any place in the country that breaches it. And I think you have the resources to do it."[219]

Commissioner Vincent sidestepped the admonition. Instead he chose to blame the media for the inability of the League to take action. "One of the ironies is that betting lines are published in virtually every newspaper...we are living with an anomaly." The newspapers remind us of it every time. Betting lines are published in virtually every newspaper in the country. And that's because the readers of those newspapers are engaged in illegal gambling."[220]

The Senator from the State of the Unrepresented asked, "You mean to say you place blame for sports transactions activity on the media because newspapers publish the odds on your games? According to you, if newspapers stopped the publication of those odds illegal sports betting might come to an end. Why didn't you respond to Senator Grassley's question about why you have not made an effort to prevent the legal sports betting industry from the use of your logos?"

The Senator turned to the NFL Commissioner. "Don't you sell your trademarks to individuals to sell your products right next to the sportsbooks where you also want to prohibit the use of your trademarks on their boards? Your trademark for the name 'Super Bowl' is on products for sale right next to the sportsbooks that can't even use your trademark name of Super Bowl. They have to call it a 'Big Game' or

---

[219] Ibid, p.64
[220] Ibid

'Championship game' or some other language because you prohibit their use of the name 'Super Bowl'."

Commissioner Tagliabue said, "We have made it clear that we would support legislation that prohibited any and all forms of gambling. We also recognize that we live in a country, a great one, which operates by consensus and that in order to take a step forward, we have to accept this form of legislation which contains a very narrow grandfather provision."[221]

Senator Grassley asked, "Why does the sports industry support this exemption (for Nevada), thus precluding from coverage the prime and most active purveyors of sports gambling in this country?"[222]

No one from the sports monopolies dared to respond. The reason for their silence was exposed by the testimony of Assistant Minority Leader of the Kansas House of Representative Wanda Fuller. She said, "The proposed bill would create a different standard of protection for certain trademarks and would undermine the cornerstone of the Lanham Act. In other words, it would exempt professional sports organizations from having to prove the basic elements of trademark infringement currently set out in the Lanham Act."[223]

"The anomaly that we are living with that was mentioned by Commissioner Vincent was not the fact that betting lines are published by newspapers, but in the fact that an anti-trust exemption had been conferred on professional sports leagues. This anomaly enabled the professional sports leagues to use the power over the right to use their trademark. This right that accompanied the anti-trust exemption bestowed monopolies to those states that had used the trademarks before PASPA had been enacted.

---

[221] Ibid

[222] Ibid, p. 20

[223] Ibid, p.10

Monopolists created monopolies in order to prohibit the extension of the use of their trademarks. This extension would have accompanied an expansion of legal sportsbooks beyond Nevada."

James Hosker, President of the North American Association of State and Provincial Lotteries responded, "Congress is creating a monopoly on legal sports wagering in Delaware, Nevada, and Oregon and encouraging the outflow of sports wagering revenue from other states to those grandfathered states."[224]

The Senator from the State of the Unrepresented said, "PASPA is an interaction between politics and economics that could challenge economic and political theories that cover the so-called spectrum of left to right. The economic payoff to professional sports leagues that was bestowed by the political system through the imprimatur of PASPA would mock theories of capitalism, free enterprise, and representative democracy."

"What about our representation in this unrepresentative democracy?" shouted a member of the profession. Other words permeated through the doors that were closed to all members of the profession. "We have not had our chance to be heard."

"You aren't the first and you won't be the last," resonated from within the walls of the Senate Chamber.

"What about our input on a matter that affects our lives?" a voice responded.

"Who said representative democracy represents the people?" shouted a representative of representative democracy.

Members of the profession would understand the response that ordered them to become part of the line with other Americans outside that door, a door that had been closed by those who owned the key. They

[224] Ibid, p. 108. Mr Hosker omitted Montana as one of the grandfathers.

might not have understood what was behind the gate that opponents would attempt to install in front of that door.

Amateur Sports Integrity Act

The effort to expand on what proponents of the prohibition of legal sports betting had begun with PASPA resumed a decade later with the introduction of legislation by another Senator from Arizona. The endeavor to prohibit sports transactions crossed party lines when Senator John McCain introduced the Amateur Sports Integrity Act (ASIA). He argued that ASIA was necessary to "cover the loophole left by PASPA." The loophole was the legal sports betting industry in Nevada that had been grandfathered by PASPA.

Senator McCain did not present evidence to support the need for new legislation because PASPA had failed to do the job. He did not present statistics that documented an increase in gambling among young people because PASPA had grandfathered Nevada.

There was no evidence that PASPA had led to an increase in the number of attempts to compromise the integrity of the game. No documentation was presented to the Committee because none was needed.

The Senator insisted that the "cover" for the legal industry in Nevada provided by PASPA had to be lifted. He relied on a conclusion from a study by the National Gambling Impact Study Commission (NGISC) to launch the effort. The NGISC had concluded that "Legal sports wagering, especially the publication in the media of Las Vegas and offshore-generated point spreads, fuels a much larger amount of illegal wagering."

Their conclusion twisted cause-and-effect in order to blame the legal industry in Nevada for the problems that came from illegal sports betting. They said, "Legal sports wagering, especially the publication in the media of Las Vegas of offshore-generated point spreads fuels a much larger amount of illegal wagering."[225]

Senator McCain latched on to the conclusion to make his argument that "...the Las Vegas sports line can be found in newspapers, on the radio, television, and the Internet nationwide. The result is a substantial problem with illegal sports betting that places our nation's college athletes at the mercy of bookies and bettors."[226]

McCain argued that passage of his legislation would "...send a message that betting on college sports by college students is illegal." He said, "A ban will help reduce or eliminate the published pointspreads on college games in newspapers, which feed illegal betting activity." But, most important, a ban will end a practice that has cast athletes as items to be bet upon, exposing them to unwarranted pressure, bribery and corruption."[227]

The Senator added, "While I agree that we need to address illegal gambling, I think they have put the cart before the horse. Let's change the law to send a uniform message that gambling on amateur sports is wrong, then work on those who break it."[228]

Senator McCain placed the blame on the legal industry in order to justify legislation that would "uncover" the protection that was provided for Nevada by PASPA. According to the Senator, there was a need for legislation that would protect amateur sports from sports transactions in Nevada, the only state

---

[225] National Gambling Impact Study Commission note 1, 3-9

[226] Amateur Sports Integrity Act (hereafter referred to as "ASIA"), Report of the Committee on Commerce and Technology on S.2340 May 3, 2000, p. 3

[227] Ibid, p. 5

[228] August 8, 2001,"It's Past Time to Ban Amateur Sports Gambling" by John McCain

grandfathered by PASPA where individual wagers on NCAA team sports was legal.

The Senator failed to mention that he chose to sponsor this legislation in order to make a payment on a debt to the NCAA for favors the organization had bestowed on the State of Arizona.[229] He also failed to mention the fact that his legislation was intended to protect the trademarks owned by the NCAA. There was no mention of the fact that the NCAA refused to participate in the testimony about trademarks during the hearings on PASPA. They were not part of the testimony about the need to defend the exploitation of trademarks of their business by sportsbooks.

Although the protection of trademarks of amateur sports was implied with the inclusion of "Amateur" in the title (PASPA), the arguments for the protection of amateur sports had focused on the evils of sports transactions for young people and the integrity of the games. Protection of NCAA trademarks should have been part of the testimony. However, an appearance by the NCAA with professional sports leagues on behalf of the protection of trademarks might have tarnished the "amateur" image of the NCAA with professional corporate businesses. Patents and trademarks had an appearance suited more for professional sports not with the NCAA and amateur sports.

This tactic allowed Senator McCain to introduce the Amateur Sports Integrity Act (ASIA) in the Committee on Commerce, Science, and Transportation. Senator Bradley had paved the way for Senator McCain with his effort to justify PASPA through the commerce clause. Justification through the commerce clause had cleared a hurdle that would avoid another conflict over States Rights, PASPA had established

---

[229] This business matter is discussed in the section of Chapter Three entitled "Pain from McCain."

federal jurisdiction. Sports transactions were defined as interstate commerce.

Senator McCain welcomed the removal of the obstacle. "While the Commission (NGISC) has recognized the traditional authority of states, through PASPA, the federal government maintains jurisdiction over sports wagering. The intent of the Commission's recommendations was to close the loophole in the 1992 Act (PASPA), a recommendation requiring federal action."

The Senator did not have to re-address the issues of states' rights and trademarks that were incorporated into PASPA. ASIA was proposed as an amendment to Senator Ted Stevens (R-AK) Olympic and Amateur Sports Act of 1978. Title II, Section 201 of ASIA would have added a "Prohibition on gambling on competitive games, including high school and college athletics and the Olympics."

Testimony from the groups that supported ASIA rehashed arguments that had been presented by similar interest groups that had supported PASPA. All of the evils that could impact young people by legal sports transactions were presented as justifications for the prohibition of legal sports wagering on amateur sports in Nevada. All of the harm to the integrity of the game that could be caused by transactions on sports was also restated only this time with a focus on amateur sports.

Senator Richard Bryan (D-NV) challenged ASIA. He argued that PASPA already prohibited the sports-based wagering schemes that were described in ASIA. He said, "Against this backdrop of a serious national problem with illegal sports gambling, this legislation (ASIA) takes the peculiar approach of targeting the only place in America where sports wagering is legal, regulated, policed, taxed and confined to adults over age 21 — the State of Nevada." [230]

The Senator placed responsibility for the enforcement of the prohibition of sports wagers on the NCAA. He argued that wagering of any kind, college or professional, was a violation of NCAA Bylaw 10.3 and enforcement of that Bylaw was "infrequent and spotty at best" according to their publicly available computer database of rules infractions.[231]

He challenged testimony from the NCAA that suggested the prohibition of sportsbooks in Nevada would deter newspapers from publishing pointspreads. "The NCAA has threatened for years to deny the NCAA-sponsored tournament press credentials to newspapers that publish betting lines, but they have never done so. Furthermore, neither this Committee nor the NGISC took testimony from newspapers to determine if, in fact, they would cease publishing betting lines if sports gambling were made illegal in Nevada."[232]

The Senator attacked the argument that ASIA would send a message to students and others that wagering on sports is illegal. "Again, there is a complete absence of any empirical evidence or fact-based testimony that America's college students (or adults for that matter) will heed such a so-called message."[233]

Blame was placed on the NCAA for problems they refused to address. "There was little testimony concerning what concrete steps the NCAA has taken to date." The Chairman of the NCAA's executive committee testified that during his ten years he has served as president of his university, he could not recall a single case of a student being expelled or

---

[230] Ibid, p. 16
[231] Ibid
[232] Ibid
[233] Ibid

otherwise disciplined for illegal gambling even though he acknowledged there are illegal student bookies on campus," Senator Bryan said.[234]

He added, "The NCAA and its members have failed to follow through on the very steps they recommended to the (NGSIC) just one year ago. There was little evidence that a new Public Service Announcement (about sports betting) was shown either frequently or during times of maximum audience exposure during the men's basketball tournament."[235]

The Senator from Nevada concluded, "For over two hundred years the federal government has deferred to the states to determine the scope and type of gaming that should be permitted within their borders. The Professional and Amateur Sports Protection Act preempted that authority as it relates to sports betting, but only prospectively. If Congress sees fit to overturn Nevada's sports wagering statutes that have been on the books for decades, it sets a dangerous precedent that should be concern for the other 47 states with some form of legal gaming operation."[236]

Senator Bryan placed the blame for problem gambling and issues with the integrity of the game on the proponents of ASIA, not the profession in the State of Nevada. His argument resonated with interest groups that supported the industry.

The American Gambling Association and its citizen action group, Americans for Casino Entertainment (ACE) became allies with the Nevada congressional delegation. ACE sent letters to members of Congress. They expressed support for the National Collegiate and Amateur Athletic Protection Act of 2001 sponsored by Nevada Senators Harry Reid, John Ensign, and others. That legislation would have increased penalties for

---

[234] Ibid
[235] Ibid, p.17
[236] Ibid, p. 18

illegal sports wagering. A prosecutorial task force would enforce the law. In addition, the Bill would have funded a study to examine gambling behavior among minors on college campuses.

This alternative was proposed after a vote in Committee on an amendment to ASIA. Senator John Ensign (R-NV) had offered an amendment that would have eliminated the section of ASIA aimed at the prohibition of wagering on college sports in Nevada. The 10-10 tie vote on the markup of the Bill shelved the measure for another time. The additional time allowed ACE to continue efforts to resist Senator McCain.

In the meantime, Senator Harry Reid (D-NV) had risen to second place in positions of power in the Senate. As the Senate Majority Whip he was able to control when legislation would be sent to the floor of the Senate for a vote.

After he had ascended to that position, Senator Reid said, "The Bill (ASIA) won't pass out of Congress. We'll kill it. I am confident. I wasn't confident last year, but I am now. People are starting to understand that 90 percent of gambling done on college sports is bet illegally on college campuses. People are beginning to realize it (ASIA) is a guise to cover the incompetence of the NCAA."

The Senator did not mention that the guise was also part of the attempt to cover the issue of trademarks. A bill that would help curtail illegal sports wagering on campuses as well as protect the integrity of the game would have had a better chance to win passage than one intended to protect trademarks such as "The Road to the Final Four," "March Madness" and "The Bowl Championship Series," among others. The business matter of trademarks could have tarnished the image of the so-called integrity behind the legislation.

With the help of then Senate Majority leader Tom Daschle, Senator Reid assured his supporters that a floor vote on ASIA would be avoided. "They can't do it directly like they did before."[237]

Tactics by Senator Reid, the soon-to-be Majority leader of the Senate, accompanied by support from Senator Ensign of Nevada prevailed. ASIA did not make it to the floor of the Senate for a vote. The alliance of corporate gaming interests and Nevada senators prevailed over the alliance between the NCAA, political opponents of the business outside Nevada, and interest groups with social and moral agendas.

If the outcome had ended with a victory for the NCAA, odds are the legal sportsbook industry in Nevada would have come to an end. An argument had been made that even if ASIA became law, the industry in Nevada would have survived on the business from wagers on professional sports. That argument went so far as to suggest that business from the NFL alone would have been enough to keep the doors open for some, if not all of the sportsbooks.

The argument failed to consider the likelihood that the professional sports leagues would have sponsored another challenge to the industry in Nevada. If ASIA had become law, there would have been momentum for legislation that would have had the political support to repeal the grandfather clause of PASPA.

The efforts of Nevada's senators kept the only legal sports wagering industry in business. Their "KO" sent the opponents of the industry to a canvas from which they would not rise to fight another battle to end the legal industry through legislation that would circumvent the guarantee of a state's right.

Senator McCain exposed his lack of integrity when he tried to rescind the grandfather payment that had been made to Nevada for the votes from the state that

---

[237] *Las Vegas Review Journal* July 3, 2001, "Reid: College bet ban finished."

made it possible for PASPA to become law. When the Senator decided to rescind the privilege that had been given to Nevada, the senators from that state were forced to end their alliance with the coalition that supported PASPA. Nevada politicians were forced to protect the economic interests of their State. No politician would blame them for they would also do.

The attempt to repeal that privilege amounted to a stab in the back with consequences as painful as those that could result from what amounted to a divorce from members of the PASPA coalition. The Senator learned another lesson about divorce he should have learned from his personal experience.

The tactics he used to renege on a deal were unacceptable to more than the politicians in Nevada. He violated one of the bottom lines for politicians. Exposure of a double-cross would make it more difficult to make deals in the future. Politicians would become even more skeptical of fellow members who had reneged on a deal after the goods had been delivered.

Even Senator McCain had to acknowledge, "The Senators from Nevada who cannot be faulted for their able efforts on behalf of their constituents have sought to derail S. 718 by introducing a separate bill that they claim targets the real problem of illegal gambling."[238]

He failed to anticipate their guile. The odds against the two Senators from Nevada might have appeared to be "off the boards"[239] to the Senator from Arizona because of the numbers of members of Congress who supported his legislation. The possibility that two Senators allied with support from their

---

[238] Press Release from Senator John McCain: "It's Time to Ban Wagering on Amateur Sports" 8/1/2001

[239] Lingo from the profession to indicate that the proposition would not make the boards of the sportsbooks because the odds for one side would be prohibitive. There would be no interest in two-way action on the other side because the outcome appeared certain.

corporate gaming interests in Nevada could prevail over an alliance of corporate, social, moral, and political interests throughout America might have led to his conclusion that Nevada could not win. If there had been a betting proposition: "WILL ASIA BE PASSED BY CONGRESS?" proponents of the legislation would have likely made "YES" the prohibitive favorite.

However, Senator McCain rolled snake-eyes in this version of Monopoly. The outcome was similar to his experiences at the dice tables in Las Vegas owned by the same casino corporations he attempted to betray by the closure of the doors to their sportsbooks.

His alliance did not anticipate one option of checks and balances that would determine the outcome. This option skewed the value of numbers in a way that made a minority the favorite. Two Senators established a deadlock in Committee that would, in turn, prevent a vote on the floor of the Senate where the advantage of numbers would come into play.

The coalition that supported ASIA lost because they tried to rescind the political compromise that had been made in order for PASPA to become law. The grandfather clause that exempted Nevada and other states was necessary to pass the legislation. Even the proponents admitted those votes were essential. They came at the expense of the grant of sports wagering monopolies to the grandfathers.

But the balance of power that led to the passage of PASPA was altered after the Nevada Senators changed sides to become opponents of that coalition. They were in a position to defeat the challenge to their corporate constituents by the corporate supporters of ASIA. Legal and illegal sports wagering would continue to co-exist in a system dictated by an alliance of political and corporate interests.

More from "Way Beyond the Fringes"

The failure to enact ASIA was a result of politics gone wrong not because the business of sports transactions had been vindicated. While both alliances could live with the outcome, the Senator from the State of the Unrepresented would not have been satisfied. A State's right had been preserved at the expense of States Rights.

"I regret that the rights of individual members of the profession were sacrificed in order to preserve that State's right. I would have supported the Nevada Senators in order to keep hope alive for the profession, but my payback for that support would have to come in the form of support for the possibility to continue to fight for the legalization of the profession throughout America."

As part of my campaign I would have had to raise the question, "How can we be responsible for the integrity of the games, if the profession is illegal outside Nevada? How can we help the sports leagues maintain integrity of the game they profess to be of utmost importance if we cannot be above board with responses to them about possible threats to integrity from everywhere in America"

The Senator would also have answered the question. "The profession in Nevada has helped you with those alerts. That is one example of how this system could be expanded to deter other attempts to compromise the games throughout America, that is, unless you don't want those threats uncovered for other reasons."

The campaign would also address the dilemma, "[y]ou have created in which a state of segregation compromises the integrity of America. The political compromises that have been necessary to impose that order are not worth the value of trademarks that could be protected through contracts with the profession for the use of your product."

The Senator would have to add, "[m]embers of the profession are not in a position to make those agreements with you. Since they are at the mercy of economic and political alliances that do not give them a voice in their own wellbeing as well as yours and the democracy that represents America, you must open the door for us."

Instead of a response that addressed the need for freedom, the opponents of the business began another effort that focused on the need to restrict the technology that would present another threat to their interests. Segregation of the profession within Nevada could not be used to restrict the technology that expanded the ways in which wagers could be made illegally. The Internet opened the door to those possibilities

Opponents of the business responded with an attempt to close that door with legislation that would expand on prohibition through an extension of segregation. They would try to segregate America from the rest of the world.

The Internet Gambling Prohibition Act

The Wire Act was a tool to help enforce the prohibition against interstate wagers over the telephone. The Information Age opened the door to the Internet as an alternative way to make those transactions. The Internet extended the possibilities beyond America. Members of the profession would be able to make wagers from states where the transaction was illegal to nations where the transaction was legal. The Internet had an international ring that differed from those with the telephone. This ring could circumvent the Wire Act.

While Senator McCain led one fight against the profession, another Senator from Arizona launched a campaign to expand the Wire Act in a way that would prohibit sports transactions over the Internet.

In 1995, Senator Jon Kyl (R-AZ) led an alliance that was organized to prevent all types of gambling via the Internet As Senator Kyl said, "From the beginning of time, societies have sought to prohibit most forms of gambling."[240]

The Senator used findings from the National Gambling Impact Study Commission to justify the Internet Gambling Prohibition Act (IGPA) of 1999. That legislation was deemed necessary because NFL studies "indicate that sports-betting is a growing problem for high school and college students." The opportunity to wager on the Internet would "entice youthful gamblers into potentially costly losses.[241]

Families also had to be protected from that evil. The Senator said, "Gambling has terrible conse-quences for families and communities. And, according to the Council on Compulsive Gambling, "five percent of all gamblers become addicted. Many of those turn to crime and commit suicide. We pay for all those tragedies."[242]

Beside young people and families, the Senator said the legislation was necessary to protect busi-nesses and the economy from the harm that would stem from Internet gambling. He intimated that gambling caused the rise in filings for bankruptcy that eliminated $40 billion in personal debt. His source for the estimate was a report from the television program "Nightline." He used the words of the host, Ted Koppel, who said, "If anything promises to increase the level of personal debt in this country, expanding access to

---

[240] Statement of Senator Jon Kyl regarding Hearing on the Internet Gambling Prohibition Act March 23, 1999, p.1

[241] Ibid

[242] Ibid

gambling should do it." Absenteeism at work and declining productivity were also included as consequences of gambling.[243]

Addiction, criminal behavior, unfair payouts, and cost were also added as reasons for the need to address a situation that "threatens to disrupt each state's careful balancing of its own public welfare and fiscal concerns by making gambling available across state and national boundaries with little or no regulatory control."[244]

Senator Kyl advocated federal intervention because "States cannot protect their citizens from Internet gambling if anyone can transmit it into their states." A precedent for federal intervention had been established by the Wire Act of 1961 which prohibited the use of telephones for wagers and gambling information, but the Wire Act could not be used to counter the technology that had added options to the ways through which people could communicate. According to the American Bar Association, "The problem with current federal law is that the communications technology it specifies is dated and limited."[245]

Senator Kyl responded that his legislation "brings federal law up to date. With the advent of new, sophisticated technology, the Wire Act is becoming outdated. The Internet Gambling Prohibition Act corrects that problem."

IGPA was proposed before the Judiciary Subcommittee on Technology. The legislation encompassed more than sports transactions. Other forms of gambling such as poker and blackjack had to be included because online casinos offered more than sports wagers. The legislation targeted the businesses

---

[243] Ibid
[244] Ibid
[245] Ibid, p. 3

that offered gambling options, not the people who played them.

Senator Richard Bryan of Nevada who had led the opposition to ASIA co-sponsored the legislation. He argued that this type of gambling was different. "Internet gambling is beyond the ability of states to control and regulate." He said the new technology opened doors so that "any youngster can gamble on the Internet." And the Internet was "a prime candidate for consumer rip-offs."[246]

Senator Bryan did not mention the need to defend the corporate interests in Nevada he represented. The Senator did not mention the need to defend the freedom of the people of Nevada he was elected to represent. He did not have to mention what is obvious in his system of representative democracy.

Mr. Frank Fahrenkopf, Jr., President and CEO of the American Gaming Association (AGA) who had also opposed ASIA, joined Senator Bryan in support of the legislation. He dismissed the accusation that the reason behind his position was because "the traditional gaming industry is fearful of the competition from Internet gambling." He said, "If the well-branded casino companies entered that market, they would quickly capture dominant market share."

He did not mention that those "well-branded" casino companies did not want potential customers to become gamblers who would prefer to stay at home. Nevada casino corporations wanted those customers in Las Vegas at their hotels, restaurants, and entertainment venues in order to reap additional profits from their presence at the properties.

Mr. Fahrenkopf also argued that "Internet gambling should not be sanctioned until demonstrable methods are shown that allow states to retain their

---

[246] *Las Vegas Review Journal* article by John Edwards, "Bryan rips into Internet Casinos" August 14, 1997, p. 1

right to set policy and enforce state law for gaming activities by persons within their boundaries."

He said there was a need for federal enforcement of laws that had been passed. Federal enforcement was necessary to protect individuals as well as the states in which they lived. "This will require the federal government to make a sincere commitment to opening diplomatic channels to assure international cooperation in the enforcement of the law."[247]

At the same time that Senator Bryan and Mr. Fahrenkopf expressed their opposition to ASIA because the legislation posed a threat to the monopoly in Nevada, they also opposed the opportunity to expand the options for members of the profession to make their transactions. Neither Senator Bryan nor Mr. Fahrenkopf would dare open the door to legal competition for the monopolies they represented.

Despite his assurance that Nevada corporations would dominate market share if they entered the competition, the sports-wagering industry proved otherwise. Offshore sportsbooks had taken the initiative to compete with Las Vegas for primacy in the industry. They had made Sin City the "ex-sports-betting capital of the world." Offshore sportsbooks made it possible for members of the profession to be able to once again "shop"[248] for different numbers on games, an option that had been curtailed by the corporate takeover of the industry in Nevada.

Offshore sportsbooks had also taken the initiative to post opening lines on games before the Stardust

---

[247] Testimony: THE INTERNET PROHIBITION ACT OF 1997 pp. 1-3

[248] Shopping for the best odds is an endeavor that is essential to success for handicappers in the profession. It is a must for Professionals to shop for opportunities to lay 6 points instead of 7 on a football game or to take 10 instead of 9. Professionals cannot allow themselves to be at the mercy of one sportsbook that only offers them one number on any game. Handicappers must have options in order to be successful. The profession is a "numbers" game in which rules must be respected or else.

Race and Sportsbook, the erstwhile leader in the endeavor at that time. "Offshores" also posted odds on more games than those that had been on the boards in Las Vegas. They also took the initiative to offer more options for wagers on games such as first half lines and propositions the Las Vegas sportsbooks were eventually forced to post on their boards. In addition, limits on wagers not only rivaled but surpassed those of most Nevada sportsbooks. Offshore sportsbooks forced Las Vegas sportsbooks to be more competitive with them in order to keep the dollars home.

The revolution in technology had changed the playing field for the business. 800 numbers became plentiful. They were less costly for the offshores. The Internet offered more. Online casinos offered more than transactions on sports. All casino games could be played from the privacy of home.

The transition from telephone transactions on sports alone to Internet transactions on all casino options helped to force the Nevada corporate monopolies that had opposed ASIA to support IGPA. They could not mention the fact that their support would preserve the legal monopoly on sports transactions that had been granted to Nevada by PASPA and through the rejection of ASIA. They could remain consistent in their inconsistency.

Other interest groups presented testimony that expanded on the need for the legislation. They argued there was a need to protect individuals from businesses in cyberspace that might exploit their customers without penalties. This testimony recommended that states should exercise control over business on the Internet.

Professional and amateur corporate sports monopolies also testified in support of the legislation. The NFL, NBA, MLB, NHL, and the NCAA reiterated arguments they had made in support of PASPA and ASIA. This testimony was supported by statistics that documented the growth of the offshore sportsbooks. "The number of Internet websites has grown from two in 1996 to over 70 today (3/23/99). It is estimated that Internet sites will book over $600 million in sports bets in 1998, up from $60 million just two years ago," said Senator Kyl.

He added a statement from the NCAA to support his legislation. The NCAA had concluded, "There is no question the advent of the Internet sports gambling poses a direct threat to all sports organizations that first and foremost must ensure the integrity of each contest played."

Although sports transactions were not the sole target of prohibition as they had been in PASPA and ASIA, the industry garnered the most attention. It had a head start on the other options that were offered by casinos outside the U.S. Those options did not have to confront the opposition of corporate sports monopolies.

In addition, telephone transactions on sports did not require the visual and physical interaction of other games. The Internet added the option to interact. The opponents of sports transactions were forced to include their opposition to include a prohibition on all games. They were not in a position to single out the business of sports transactions.

Unlike the Wire Act, concerns about enforcement measures against Internet transactions raised questions about IGPA. There were questions as to how far the federal government could intrude in the lives of individuals in order to stop them from making transactions through the Internet. No one would advocate federal intervention that allowed the enforcers to enter the homes of players. And at the other end of the spectrum of enforcement, the federal government could not enforce prohibitions on other nations that had legalized the operation of gaming businesses.

Resolution of the issues that accompanied enforcement could not be resolved. Only the questions of whom and what to target were settled. IGPA targeted casinos that offered gambling not the gamblers. All of the gambling options offered by offshore casinos were included. Exemptions were made for state lotteries, fantasy sports leagues and certain activities legitimized by the Interstate Horse Racing Act of 1978.

There was little testimony to oppose the legislation as there had been with PASPA and Asia; however, E-Lottery attempted to derail the legislation. E-Lottery sells lottery tickets online. They hired a lobbying firm run by Mr. Jack Abramoff to help them defeat the legislation. His efforts prompted Majority Whip Tom DeLay (R-TX) to vote against IGPA. Mr. DeLay then placed the legislation on a suspension calendar which banned amendments and limited debates. The legislation could not generate support of the two-thirds majority that was required by rules of the suspension calendar. As a result, the legislation was placed on hold until further notice.

House Rule 4419, the Internet Gambling Funding Prohibition Act (IGFPA) was proposed as an alternative. This legislation applied "only where such bet or wager is unlawful under any applicable federal or state law in the state in which the bet or wager is initiated, received, or otherwise made." This legislation also failed to pass a vote in the House.

In 2003, IGFPA was resurrected. The legislation focused on the use of credit cards that would be used to make wagers. IGFPA required financial institutions to identify and prevent wagers that were made through their payment systems.

Those financial institutions would have been monitored by the Office of the Comptroller of the Currency, the Board of Governors of the Federal Reserve System, the Federal Deposit Insurance Corporation, the Office of Thrift Supervision, and the

National Credit Union Administration. The Federal Trade Commission and the Department of Justice would have been responsible for additional enforcement. In addition, the legislation would have established the Office of Electronic Funding Oversight in the Department of Treasury.

Once again, protection for young people and problem gamblers was offered as justifications for legislation that was intended to prohibit what proponents called the "crack cocaine of gambling." Money laundering by criminal organizations was also included as part of the justification. For some reason, no one mentioned the integrity of the game as a justification.

This time those who opposed the legislation were allowed to present their arguments. The former Attorney General of Indiana and the President and Chief Operating Officer of MGM-Mirage Online expressed concern about the ability to enforce the provisions. Both witnesses supported the alternative legislation proposed by Representative John Conyers (D-MI). His legislation would have established a Study Commission on Internet gambling.

Lobbyists also contributed to the defeat of this version of the legislation. They were supported by congressional opponents of the attempt to use government to intrude into the lives of individuals in their homes. The inability of Congress to reconcile the Senate and House versions of the Bill kept the legislation in limbo. Conflicts between the motives behind legislation that would either prohibit or regulate actions by businesses or individuals could not be reconciled.

Uniform Internet Gambling Enforcement Act

Ten years after Senator Kyl had introduced IGPA Congress passed the Uniform Internet Gambling

Enforcement Act (UIGEA) of 2006. While the name of the legislation was different, the intent was similar. The Bill was able to pass the House of Representatives through a political version of the "back door cover." UIGEA did not have the votes to pass. The legislation would have been shelved had it not been for supporters who were able to pass the Bill as an attachment to the Safe Port Act.

Most of the usual proponents expressed most of the usual arguments to support the legislation. Opponents who had not testified before the legislation arrived at that Safe Port were unable to express their concerns until hearings were held on the implementation of UIGEA.

At those hearings, officials from the Federal Reserve and the Department of Treasury voiced concern about the development of regulations that would implement UIGEA. They said the law was not clear about which types of gambling were illegal online.

"The challenge we have is interpreting...federal laws that Congress itself isn't sure what they mean," said Louise Roseman, Director of the Federal Reserve Department of Bank Operations and Payment Systems. She added, "It will be very difficult to shut off payment systems for use of Internet gambling transactions. The implementing statute will not be iron clad at all."[249]

Institutions that would be responsible for enforcement also opposed the law. A member of the American Banking Association said the law "makes financial institutions the police, prosecutors, and judges in place of real enforcement officers. The path leads to an increased cost and administrative burden to the banks and erosion in the performance of the payments

---

[249] "UIGEA too ambiguous to work, say hearing witnesses" bestage.com, 4/04/2008, p 2

system, but it will not result in stopping illegal internet gambling transactions."[250]

A member of the Financial Services Roundtable which included Visa, Master Card, and Wells Fargo among its members pointed out that 100 billion payments are processed by financial institutions each year. That alone would make it difficult to identify which payments were related to gambling. "They cannot know if a transaction is restricted unless they have in hand specifics of the transaction in almost all instances they will not have." And enforcement "could impose significant compliance burdens on financial institutions by increasing their role in policing illegal activities to determine whether a transaction is illegal." He added that monitoring of websites was "...inappropriate to include in a financial institution's monitoring activity."[251]

The Poker Players Alliance opposed UIGEA. Their lobbyists argued that the law should not include poker. They claimed that poker is a game of skill, not chance. According to them there is a difference between games of skill such as poker and games of chance such as dice and roulette. They said games that require skill were not gambling as other games of chance.

One of their lobbyists added his two cents. "Online poker is a legal, thriving industry and poker players deserve the consumer protections and the freedom to play provided for in this legislation," said Alphonse D'Amato, head of the Poker Players Alliance.[252]

Members of Congress also had reservations about the Bill because of the possible implications for gaming corporations that might choose to operate online in the

---

[250] Ibid

[251] Ibid

[252] Barney Frank Introduces New Gambling Bill" by Allan Moody, About.com: Sports Gambling

[252] Wikipedia Online gambling p.3

future. Congresswoman Shelley Berkeley (D-NV) proposed alternative legislation that would have called for a study of online gambling. Nevada corporate casinos supported that alternative.

Opposition from other interest groups led to exemptions in the legislation for horse racing and fantasy sports. The NFL lobbied for an exemption for fantasy sports. Corporations that paid for the right to televise NFL games would have the right to benefit from their fantasy sports leagues. Since the television networks paid for the games, the NFL supported the exemption for fantasy sports.

The Wire Act of 1961 was also excluded from the legislation. There was disagreement among law enforcement officials as to whether the Wire Act could be included because the legislation had been directed at the prohibition of sports wagers over the telephone between states.

In 2002, the 5th Circuit U.S. Court of Appeals had decided that the Wire Act applied only to sports wagers. The Justice Department disagreed. Officials argued that the Wire Act applied to all forms of gambling over the Internet.

In 2004, the 5th Circuit Court of Appeals supported the Justice Department. The Court upheld a decision by a District Court for the Middle District of Louisiana. Judges said, "The government's interest is specifically directed towards the advertising of illegal activity, namely Internet gambling."

Rather than test the waters for the application of the Wire Act to the Internet, proponents chose to exclude that piece of legislation. The law had already been justified by the prosecution of Jay Cohen.

Mr. Cohen had lost a gamble that his return to the U.S. from Antigua would set a precedent. He bet that the Wire Act was not applicable to operators of offshore sportsbooks that were licensed in nations where sports transactions were legal. But a "backdoor" cover by the prosecution in which the rules of the game were rigged in their favor led to Mr. Cohen's prosecution. The verdict sent a message to other U.S. citizens in a similar position as Mr. Cohen who might have also considered a return to the U.S. The verdict left these members of the profession with the choice of freedom in exile or a sentence to prison in their homeland.

Despite the fact that the Wire Act had been removed as an obstacle to passage of the legislation, proponents had to ride the coattails of Homeland Security to sail it into a Safe Port. Homeland Security became as relevant to UIGEA as the Commerce Clause was to PASPA.

UIGEA had been scheduled to become effective in 2009, but the implementation was delayed because the Regulation for UIGEA that was published in late 2008 did not define "unlawful internet gambling."[253]

Interest groups that claimed exemptions to the law had appealed to the Federal Reserve and the Treasury Department for a delay in the implementation. An alliance of poker players, the thoroughbred horse racing association and greyhound track operators were granted an extension on the implementation of the regulation until December 2010.

Internet Gambling Regulation, Consumer Protection and Enforcement Act

In between the delays to implement UIGEA, Congressman Barney Frank (D-MA) proposed to repeal the legislation. He described UIGEA as a "bizarre piece of legislation." He said, "It is a terrible idea and there are a large number of people who think it is a terrible idea. The worst that happens is that enough anti-gambling busybodies will be less inclined to interfere in people's lives."[254]

The Congressman proposed the Internet Gambling Regulation, Consumer Protection and Enforcement Act (IGRCPEA) as an alternative that would regulate instead of prohibit online gambling. This bill "provides for the licensing of Internet gambling activities by the Secretary of Treasury, to provide for consumer protections on the Internet, to enforce the Tax Code and for other purposes," he said.[255]

But the complexities that surrounded the enforcement of his legislation led to a situation similar to the one that had caused the delay on the vote for UIGEA. IGRCPEA stalled in the House of Representatives. There was speculation that IGRCPEA might have to be added as a rider to another bill the same way UIGEA had been added to the Safe Ports Act.

Opposition from the NFL also helped to keep the Bill in limbo. After their success with the exemption for fantasy football from UIGEA, NFL lobbyists stretched their tentacles. They lobbied for the inclusion of a prohibition against sports transactions in IGRCPEA. Congressman Frank intended to legalize the business. He attempted to take advantage of the exemption of the Wire Act from UIGEA. But the Congressman caved in to the opposition of the NFL to the version of the Bill he introduced in 2007. He removed the option for sports transactions from subsequent versions of the legislation.

That did not satisfy the NFL. They remained opposed to IGRCPEA until 2010 when Representative Peter King (R-NY) attached an amendment that would prohibit sports transactions as an option for the companies that would be licensed under the law. The

---

[254] "Barney Frank Introduces New Internet Gambling Act" Gambling911.com 4/26/07

[255] Barney Frank Introduces New Gambling Bill" by Allan Moody About.com: Sports Gambling

amendment stated, "No provision of this subchapter should be construed as authorizing a Licensee to operate an Internet gambling facility that knowingly accepts bets or wagers on sporting events from persons located in the United States in violation of section 3702 of Title 28, United States Code, except for fantasy of simulation sports games."

"We don't oppose (it) now since it includes language we had hoped for. The amendment language adequately addressed our specific concern. We are pleased with the outcome," said Brian McCarthy, Vice President of Communications of the NFL.[256]

"Unfortunately, they do have a strong lobbying presence," Congressman Frank said. "I'm going to say it's a little odd for them to learn that...well actually what they're saying is if you let the bill go through, people might start betting on sports games. I mean the hypocrisy of acting as if they don't know that already happens and not at all troubled by it a little bit disappointing."[257]

The decision by the NFL met with the approval of the Poker Players Alliance. They lobbied in support of the legislation despite the fact that the King Amendment would prohibit transactions on another game of skill. Their definition of a game of skill would also be applicable to sports transactions, a business in which poker players also participate. But self-interest prevailed over integrity, when they allowed the NFL to do the dirty work that would legitimize poker, but prohibit sports transactions.

The Poker Players Alliance did not want to test the possibility that opposition to the Amendment could have rekindled a debate about the prohibition of all types of gambling. They did not want to kindle an

---

[256] "NFL Drops Opposition to Internet Gambling Regulation, Consumer Protection and Enforcement Act"Pokernew.com 8/10/2010
[257] "Barney Frank on Legalized State Online Gambling" Gambling 911.com 9/01/2009

argument that would compare degrees of skill that legitimize what they do in comparison to other types of gambling. The odds against winning that debate would have been worse than the odds for keno.

Despite this tactic by the Alliance, the prohibition of sports transactions in the legislation opened the door for politicians to attempt to overcome the odds against comparisons. They tried to amend the legislation with the Game Protection Act and the Internet Skill Game Licensing and Control Act. Those amendments would exempt games such as poker, bridge, chess, and other so-called "games of skill" that did not include sports.[258]

Congressman Frank added to the confusion when he decided to limit the legalization of online gambling to poker even though that profession had already been equated with the business of sports transactions through enforcement measures taken by the U.S. Department of Justice. In 2009, the Justice Department seized over $34 million from 27,000 individual accounts of online poker players. The Justice Department had redirected its enforcement from gaming companies to individual poker players.

Despite this endeavor by the Justice Department, the enforcement of UIGEA has not been implemented. The debate over whether the enforcement agencies would have to focus their efforts on individuals as well as gaming companies could not be resolved and questions about which forms of gambling amount to games of skill rather than chance have not been answered, except for the profession of sports transactions.

Although sports transactions are only one among all of the other options offered by online casinos, the

---

[258] Thanks to the late Lois Ann Williams Czuchra for a reminder from her poetry about the consequences of comparisons. "...in comparisons we can lose something, mostly ourselves."

profession has been singled out for prohibition the same way it had been by PASPA and ASIA. Even though poker has not been a target of that prohibition, that profession was lumped together with sports because of its prohibition on the Internet along with other casino games. All types of gambling had been either directly or indirectly equated with sports until Congressman Frank singled out the profession for prohibition after he caved in to the demands of the NFL.

The issues with definitions and comparisons have become part of another problem for the legislation, a problem that transcends the borders of America into international politics and economics. Whatever the definitions and comparisons that are in vogue at the time, the legislation has had an impact on the sovereignty of nations that have legalized wagers on all types of gambling without regard to whether they are games of "skill or chance."

PartyGaming.Bwin, Casanova Enterprises, and Sportingbet and other offshore gaming operations were forced to suspend their money transactions for U.S. customers. Even though those companies are legal in the nations that license them, they were forced to respond to the long arm of U.S. laws.

The government of Antigua and Barbuda had welcomed those companies after a decision was made to diversify its economy in order to accommodate the business of Internet gambling. In 1999 they licensed 119 operators. These operators paid the government $7.4 million in licensing fees. Those revenues amounted to more than ten percent of the gross national product for that nation.

Antigua was forced to impose additional regulatory restrictions on these businesses after the U.S and the United Kingdom warned investors to be wary of transactions with the financial institutions in that country. The warning implied that those institutions might be involved in money laundering and associations with organized crime.

As a result, 35 banks were forced to close between 1999 and 2004. There were estimates that the number of Internet and gambling operations had decreased by as much as 710%. The number of people employed in the businesses had decreased by 750% and licensing revenues decreased by approximately 410%.[259]

Antigua and Barbuda interpreted this threat from UIGEA as the final touch that would put a nail in the coffin of its Internet gambling business. In 2003, they appealed to the World Trade Organization (WTO) to protest the prohibitions in UIGEA that would restrict access to their free trade with other members. The appeal asserted that the U.S. ban on Internet wagering violated the rights of Antigua and Barbuda as a member of the WTO. That nation argued that the ban was a violation of the Treaty signed by all member nations of WTO. They sought compensation of $3.4 billion from the U.S. as well as an exemption from U.S. patent and copyright laws.

In 2007, the WTO ruled in favor of Antigua. That nation was awarded $21 million in trade sanctions that would allow them to penalize U.S. trademark and copyright laws. The U.S. admitted the violation, but argued that the penalty should have been less than $1 million. In addition, the U.S. decided to withdraw its commitment to the gambling and betting services sector of the WTO General Agreement on Trade in Services. That decision would remove the U.S as a target of future challenges from other members of WTO against prohibitions on Internet gambling.

One factor complicated the United States' position. Wagering on horses on the Internet in the United

---

[259] The Trade of Cross Border Gambling and Betting: The WTO Dispute Between Antigua and the United States" by James Thayer Duke Law and Technology Review no.0013 11/05/2004

States remains legal. The WTO decided the trade sanctions would continue until the U.S. decided to allow Americans to either wager on horse racing with foreign gaming operators or to prohibit those transactions over the Internet.

The U.S. tried to settle the issue with concessions in other trade-related areas. Those concessions did not satisfy European nations. They argued that the U.S. targeted specific websites and ignored others. A report by the European Commission stated that U.S. laws on gambling discriminated against foreign Internet gambling operators. The report concluded that those laws denied European companies the right to compete for customers in the U.S. The Commission left open their option to file a complaint against the U.S. with the WTO.

However, even if the U.S. decides to comply with the recommendations of the European Commission and the decision of the WTO, sports transactions will remain the exception to freedom of trade on the Internet. Poker and other forms of gambling may be approved for the Internet because they do not have to confront the opposition from corporate monopolies. There are no corporate versions of the NFL, NBA, MLB, NHL, and the NCAA that oppose those the people who engage in poker, blackjack, or craps.

While the corporate sports monopolies have been able to hold serve against sports transactions through the legislation, their attempts to prevent the transaction cannot be implemented. The inability to formulate regulations reflects the inability to enact what cannot be done.

Members of our profession have always found ways to get around the attempts to prohibit them from doing what they want to do. Even though there is an exit sign for sports transactions on the road to cyberspace, corporate monopolies cannot keep the members from the detours that bypass those exit signs.

And, even if the regulations reduce the number of transactions, they will confront another situation that will reshape a picture definitions cannot control. "Trickle down" from the domestic and global recession will impact the need for Tax revenue. That "trickle" has already opened the door for allies to side with the profession out of economic necessity. They know the outflow of revenue to other nations from sports transactions will continue despite UIGEA and IGRCPEA.

The Land of Make Believers

These efforts to contain the business contradict the principles that are supposed to distinguish America from other nations. Principles that are supposed to be the foundation for freedom and justice for all were swept aside by a coalition of economic and political interests. They decided sports transactions would be prohibited even at the cost of legal segregation.

This effort dictated an 11th Commandment to people in the business. "Thou shall not use what we have taken from the freedom created by "We, the people". We shall preserve our benefits whatever the cost. 'You, the people' who have made it possible for us to profit from America must now abide by the limits we impose on your freedom.

Corporate sports monopolies justified their legislation with moral arguments that are a cover for the bottom line of corporate sports monopolies. They used this cover to enact legislation that would prevent a trickle down of benefits to people in the business. Their lack of morality was exposed by the legal segregation to which they lowered themselves in order to retain their home field advantages.

Morality was center stage for the justification of PASPA, but morality alone would not justify the use the Commerce Clause of the Constitution to prohibit sports transactions. Use of the Commerce Clause exposed the economic reasons behind the PASPA. The Commerce Clause became the tool for the corporate sports monopolies to exercise control over their patent rights. The make believers would have had Americans believe otherwise.

Proponents of ASIA attempted to extend this illusion. PASPA had left the door open for the NCAA to sponsor legislation that would finish what the legislative effort had started. ASIA would have prohibited one of the "grandfathers" in PASPA from the exploitation of the patent rights claimed by the NCAA.

The NCAA employed moral arguments to justify the need for ASIA. The legislation would help to protect the integrity of young people who play their games. The umbrella of morality would cover the motive of patent rights that was behind the legislation.

Promises of payoffs from the NCAA to the State of Arizona led to sponsorship of legislation by Arizona Senator John McCain that would have prohibited sports transactions on their games. In return, Arizona was rewarded with sites for the Road to the Final Four, for BCS games, as well as for other Bowl games. But morality could not prevail over the politics that had led to the creation of the "grandfather." The make-believers were not able to make believers out of those who benefitted from the constitutional guarantee of Nevada's states right.

Morality faded into the sunset with legislation the make believers proposed for the Internet. The alphabet soup of legislation attempted to exercise control over the technology people in the business could use to circumvent the prohibitions PASPA had not addressed. Internet legislation would have extended the control of the make believers beyond what the Wire Act had established for transactions across state borders. Internet legislation would extend the prohibition to transactions across international borders.

The technology of the Information Age expanded the efforts of the corporate sports monopolies to protect their patent rights from exploitation by other nations. Internet legislation led to conflicts with other nations over free trade. Whether it was moral for people in America to make transactions on sports evolved into a conflict over whether those people could engage in free trade with other nations. The right of people in the business to engage in free trade would be challenged by Internet legislation designed to protect the patent rights of corporate sports monopolies.

Proponents of the Internet legislation were confronted by the fact that the enforcement of the prohibition on sports transactions is easier said than done. The need to protect patent rights from the exploitation by the technology of the Information Age created opposition from people who would have to enforce the legislation.

Business and government agencies voiced opposition to the regulations that were necessary to enforce the alphabet soup of legislation. They rejected the burden of responsibility other make believers attempted to impose on them. Once again, people in the business were supported by people outside the business. Since people in the business refused to organize to protect their interests, they had to rely on others to help keep them in business.

One of the reasons they have not organized is because handicapping and oddsmaking have prevailed over the need to make time to use those skills to contest the system that segregates them. The sound of silence from people in the business has handed the ball to the make believers to define them and their business. They defined the business as "gambling." People who engage in the enterprise were defined as "gamblers." All of the evils that accompany that word were incorporated in the moral persuasion that was used as cover for all of the attempts to prohibit the business.

Arguments that highlighted the immorality of gambling and the association of the business with organized crime suffice by themselves at the outset of this conflict. They evolved into cover for the protection of business interests. People who benefit from those business interests used the definitions that had been imposed on the business by their predecessors in this conflict. Time had proven that terms such as betting and gambling could serve their purposes. Corporate sports monopolies solidified the home field advantage they had inherited from the moralists. This edge was necessary to reinforce definitions that distinguished the business from Wall Street and other businesses that gamble on the future. Definitions also separated people in the business who "shop" for the best numbers from people in other businesses who were defined as "bargain hunters" who shop for the best price for whatever item they want to purchase. Make believers censored the facts of our business in order to make their definitions. They do not mention the fact that the transaction is one that can be made face to face. It can also be made via the telephone and through cyber-space. Transactions can be made on credit or with money left on deposit. Definitions imposed by the make believers do not acknowledge the fact that all of these methods are safe. The method by which the transaction is made does not present a physical danger to the parties involved or to anyone else.

Make believers attempted to ignore the facts when they imposed the 10% poll tax on the transaction. If they could have made the legal transaction unprofitable for both parties the business would be out of business. The facts of the way business is conducted refuted this effort. People in the business deemed the business safe enough for them to warrant their effort to circumvent the tax. Their definition prevailed over the one that made it a part of organized crime.

If the business had not been defined as one that is a part of organized crime, the Wire Act would not have been necessary to target the communication of transactions over the telephone. The Wire Act attempted to extend what make believers had started with the tax. The business became part of organized crime because the make believers made the transaction illegal. Make believers created a definition of illegality that did not fit the definition of the transaction.

Make believers had to change their tactics to support their definitions. PASPA and ASIA defined the business in a way that made it a susceptible to federal prohibition. If the business were defined as commerce prohibited by the Constitution, then the make believers would be able to have their way. However, their definition confronted a definition established by the State of Nevada. This state's rights reaffirmed the definition of sports transactions as a business that could be regulated by the state. Revenue for the state reaffirmed that definition. The facts prevailed over the definitions Senators Bradley and McCain attempted to impose on the business.

Make believers behind the Internet legislation attempted to impose their definition on the business another way. Their alphabet soup of legislation would deny people in the business the use of computers to make transactions. Perhaps they envisioned a future George Orwell had described in "1984." In this version of that story the right to privacy would be compromised by need to protect patent rights. But even "Big Brother" has been unable to define this situation in a way that to get around the facts. Attempts to redefine a situation to fit their facts has kept the regulations in limbo.

People in the business have proven that the facts speak for themselves. The business is not what others have defined it to be in order to protect their interests. People in the business can use the facts they have created to define themselves. They must be the authors of what is in Oxford's, Merriam-Webster and other dictionaries.

CHAPTER SIX

TO BE FREE

The worst tragedies are those that the victims inflict on themselves.[260]

The words, the language...

"A definition is a passage that explains the meaning of a word... or a type of thing. A term may have many different senses or meanings. For each such specific sense a "definiens" is a cluster of words that defines it."[261]

"Definitions of definition meaning of word: a brief precise statement of what a word or expression means, e.g. in a dictionary act of defining word: The act or process of defining what a word or expression means..." [262]

"Definitions of definition ... 2c: a product of defining... 3: the action or process of stating the meaning of a word or a word group."[263]

The people who engage in sports transactions meet the standards that qualify them to be included in dictionaries. Publishers of those dictionaries have not met the standard that should require them to use the words and the language that define the business. Instead, dictionaries incorporate the words and the language used by those who have criminalized the business. The "process of defining what a word or

---

[260] From the *Poetics* by Aristotle
[261] Definition from Wikipedia, the free encyclopedia
[262] Definitions of definition-Bing
[263] Definition - Merriam Webster

expression means" has excluded the input of the practitioners of the business.

The victims of the "process" that established their criminal status have suffered consequences that dictate where they must live in order to be legal. There are no footnotes in the dictionaries that state "the process" that led to their segregation was determined by those who have the power to make the distinction.

Consequences of this "process" intruded into the sanctuary of the enterprise where people in the business escaped the definition of criminality. However, owners of those businesses in Nevada have had to pay a price for this pardon. This "process" permits the make believers to exploit the "patent rights" of the business. The words, the language are translated to make them acceptable to the corporate sports monopolies and the corporate networks. They have no obligation to the creators of the language to "tell it like it is" when the discussions change from "who will win" to "who is favored to win and by how much."

Announcers disguise pointspreads and odds with terms such as "favorite, huge favorite, and underdog" to meet the satisfaction of their sponsors. Those terms and others that ignore the numbers behind them distance these exploiters from the business that creates them. There is no obligation on the part of those outside the business who use our products to acknowledge the fact that pointspreads and odds make it possible for them to talk about "chalks" and "dogs."

Prognosticators on the airwaves are free to pontificate about winners of games without the need to acknowledge the equalizer of the odds that legitimate forecasts of outcomes. The terms favorite and underdog allows them to make predictions without the numbers and without the need to put their money where their mouths are.

Odds had been relegated to the status of four letter words until the corporate networks faced challenges from the media that forced them to allude to a "spread." At times, so-called "prognosticators" were forced to acknowledge "numbers" on games while they excluded any mention of their origins and contexts.

Those who have had the power over the words and language that helped to criminalize the business also exercise control over the language that can be used by sportsbooks in Nevada. They cannot post the odds for the Super Bowl under that name. They must use the term "Big Game" or "NFL Championship" or other words that describe the event. The make believers exercise their power over freedom of speech in Nevada through patent rights. Their government allows them to control "freedom of speech."

The need for the business in Nevada to create words such as "Big Game" and others is lingo that is free to everyone. This "foreign" language of the business adds to the lingo of the enterprise that coined terms such as "New Haven special," "backdoor cover," "Captain hook," "teasers," "push," "nickels," "dimes" and others that could fill a dictionary.

The words, the language are assets that can help empower people in the business to exercise control over the definitions of their business. This dictionary can become part of the "process" of the definitions of definitions. This "process" will help expose the "process" of the make believers for what it has been.

Instead of a language that describes criminality, people in the business could launch a rebellion against those who have imposed that definition. This rebellion would reframe the challenge to the system by offshore sportsbook owner Jay Cohen. This fight would challenge the foundations of the system that created the criminality of the business rather than one where the outcome of a trial was fixed by that system.

The ramifications of a commitment to redefine the enterprise might inspire others who have been or may be subjected to the judgment rendered to Mr. Cohen. The failure of people in the business to help organize a challenge to the system that renders their verdict has contributed to the persistence of the criminalization of the enterprise.

Despite the consequences of the failure to organize this challenge there is hope. Victims in the business have found ways to survive the attacks against them. Those who have endured the judgments of this system are among the "fittest of survivors," a species with the genetics to "buck the system."

Those judgments have been directed at practitioners of the business who are defined as bookmakers. There are two definitions of the word "bookmaker." One definition describes a person who designs, prints, and or binds books.[264]

Two words would be appropriate for them, but even two words would not describe their specializations and besides, specialists who engage in the making of a book would prefer to be called designers, printers, or binders rather than bookmakers.

The spoken word might associate them with the second definition of a bookmaker as a person who takes bets. Specialists who help to create a book would not choose to be included in a term that could be misconstrued to imply they are "bookies."

Nevada and casino corporations chose to avoid that comparison. "Bookie" was stricken from language of the business. They chose the term sportsbook. The term alone helped to distance the business from the criminality associated with bookmakers.

The means by which business is transacted also helps to establish this class by itself. Cash transactions distinguish sportsbooks from "credit" trans-

---

[264] Bing dictionary

actions of bookmakers. Cash deposits that are a pre-requisite for telephone transactions with sportsbooks also helps to distinguish legal from illegal.

Cash transactions do more than add to an appearance of legitimacy. They are documented with receipts that avoid disputes between the parties over what transpired. All of those transactions can be reviewed by government if there is a need to investigate "suspicious" behavior.

The definition of a sportsbook is amplified through job descriptions of those who are employed to work there. Employees are defined by State regulators and corporate owners as writers, cashiers, supervisors, and managers. Position descriptions describe the work they are hired to perform and the compensation for the position.

Although one "bookmaker" may do all of the types of work performed by the personnel at a sportsbook, that person is still defined as a "bookie" outside Nevada. They do not have the power to define all the jobs they must perform. Those who have that power relieved them of that additional responsibility.

Although offshore sportsbooks bear similarities to those in Nevada, transactions with them from America are defined as criminal. Even though transactions are made by cash with licensed businesses that employ people to work for them, offshore sportsbooks are "bookmakers." Those who have the power to define the enterprise in America have also attempted to impose that definition on nations that define their licensees as sportsbooks.

But the people who make transactions with off-shore sportsbooks or with bookmakers are not tar-geted for prosecution to the same extent or for the same reasons as Mr. Cohen. Their numbers alone, along with the privacy of the transaction, alters the playing field of enforcement. The people who are defined as bettors, gamblers, players, or investors, who may prefer chalk, dogs, pointspreads, money lines, parlays, teasers, or "props" are usually able to make their transactions without repercussion.

Regardless of how these people describe themselves or how others may define them, sportsbooks and bookmakers regard them as customers. They do not need definitions imposed on them by outsiders to know what they must do to keep them as their customers.

Dictionaries do not include the word "customer" among the definitions of those who make the transaction. Of the twenty-six definitions of the word "sport" as a noun, adjective, or verb, none link the word with transactions that are initiated by customers at a sportsbook or with a bookmaker.[265]

Among the persons defined as "gamblers" are those persons who "wager money on the outcome of games or sporting events...play games for money or some other stake...or takes a risk in order to gain advantage." The words "sports bettor" is defined with redundancy as "someone who bets."[266]

"Gambling" also has a range of definitions from "to play a game for money or property"... "to bet on an uncertain outcome," ... "to stake something on a contingency: take a chance."[267]

The words "sports" and "gamble" are linked into the redundancy "...a gamble at sporting events."[268]

The two words "sports betting" refers to a type of wager that can be made on sporting events.[269]

Gambling or betting is defined as "any behavior involving the risk of money on the outcome of a game,

---

[265] Dictionary.com
[266] The Free Dictionary and Merriam Webster
[267] Merriam Webster
[268] The Free Dictionary
[269] Sports betting from Wikipedia

contest, or even in the outcome of an activity that is partially or totally dependent upon chance.[270]

None of these definitions suggest that the people who initiate the transaction are criminals, nor do they suggest the transaction is criminal. None of the definitions connect the transaction in and of itself with criminal activity such as money laundering or to organized crime or to illegal bookmakers.

Criminality enters when law enforcement imposes their definition in order to make examples of the people who make the transactions. Individuals may be targeted if they are affiliated with a syndicate that makes transactions across state lines. If that syndicate has ties to organized crime, there is an incentive to prosecute individuals so that they might serve as examples of what might happen to other syndicates. This tactic may also be used against persons in the sanctuary of Nevada who are a part of syndicates or who choose to make transactions with bookmakers within that state.

The right to do this by law enforcement challenges a constitutional vacuum that allows people in Nevada to do what is criminal outside that state. Nowhere in the Constitution are there clauses or provisions that allow for the same transaction to be defined as both legal and illegal depending on where the parties reside.

The contradiction is magnified by the situation where people in Nevada are free to speak about their endeavors. They can discuss their business with others in public without fear of prosecution. Public acclaim for wisdom, judgment, ability, acumen, and other attributes that describe their success accompanies that freedom.

But public proclamations about the business where it is illegal can lead to jail time. That time will not be tempered with repentance that allows the

---

[270] Word IQ

defendant to reveal the secrets of their success. Leniency in sentencing may accompany lectures to others about the evils of the business. The right to freedom of speech differs for people in the business outside Nevada.

Yet the Constitution protects the freedom for people to speak about the products of the enterprise they sell wherever they reside. "Line" services that sell information about odds on games and "tout" services that sell opinions about winners of those games are protected by the Constitution. The Constitution protects their speech even though the information they sell may be used to make transactions that are illegal outside Nevada.

Where the business is legal, the Constitution empowers the State of Nevada to exercise its State's right to publish monthly and yearly reports that document profit and loss for the business. Details on these reports distinguish profits and losses by county and by the type of sporting event.

The State also has a right that allows state universities to offer courses on handicapping and oddsmaking. Those courses may be taught by "professors" who work in the business.

Freedom of speech in Nevada also means that corporate owners of sportsbooks can compete for customers through advertisements in the media. They are free to offer comps, contests, points for club cards, lower "vig"[271] along with other incentives to attract customers to their sportsbooks. The freedom to use this speech is at the discretion of the corporate owners

---

[271] "Vigorish" ("vig") is also known as "juice" and other terminology better left to the imagination.
A sportsbook may lower the "vig" in order to reduce the cost of the transaction to customers. Instead of a charge of ten cents for each dollar invested, the sportsbook may choose to reduce that charge to five cents or less in order to attract business.

of the sportsbooks who are granted that privilege by the state government.

But the "customers" who helped to create this legal business have been excluded from the "process" that governs them. There are no associations, syndicates, interest groups, unions of independent bookmakers or other types of organizations with the power to have a voice that represents their interests in this system. In Nevada, those who participate in the enterprise are defined as "customers" or "employees," not professionals or associations or business people who have a status with interests that must be served.

We are relegated to the sidelines of this playing field. Although we have been allowed on the bus, we are relegated to the back. Our self-definition has not reached a level of importance that would be essential to move to the front of this bus, the destinations of which may reach people in the business beyond the borders of Nevada.

In order to influence the direction of that bus, we must begin to jump-start the "process." That could begin by shedding the definitions that were imposed for others that would "tell it like it is." We are American citizens with rights guaranteed by the Constitution that protect what we do.

People in the business might choose to describe what we do as a profession. There are adjectives which define the word professional(s) as: "businesslike: conforming to the standards of skill, competence or character normally expected of a properly qualified and experienced person in a work environment" or "very competent" showing a degree of skill or "competence" or "doing something habitually" habitually and usually annoyingly indulging in a particular activity."[272]

Nouns that might be apropos include:

---

[272] Bing Dictionary

➤ "Somebody very competent: somebody with a high degree of skill or competence;[273]

➤ "A person having impressive competence in a particular activity;

➤ "Expert and specialized knowledge in field which one is practicing professionally";

➤ "High quality work in (examples)...primary/other research..."

➤ "Participating for gain or livelihood in an activity or field of endeavor often engaged in by amateurs..."[274]

Another option might include definitions that describe a vocation or an avocation. They are defined as a:

➤ "...special urge, inclination or predisposition to a particular or career"[275]

➤ "...occupation: a calling or career"

➤ "...hobby or pastime"

Additional examples would illustrate that the people in the business are diversified beyond the labels that have been imposed by law enforcement, corporate sports monopolies, and politicians. "We, the people" will have to flex our muscle as American citizens in order to rid the profession of the definitions that serve the business interests of those who imposed them.

Then it might be possible for an individual or group to become a sportsbook that could compete with those of the casino corporations. The freedom to make transactions with these sportsbooks could open the competition for business with offshores, some of whom may choose to relocate within America. The corporate casinos might then find themselves in a position to justify what they would have preferred to do long ago, namely, close their sportsbooks.

---

[273] Ibid

[274] Wikipedia: the free encyclopedia

[275] Free online dictionary

They chose to keep them open because they have profited from their monopoly on the business conferred by federal and state statutes. The State of Nevada and their corporate casinos have become allies with those who criminalized the business outside the state. Even those who never included Economics 101 in their curriculum know that conferred monopolies guarantee profits for their investors.

"Them times though they are a changin'." The need for revenue at all levels of government opens the door to possibilities for people in the business to change the system. The economic recession has kindled interest in the business by other states. They have expressed interest in the revenue that could be derived from the business. If "we, the people" who comprise this business can find a way to meet those interests we may be able to make "room at the top" for ourselves.

An observation from a publisher of definitions argues that "the crude all-or-nothing categories of amateur or professional should be reconsidered." A historical shift is occurring with the rise of Pro-Ams, a new category of people who are pursuing amateur activities to professional standards."[276]

This reference is to definitions of those who play professional and amateur sports. The comment is also applicable to the people who make the transactions that contribute to the success of those businesses. People in the business have also been the subject matter of definitions that ignore the "historical shift" that has transpired.

The numbers of people who comprise the business, the revolution in the technology of the business and the growth of the business beyond the borders of America demands that the "crude all-or-nothing categories" that were made by those who

---

[276] Wikipedia, the free encyclopedia

criminalized the enterprise be ended. The time has come for the people who comprise the business to rid themselves of the definitions that have been imposed by the interest groups that have created our sea of troubles.

Then our words...our language can be scrutinized, kept as is or redefined through procedures that meet with our approval. We can shape the "process" to complement the interests of those at the top who would prefer to change the system in order to benefit from the new world.

The need to redefine ourselves is as essential to change this system as it was for the "Freedom Fighters" who ended the segregation of African-Americans. Their words, their language led to the action that began the revolution to rid themselves of the definitions that created the institutionalization of "separate and unequal."

In Other Words

This journey to freedom must also be led by the people who are "separate and unequal." "We, the people" can determine whether, when, and how the "process" changes the system. Until that time comes we will remain the "dogs." In order to become the "chalk" we must MAKE THE ODDS BE WITH US.

Just as we determine who is on the boards, just as we determine who is favored and by how much, just as we determine whether or not to challenge those odds, we can also make the determination to shape the future of the business. Even though we cannot control the outcome, we have the power to put it on our "futures board." If we don't "put up" the outcome of that future will be a "lock" for our opponents.

Excuses for inaction abound. Even though this "system" may be beyond our control it does not preclude the effort. People in the business "put up" despite the fact that they have no control over the outcome of the games. The inability to control the outcome of the future of the business should be no more of a deterrent to "put up" than it is for the games on the "boards."

The "cop out" about the lack of time and all of the other excuses that have led to the failure to take action can be confronted by the "juice" that accompanies the action to MAKE THE ODDS BE WITH US. Action begins with the control of the dialogue. The words, the language will help us create the ODDS.

Those ODDS can make it "over" for whether PASPA will remain the law of the land. People in the business have the power to control the double entendre for the meaning of "over" for this future on the future of the business.

CHAPTER SEVEN

FUTURES ON THE FUTURE

"In the meantime, in between time,
ain't we got fun?"[277]

If it were not for the "fun" that is generated by the action from the transaction, it would have been "over" for "in the meantime, in between time" as an excuse for inaction. If it were not for the action from the transaction it might have also been "over" for the system that segregates "We, the people" who engage in the business of sports transactions.

Corporate sports monopolies have been able to cash in on "in the meantime, in between time" in while they play another game that dwarfs the Super Bowl.[278] They learned the hard way that "it ain't over 'til it's over." They were unable to stop the clock that has extended the time for people in the business to determine the outcome of this game. Time remains on this clock to take advantage of "in the meantime, in between time" to make the freedom of our enterprise the business of America.

The tools of the enterprise can help to hasten that time. They will help to define the playing fields for this game. The analysis will redefine the playing field. Then the "road dogs" can become the "home chalk." Tools of the business can begin the offensive against the visitors to the Constitution.

---

[277] Lyrics from the song "Ain't We Got Fun?"
[278] The NFL did not give permission to use this term.

The payout for this endeavor is an incentive for people in the business to "get down" on the action. A payout that is greater than the "true" odds would be hard to resist for "sharps" in the business. That payout would include a march to the front of the bus accompanied by the chorus of "You Got to Have Freedom."[279]

If the people in the business become organized to contest this playing field, we would become competition for what has been the worst nightmare for corporate sports monopolies. That box score for tomorrow's game that appeared to Michael J. Fox in the movie *Back to the Future* would take a back seat to the nightmare in which the power to segregate the people in the business is history.

The ability to forecast tomorrow's box score is the dream for everyone in the business.

The ability to create the nightmare for corporate America in which our segregation ends is a dream that can be made to come true. People in the business can create a nightmare for the corporate sports mono-polists that would awaken them from the dream world they created for themselves.

Methods in the Madness

The tools of the trade will be used to end this nightmare. Those tools mandate integrity. Conse-quences accompany them. People who use them to "put up" confront the consequences of "money in the pocket."[280] The tools either "tell it like it is" or else. There is no mercy from the bottom line for those who try to fudge their way to conclusions that do not fit the facts.

---

[279] Thanks to the composition by Pharoah Sanders for the inspiration.
[280] Thanks to Cannonball Adderly for the expression.

The tools employ the scientific method. This method leaves no room for waffles in the language. Words such as "luck, maybe, perhaps, if only, woulda, coulda, shoulda" and other others are excuses. They are cop-outs that attempt to reconcile the failure of the analysis with the outcome. They cannot "tell it like it is." They are suited for performances of the "Oh, woe is me soap opera" that is featured everyday in every sportsbook.

To be scientific, the method must rely on words that show rather than tell. Adjectives and adverbs fit the bill for the latter. They lack precision. Words such as "very, really, many, possibly, good, bad, almost, and others should be left to those who express opinions they would not back with money.

Words that end in "ing" can also become shortcuts to avoid the effort it takes to show. Without the easy way out from words that end in "ing" the analysis will be forced to elaborate with language that shows what happened. Then why it happened can make the connections with the future.

Nouns, verbs and numbers are the ingredients for this method. They document outcomes. Documentation is essential for people in the business who use history to forecast the future.

Forecasts of what is likely to happen in the future should not to be confused with predictions. Prediction is a word suited for people who have products to sell. If these con artists could predict the future they would use that ability to benefit themselves rather share that knowledge. Instead they "predict" in order to profit from the sale of what they don't know. Their predictions amount to "hot air" generated by the motivations behind them.

People in the business learn to avoid the temptation of hot air that is guised in comparisons. Comparisons tempt the user to draw conclusions from situations that are not comparable. Success from the forecast of one outcome can lead to the temptation to extend that success to another situation that is not comparable.

Language includes the tool of "numbers" that reinforce the integrity of the method. A proposition that establishes the Bears as a 3 point favorite over Green Bay at Soldier Field must probe history to arrive at that conclusion. That history will focus on the pointspreads that accompanied the final scores from this matchup at Soldier Field.

Other factors that could influence a number include team records for the season, the schedule, injuries, weather, power ratings and pointspreads for this matchup at Lambeau Field. Moves off the pointspread at both sites would also be examined.

The tools employed by the oddsmakers create propositions that are intended to elicit a response from handicappers. Handicappers respond through their own version of the language.

Handicappers may accept, dispute, or ignore the value attributed to home field advantage by oddsmakers. They may relegate the pointspread behind other factors that translate into their numbers for a game. Matchups on offense and defense might take precedence. Or their analysis could be influenced by a combination of factors that proven to be successful.

This method also concludes with numbers. Those numbers translate into power ratings that document their evaluation of the strength of a team. Power ratings move the language to a dialogue between the handicappers and oddsmakers. That dialogue leads to action where handicappers "shop" for the "best" number. "Shopping" for the "best" number can be the difference between a win, a loss, or a "push."

Oddsmakers also "shop" for the best number to post. They scrutinize what happens to numbers that are first to hit the boards. Those who post first might limit the size of the transactions to test the waters before they open to everyone. They understand that "shopping" for the "right" number is an exercise for longevity. Oddsmakers might prefer to start with a "safe" number of 3 on an NFL game instead of one that could expose them to a side or middle from -2 ½ or -3 ½. More NFL games end on the number 3 than on another number. Oddsmakers would prefer to change the money line on the 3 rather than move off the number.[281]

This cat-and-mouse game between oddsmakers and handicappers is a dialogue that translates into what becomes the "right" number for the proposition. Odds will then fluctuate according to interest from the markets.

The method that leads to the conclusion of the dialogue on the game between the Bears and the Packers can be extended to create a dialogue on the total points scored by both teams. The "over and under" was followed by dialogue on outcomes while a game is in progress.

The method has also been applied to situations where time is extended beyond one game. Dialogue includes propositions on the total number of wins for both teams for the season. The dialogue includes propositions with odds on whether either team will win their Division, a Conference, or a Super Bowl. The methodology is adaptable to time and place. The method is adaptable to other venues. Oddsmakers and handicappers face off on elections, the Royal Wedding, the Oscars, and other venues where there is an interest for investors to put up or shut up.

Projections into the future of the business in America will employ this methodology. The words, the

---

[281] The sportsbook could be "sided" if the game moved from -3 to -3 ½. They could be "middled" if the game moved from -3 to both -2 ½ and -3 ½. Moves off the number 3 for NFL games have become rare. Sportsbooks prefer the "push" from adjustments on the money line on -3.

language, the conclusions might provoke a response from those who are responsible for this in-running game. Perhaps the method that contests their madness can force them to shut up because they cannot put up...with us.

Odds and Ends

The tools of the trade will be adapted to three in-running games[282] that project into the future for the business. These in-running games are extensions of the in-running game that began with the imposition of the ten percent tax on the business in Nevada. The factors that led to the outcomes of that game, as well as all of the contests that followed will be applied to handicapping three possibilities for the future.

➤ Will Congress repeal PASPA?
➤ Will the Courts declare PASPA unconstitutional?
➤ Will PASPA remain "The Law of the Land?"

This phase of the in-running begins with a revisit to the contest between FEDERAL LEGISLATION vs. "WE, THE PEOPLE" IN NEVADA.

This game began in a climate in which organized crime was raised to the top of a list for containment by government. The business of sports transactions was defined as one of the businesses of organized crime. The definition organized crime justified intervention by the federal government into the business. Intervention into the legal business in Nevada was justified because the government made the case that those businesses were also a part of organized crime.

---

[282] Games within a game. Propositions are posted with odds on what will occur next at future points in time until the game concludes. Propositions may be posted with updated pointspreads at any point in time. Propositions may also offer "overs and unders" on the performance of a player or on a score at a particular point in time. Odds may also be offered on the outcome of the next play or on whatever else might connect the present to the future.

Paul Czuchra

The federal government expanded on state control of the business through a ten percent Tax on sports transactions imposed by the Kefauver Commission investigation into organized crime. Failure to pay that Tax by the turf clubs in Nevada could have led to legal action that would close the business irrespective of whether or not the owners were members of organized crime. Since it was presumed that "organized" crime also controlled the legal businesses in Nevada, the tax would also be used to monitor the activities in and around the sportsbooks.

The ten percent tax began an effort by the federal government that would lead to additional legislation to control the business. The Wire Act of 1961 and the Organized Crime Control Act of 1970 added to the game plan for the federal government to close the businesses in Nevada.

The tax began an offensive that forced people in the business to find ways to circumvent a tax that would make the transaction uneconomical to both sides. People in Nevada either had to find the ways to circumvent the tax or lose business to illegal businesses that were likely to exclude the tax from their transactions. Players would go elsewhere before they paid a tax beyond the *11 to 10* "juice" they paid on each transaction in Nevada.

Resistance to the tax in Nevada began an effort by people in the business in Nevada to change a coin toss where the coin offered the federal government the advantage of a call on a two-headed coin. Resistance changed the image on the coin to "heads or tails, a 50-50 proposition instead of the "lock" for the feds where two heads were better than one.

Implementation of the tax depended on the compliance of people who would be out of business if they complied. People in the business in Nevada exploited their home field advantage. They found the ways to resist the tax. They put their money where their mouths were in order to continue business the way it had been. Self-interests of the owners and their customers would challenge the outside interests of federal law enforcement.

Those who imposed the tax did not have to put their money where their mouths were. The tax did not have to be justified to anyone on the federal side of the conflict even though the costs of enforcement could be greater to taxpayers than the revenue generated from the tax.

Support from opponents of the business that accompanied the ten percent tax on "organized crime" was value that exceeded the chump change from tax dollars. The ten percent tax was part of a political game. Proponents of the tax could claim victory against "organized" crime because they passed the law. There was no need to prove to the public that the tax had impacted the business in Nevada.

People in the business responded with defensive measures that would counter this offensive by the feds. Their game plan focused on extending the time for this game. They would test time on the playing fields inside and outside the sportsbooks. The longer it would take for the tax to show results, the greater the likelihood the tax would become irrelevant. That would make the tax expendable.

Federal agents were assigned to help make the tax work. They were present in the sportsbooks to send a message. Their lineup cards identified people in the business who did what in and around the sportsbooks. Agents attempted to intimidate them by their presence to deter them from business. Owners of the business were also scrutinized by agents for what they might try to do for their customers.

Federal agents were confronted by the "street smarts" of the patrons and owners who knew the business better than these outsiders. People in the business shared their lineup cards of agents who circulated from one turf club to another. People in the business knew them as well as their tactics.

Customers and owners who knew each other developed a code language to get around the tax. Tickets for the transactions were written in a way that could make a $1,000 transaction appear as $10. These teammates invented their version of a "prevent" defense against an offense that could not penetrate their end zone. "Street smarts" would keep the game alive for decades after the tax was enacted to end it.

If the proponents of the ten percent tax had been required to put their money where their mouths were on the success of this endeavor, they would have had to pay. British bet shops would have paid their freight to England to take their money after the pattern of the game had been established.

The longer their proposition: Which will survive to win this contest? Sportsbooks v. the ten percent tax remained on the boards the minus behind the odds on the sportsbooks would rise. There would be few, if any, takers for the plus behind the odds behind the ten percent tax. Even those who enacted the tax would have known better than to put their money on themselves.

Time also worked against proponents of the Wire Act who hoped to use the legislation as a tool to stifle the legal business in Nevada. Federal agents assigned to work inside sportsbooks performed double duty as stakeouts beside the public pay phones outside the sportsbooks. They were assigned to listen to conversations of those who might attempt to conduct business outside Nevada.

This tactic was compromised by a court decision that protected the transmission of information as "free speech." The Constitution protected speech, *not* the transaction.

Agents would have to prove that speech on the pay phones was the transmission of a sports transaction.

The court decision forced the agents into a position where they would have to determine whether calls had been made to transmit wagers or information. This effort was also compromised by a code language that could translate what appeared to be information into language for a transaction.

Wire taps were necessary to break the code language; however, wire taps on public pay phones could not produce the results that could be had from taps on private phones at homes or offices. The court decision on freedom of speech raised the odds in favor of the people in the business to continue their business at pay phones around the sportsbooks.

The ten percent tax and the Wire Act did not lead to victory for the federal proponents of the measures. Two decades after the tax and one decade after the Wire Act business remained as usual at most of the sportsbooks. "Street smarts' had bought time for people in the business to hold their own. People in the business used their home field advantages to keep their chances alive against those who attempted to use laws that would be difficult to enforce on this playing field.

Propositions on the future course of this in-running game would change. As the game continued, propositions would shy away from the conclusion of this game to documentation of the progress of the game. They would offer "overs and unders" on numbers and time frames on whether a sportsbook would close during a year because of the tax, whether revenue from sports transactions would decline each year and how much would sports revenue decline.

Although there are no records about the amount of revenue generated by turf clubs, the number of sportsbooks that remained in business would be an indicator. The number of turf clubs increased from three in 1960 when the tax was imposed to eleven in

1975, fifteen years later.[283] People in the business would have had reason to rejoice over the success of their efforts to keep the business alive.

Props that focused on what could be documented would have kept the in-running game in motion until changes in the climate that generated the tax would alter the playing field for the contest in Nevada. "Organized" crime would be contested in the next phase of this in-running game by the interest of Casino hotels in the business of sports transactions. Owners of turf clubs that housed sportsbooks would face challenges to their survival from "big" business, not the ten percent tax. The addition of hotel casinos to the lineup of owners created distance between sportsbooks and their association with "organized" crime. As the timeframe for this in-running game moved into the decade of the '70s, there would be reasons for oddsmakers to make survival of sportsbooks the favorite against the success of federal intervention in Nevada. Despite the change in the odds in favor of the survival of the business, speculation on when the game would end remained in doubt. Although the people in the business had earned a "TKO" at the end of the decade of the '60s, the climate had not been altered to where it could be declared a "KO" of the effort by federal opponents of the business.

Until the climate changed to one where the tax would be challenged by other players in Nevada, speculation about this phase of the in-running game would have been limited to outcomes that could be documented. Life and death propositions about the business would be on hold until the end of a "commercial" break that would last for years.

During that time, changes in the big picture for the business in Nevada would force the federal government to reassess the use of the tactic of

---

[283] Data from the Nevada Gaming Control Board

organized crime as the game plan to impose controls on the business. As the time for this in-running game approached 1972, oddsmakers would have started to "get the feel" to speculate about odds for the proposition: Will the Ten Percent Tax on sports transactions be reduced?

That "feel" would have come from changes in the climate. The Nevada Gaming Control Board became a player in the game. The importance of business of sports transactions forced them to reformulate regulations in order to reflect the embrace the interest in the business expressed by owners of hotel casinos. The Stardust, Castaways, Union Plaza, El Cortez, and other hotel casinos joined a lineup of players with interests in the business. They became competitors of the turf clubs.

Change in the climate forced the Nevada Gaming Control Board to reexamine the Regulations that had governed the business for decades. New Regulations were necessary to accommodate the interests of hotel casinos.

These Regulations would also have to address the interests of the federal government. Regulations for telephone wagers as well as wagers from "messengers" responded to the federal concerns about sports transaction that had been expressed in the "Wire Act" and the Organized Crime Control Act.

Even though Nevada Regulators were likely to have known the Regulations could not be enforced, their attempt created an appearance of compliance with federal interests. These Regulations would create a climate for repeal of the ten percent tax. Repeal of the tax would then open the door for hotel casinos to incorporate sports transactions into their business.

These Regulations enabled another player to join the lineup of supporters of the business in Nevada. After almost fifteen years of service in the United States Senate, the time had come for Nevada Senator

Howard Cannon to begin the effort to repeal a tax that stifled the growth of business within his State. He had earned the clout for Congress to accept his word that the new Nevada Regulations had addressed federal concerns about organized crime.

Despite his assurances, it was no "lock" that the Senator would be able to gain the support of Congress to eliminate the tax. Nevertheless, the change in the climate for the business in Nevada would have aroused speculation among oddsmakers about whether the tax would be reduced, by how much, and when.

Speculation about the odds on "YES" vs. "NO" for the proposition would have fluctuated as the legislation moved through the Senate for a vote. Props on the ability of Senator Cannon to maneuver passage of the legislation through amendments to other legislation would have been as much of a challenge for oddsmakers and handicappers as they would be on the success of a quarterback on a last minute drive to win a Super Bowl. Will amendments by Senator Cannon to the ten percent tax be approved by Congress?

Senator Cannon's ability to reduce the tax to two percent would open the door to speculation about additional reductions in the tax. After the approval of this reduction, the Senator expressed his interest in the elimination of the tax.

The factors that had led to the reduction to two percent could be used to help with forecasts on what more it might take to eliminate the Tax. The interaction of the economic and political interests that led to the reduction of the tax could have led to further reductions. While the reduction to two percent breathed life into turf clubs, that number would not satisfy hotel casinos. They regarded the two percent as taxation without representation.

The reduction in the tax bought time for the Gaming Control Board to address Regulations that had created the playing field for the turf clubs. The change in the climate for the business made those Regulations rules for the past.

The outcome of the proposition that cast "We, the people" against the ten percent tax evolved into another that would pit them against competition from the hotel casinos. Their victory came with the reminder "to be wary of what you wish for." Unforeseen consequences accompanied the winds of change. "We" the people" could not have foreseen that their victory would lead to a playing field where they could no longer compete.

Any oddsmaker or handicapper who forecasts this outcome two decades before this game had ended would qualify for the seat at the right hand of the Almighty. That person would have had the "feel" to forecast the change in the climate from "organized" crime to big" business. The fortitude of "We, the people" that led to the change in this climate that enabled Senator Cannon to repeal the tax would have had to accompany that "feel."

Anyone who in 1950 could have parlayed those factors into an outcome that would become the basis for the next phase of this in-running game would be a challenger to the Almighty. That person would have had to have foreseen the interaction of the factors from the previous phase of the in-running game that led the Gaming Control Board to dictate the next phase.

The Contest For Home Field Advantage

While "We, the people" had been able to hold their own in the effort against the ten percent tax, the time it had taken to win that contest led to changes in the climate that would force the Nevada Gaming Regulators to reconcile the present with the past. While "the people" had broken a law that was meant to be broken, the reduction of the tax created an environment that would not be favorable for them to continue business the way it had been. Even though they contributed more than their two cents to the argument that the law was meant to be broken, the reduction in the tax had consequences for them. Other players in Nevada reaped the benefits from their efforts.

These players did not need the "street smarts" of "the people" to play this game. The importance of those "smarts" had been diminished by the environment "We" had helped to create. In order to remain in business the turf clubs that were saved by those "smarts" would need salvation from State Regulators in order to remain open. The economic environment that had been created by the reduction in the tax aroused the interest of hotel casino owners in the business. They would become competitors with the turf clubs for customers. The reduction in the tax opened the doors for them to compete for customers who patronized turf clubs who might also be interested in casino games. Hotel casino owners would then have to compete with each other to keep those customers from those who had the audacity to include sportsbooks as part of their business. The owners of hotel casinos would compete among themselves for customers.

Before hotel casinos owners would become players in this game, they asked for more. They demanded a reduction or elimination of the tax. If that demand was met it would maximize the bottom line from the sportsbooks that would occupy space in the casino.

Nevada politicians responded to their constituents. In 1983, Senator Cannon was successful in his effort to reduce the two percent tax to .025%. "We, the people" defeated the people who had imposed the ten percent tax.

The reduction of the tax to .025% also met the demands of hotel casino owners. The reduction of the tax forced the Gaming Control Board to create a home field advantage for them that would eliminate competition from turf clubs. The Senator's victory on behalf of the home team in Nevada moved the playing field for the next phase of the in-running game from the Halls of Congress to Carson City, Nevada.

Parlay specialists would have made a connection between the outcome of the contest with the ten percent tax and the need to change the Nevada Gaming Regulations in order for owners of hotel casinos to include sportsbooks in their casinos. That connection would have led oddsmakers to speculate about whether turf clubs would remain open for sports transactions.

Oddsmakers would have made NO the favorite. They would bet that the Gaming Control Board had to respond to what Senator Cannon had delivered to Nevada. The response would come in the form of regulations that would terminate turf clubs.

Speculation by oddsmakers would focus on *when*, not *whether* they would close. The time factor would depend on when members of the Gaming Control Board would be able to complete their agenda to revise the Regulations that had governed the business for decades. Before they could begin, Regulators would have to confess to the hypocrisy about the business that previous members had established in their Regulations. Those Regulations stipulated that sports transactions would be the exclusive business of turf clubs. The business had been confined to turf clubs after Regulators determined that sports transactions were different from other casino games. They made the determination that sports transaction posed a threat to "public health, safety, morals." In order to reduce the effect of those evils on the patrons of turf clubs, Regulators prohibited the sale of alcohol on the premises.

The Regulation had to be revisited after owners of casinos and hotel casinos became interested in the business. Regulators were in a position where they had to decide whether hotel casinos could survive the threat the business posed to "public health, safety and morals."

After the ten percent tax was reduced to two percent, the Gaming Commission proceeded to document their hypocrisy. They approved a Regulation that opened door for owners of the Castaways, Little Caesar's, and the Stardust, among others, to expose their customers to the threats of "public health, safety, morals" in an environment that would include alcohol.

After the intensive care that would have been necessary for oddsmakers and handicappers to recover from the strangulation caused by their regurgitation of this hypocrisy, they might have been able to focus on speculation that would narrow the timeframe for when turf clubs would come to an end. Their inability to attach a time or date for when it might happen would have kept propositions off the board until 1985 when Regulations were formulated to stipulate how the business of sports transactions would have to be conducted.

The "street smarts" that had saved the business from the ten percent tax at the turf clubs would no longer be part of the way business was conducted at sportsbooks in casinos. Technology that helped define the "Information Age" would replace those "smarts." A cost factor accompanied the regulations that would impose this technology on business conducted at the sportsbooks. This technology became part of the home field advantage for owners of casinos. The climate had changed from one where economics led to the politics that eliminated the Tax to one where economics led to the politics that reformulated the Regulations that governed the business.

The announcement that Churchill Downs Race and Sportsbook would close on June 30, 1987 ended this phase of the in-running game. "NO" was the answer for the proposition:

Will Turf Clubs remain open for business?

That outcome would have led to another prop:

Will hotel casinos remain open for sports transactions?

While the turf clubs were targeted for closure by the Regulations, the economic climate also whacked the beneficiaries of this change. Time had shifted to fast forward when corporations became players in the business of gaming. They posed a threat to the survival of "Strip" properties such as the Castaways Hotel and Casino. Speculation about the survival of that property ended when the owners announced they would close the on June 30, 1987. The Castaways and Churchill Downs would no longer occupy the turf that been sold to corporate casinos.

Sportsbooks had become "Wanted" by "big" business on the "Strip. The Regulations that helped to bring about this situation blended into the economic climate to change the playing field for the rest of this in-running game. Home field was determined by those who could afford to pay for it. This field had taken the shape of dollar bills that extended the zeros for the money it would take to play this game.

Changes in the roster for the home team accompanied the changes in the playing field. Although several hotel casinos remained as players, speculation would begin about how long they would be able to compete with the corporations.

Little Caesar's Casino also occupied the turf that housed Churchill Downs Race and Sportsbook. The Casino remained open for business until 1994 when the climate became ripe for Bally's to extend its corporate presence into the shopping center formerly occupied by Gene Mayday, the owner of Little Caesar's Casino. The Paris Hotel and Casino would house a sportsbook in the space formerly occupied by Little Caesar's.

The last survivor of the game that began in the 1970s remained in business until 2009. The Stardust Hotel and Casino had the property rights to the land as well as the financial resources to remain competitive with corporate casinos on the "Strip," but the expansion of the business to the offshores relegated the Stardust sportsbook from the place "to be" to another player who would have to retire because of "old age."

This phase of the in-running game ended with a home field advantage for players who paid for the rules Nevada Regulators would dictate for the business. The details that led to this outcome were documented. Oddsmakers and handicappers would use them to begin the next phase of the in-running game.

That documentation would also include the changes in the climate for the legal business from organized crime to big business. "We, the people" had lost control because of factors that created the change in the climate from organized crime to big business.

The alliance of Nevada Regulators, politicians, and corporate casinos established control over the business in Nevada. The tactics used by law enforcement to contest the legal business in this climate were no longer appropriate. They had to make adjustments in order to continue the in-running game as a contest between:

SPORTS TRANSACTIONS IN NEVADA
vs. FEDERAL REGULATIONS.

Nevada Regulators paid an IOU to Nevada politicians and corporate business interests with Regulations that redefined home field advantage.

A political IOU remained on the books for politicians in Washington who had supported Senator Cannon's efforts to end the ten percent Tax.

NO BS CHAMPIONSHIP SERIES
Federal Regulations vs. The business in Nevada

Even though the ten percent tax had been repealed, the coalition that supported the tax would continue their effort to impose federal control over the business in Nevada. This coalition regrouped from the defeat of the Tax with a strategy that would enable them to impose control through federal regulations.

Nevada Regulators would assist them. Federal interests were included in a "huddle" where they could call the plays that dictated how people in the business would have to conduct their business at the sportsbooks.

Regulations would challenge the technology of the "Information Age" that could be used to circumvent the Wire Act. Nevada Regulations attempted to force compliance with a Regulation that prohibited the use of cell phones in and around sportsbook "areas."

This federal interest that stemmed from the Wire Act trickled down to where owners of the sportsbooks were forced to assign their employees the responsibility for the enforcement of this attempt to exercise federal control over the business.

Once again, "people" in the business were pitted against the attempt to exercise federal control over the legal business and once again, "the feds" attempted to impose control over "people" on both sides of the counter. This time owners of the sportsbooks were forced to assign their employees the responsibility to enforce the Wire Act.

The tools of the business would have flagged the factors that led to the outcome of the ten percent tax to apply them to this contest between:

PEOPLE IN THE BUSINESS
vs. CELL PHONE REGULATIONS

Experiences from the previous contest over the ten percent tax would have led to the call to bet that "the tactics of the people" who had kept the business alive at the turf clubs would also hold sway in this game of Regulations. People in the business would be the favorites over the opponents of their business.

No one with the "street smarts" of the business would jeopardize themselves with suspicious behavior in front of an audience at the sportsbooks that was primed to detect them. They could take their cell phones to wherever it was safe to do whatever they needed to do. Information from the boards of the sportsbooks could be transmitted from safe havens throughout the casino. A regulation on cell phones could not keep people from what they had previously done from pay phones outside sportsbooks.

This regulation did not take into account what be necessary to enforce it. Employees who were assigned the duty of enforcement might be sympathetic to their "friends" on the other side of the counter. These employees would allow their friends to "act" their way through scenarios so that both could pretend to comply with the Regulation.

Other employees who did not have friends on the other side ignored the assignment. They would turn their heads the other way rather than accept an assignment for which there was no additional compensation.

At times when the business of the sportsbooks consumed all the time of the employees, hotel security staff would be assigned the job of enforcement. Hotel security would not make that assignment a priority over other matters that demanded their attention. If they had the time and the interest all they would do is "shoo" people elsewhere.

People assigned to enforce the regulation were satisfied to go through the motions. This attitude, along with the inability to enforce a regulation designed for the sake of appearances, would have led oddsmakers and handicappers to solidify their speculation about the outcome of this contest. They would ask: "Will The Cell Phone Regulation be repealed?" Time would change the speculation to: "When will the Regulation be repealed?"

The right to free speech along with the inability to monitor the conversations of everyone who weaved in and out of the sportsbook area led to a decision by the Gaming Control Board on August 21, 2008 to rescind the Regulation. The decision ended this portion of the in-running game in which state regulators caved in to the federal interest to prohibit the use of cell phones in one "area" of a casino.

The outcome of this phase of the game connected with the outcome of the contest over the ten percent Tax. Regulations imposed by federal interests were "dogs" against the home field advantages of the people in the business in Nevada. The legal business was not susceptible to prohibitions imposed by outsiders that had no clout.

Even though the environment for the business had changed from turf clubs to corporate-owned sportsbooks, the people who comprise the business won in both of them. Even though the "people" who comprise the business were different in these environments, they had the smarts to win their contests.

These "smarts" were reflected in another contest in this in-running game: Federal Control vs. "Suspicious Behavior" in the business.

People in the business were smarter than the fifth graders the Gaming Control Board had assumed them to be when Regulators attempted to extend federal control over the business through transactions at sportsbooks that were defined as "suspicious." Nevada regulators attached the word "suspicious" to transactions made by one person that exceeded an amount of money that was deemed worthy of suspicion. They responded to federal demands for a tool they said was necessary for them to combat money laundering.

Whether this regulation could be implemented or how long it might survive would not have been worth the time for oddsmakers and handicappers to consider for speculation. The outcome of this contest would have been engraved in the files of the past. Those files had documented the factors that would have led to the results for this one.

The people in the business will always know more about the business than their opponents. Sportsbook employees are always wary of wagers that might appear to be "out of the ordinary." Their perceptions of "suspicious" are part of the business. They preceded the "invention" formulated in the Regulations. Suspicions about "fixed" outcomes have always accompanied transactions that reach the limits on the amount a sportsbook will take on a transaction.

A limit on that amount is one way for sportsbooks to exercise control over suspicious transactions that could be a disaster for the takers. That's why sportsbooks keep limits on transactions lower for "strangers." Their transactions remain "suspicious" until they become "regulars."

There was no need to remind people in the business about suspicions aroused by paperwork imposed by regulators. Transactions into four figures by "strangers" would be at the top of their list of "suspicions" for all sportsbooks. Whichever way those suspicions might lead could depend on whether the transactions would help to balance the books on a game.

Proponents of the Regulation also defied the reality that people engaged in money laundering would have the smarts to avoid their detection by a regulation that targeted their transaction. Only those who did not have the smarts of a first grader would have used sports transaction to launder their money. Regulators were content with their effort at public relations for the feds. They could live with the fact that no one could ever "prove" that the regulation had an impact on money laundering.

The renewal of a conflict that would subject the business to federal control through a regulation rather than a tax would have led oddsmakers and handicappers to make the people in the business prohibitive favorites. Their time would have been wasted with speculation about whether this regulation would exercise "control" over the business. They might have amused themselves instead with an over and under about how much time would be wasted by people in the business to comply.

Speculation about the outcome of this contest could have focused on when the State would end its involvement in the reports on suspicious behavior. The "paperwork" for the State included reports on all casino games. The resistance to the attempt to make "suspicious behavior" a code word for organized crime differed from the tactics that were used to defeat the ten percent tax. The people in the business who resisted were different from those who fought against the ten percent tax. The outcomes were similar even though they differed. The regulation could not be repealed the way the ten percent tax had been, but Nevada "repealed" its participation in the process of reports on the regulation. The result of the matchup for this contest would have been posted as a new report. "'Suspicious behavior' lost by TKO to people in the business in Nevada."

Nevada Regulators repealed Regulation 6A. The State no longer reports "suspicious" behavior from sports transactions to the federal government as it had been required to do by Regulation 22.121. The State withdrew from its participation in this process.

Despite the failure to keep the State of Nevada involved in its dirty work, the federal government kept the formality of the game alive with reports from the casinos directly to them. Casino owners remained reluctant to continue this charade. Several were penalized for their failure to file the required reports on time.

While this battleground with the sportsbooks would continue as a formality, another conflict between the business and the federal government played out its own way. Promoters of this contest could have headlined the conflict as "A Blast from the Past."

Federal concerns about telephone wagers at sportsbooks would become the second game of a double-header. People in the business won the opener when they found the ways to circumvent the restrictions of the Wire Act for the game that was played at the pay phones outside the turf clubs.

The proposition for this game would have been posted: "Will sportsbooks be allowed to accept telephone transactions?"

The odds on "YES" as the favorite would rise as technology made it possible for the business to comply with the Wire Act. Whether or not telephone transactions would become part of the business was contingent on technology that could preclude calls to sportsbooks from out of state. After it was proven that the technology could prevent those calls, the door was opened for customers in Nevada to make transactions.

Despite the guarantee that telephone calls to sportsbooks could be restricted to Nevada, that technology was irrelevant to people in the business who received money from out of state to make transactions. While technology could prevent telephone connections to sportsbooks from out of state, it could not close the door on "runners" with money from their partners out of state.

"NO" would have been a prohibitive favorite for the proposition "Will the technology prevent transactions from out of State?" Residents of Nevada were able to use the telephone to "run" for their partners who resided outside the State. The technology that made it possible for Nevada regulators to approve telephone transactions also transported people from outside the state to where they could be as close to the sportsbooks as the people who were on the phone to make the calls to the "books." The gun would have sounded to end the game before it started.

Telephone Wagers vs. The Wire Act

People in the know knew the technology would extend the option to all people in the business who had connections in Nevada. Technology was the "cover" that was necessary to satisfy an appearance of compliance with the Wire Act. That technology could not keep people in the business from circumventing the intent.

People in the business had the "smarts" to outwit opponents of the business who had not learned from their past experiences. This outcome dictated by "the people" was similar to the outcome of the ten percent tax. This lineup that comprised "the people" was up to the task to perform as necessary in the climate of big business.

Oddsmakers and handicappers would not have wasted their time with speculations about who would win this contest. Savvy about which way the one-way action would go would have been enough to keep the propositions off the boards.

They would have noted that the political IOU from Nevada for the support that ended the ten percent tax was paid by Nevada regulators. This phase of the in-running game between federal regulators and Nevada ended with a TKO by "We, the people in the business." They had defeated the feds in the first two games of what oddsmakers and handicappers could agree would become a series. The number of games for this series could engender a debate. Speculation about that number would stress the importance of the home field advantage in Nevada that allowed the guile of "the people" to determine the outcome.

Whatever the number, the analysis would stress the need for opponents of the business to reassess the game plans of taxes and regulations that created the home field advantage for "the people" in Nevada. In order to continue this in-running game, the playing field would have to change to one that kept "the people" on the sidelines.

The site for a third game of this series would have to change. Home field advantage for the opponents of the business would have to accompany this change. They would then become the favorites in the game and would have to bestow home field advantage on the opponents of the business in the game between:

PASPA vs. NEVADA

The outcomes from the previous contests were unacceptable to the opponents of the business. What had been chump change to the federal interests had grown into "big business" for the corporate sports monopolies. People in the know about the reasons behind the assault on the business would have bet their lives this game would continue. Speculation would have focused on when and how, not whether.

Opponents of the business needed a game changer for another contest that could extend this into a series. A tool of the business could be employed by handicappers and oddsmakers to help forecast the "game changer" that would prolong this in-running game. The "Zigzag" theory[284] could help to show the way. This theory argues that the losers of the previous contests would have to make adjustments in order to make it possible for them to win the next game.

Outcomes of the previous contests had proven the limitations in their game plans for the ten percent tax and federal regulations. Those game plans could not lead to victory on the home field of Nevada where people in the business held the advantage. "Zigzag" would argue that in order to win the next game they would have to make an adjustment that would take home field advantage away from the people in the business in Nevada.

The inability of the opponents to win the previous contests helped to reconfirm the legitimacy of that business in Nevada. Another attack on that legitimacy would have to incorporate a strategy that removed control of the game away from "the people" in the business. They would have to be excluded from the field of play.

This adjustment would have to remove their "street smarts" that had been used to defeat the game plans of taxes and regulations. The decision to move the playing field from Nevada to the halls of Congress

---

[284] "Zigzag argues that transactions should not be made on the first game of a series. Transactions should be made on the team that lost that game and against the team that wins each successive game.

in Washington opened the door for the opponents to use their political "smarts" as the game plan that would give them the advantage on their home field. This move to change the home field fit with the change in the climate for both businesses.

Turf clubs had been replaced by casino sportsbooks which, in turn, gave way to corporate casino sportsbooks. The Information Age had contributed to the explosion of interest in football and basketball. The business had grown to "big" business where the monetary stakes for corporate casino monopolies dwarfed those of the turf clubs.

Big business also defined the opposition. This lineup had changed from law enforcement to the corporate sports monopolies. They had the power to change the playing field for the next contest. Their "Big Game" in Washington would replace the two Las Vegas Bowls for the previous contests. On this home field, they could expand the role of the federal government beyond the previous limitations of taxes and regulations. In the halls of Congress they had the power to redefine "representative" government. In Washington they could buy sponsorship for this contest from their political representatives.

"Zigzag" assumes the team that lost the previous game will make adjustments that will raise the odds in their favor. At the outset, the theory had statistical support, but oddsmakers used those results to make adjustments in the odds. They made the adjustment that reduced the theory from a "lock" to one that was closer to 50-50.

The Professional and Amateur Sports Protection Act (PASPA) became the game plan employed by this coalition. PASPA redefined the role of the federal government. Its intent was to hammer a "closed" sign on the legal business in Nevada. It would end the need for another contest in this in-running game. This win would overcome the defeats of the previous two.

There were enough political and economic factors to handicap to send people in the business into overtime with speculation about the way this game would play out. At the outset, speculation would have focused on the battleground between the Commerce Clause of the Constitution vs. States Rights.

Odds on the outcome of this conflict would fluctuate. The numbers would be contingent on whether states that had legitimized various versions of the business had the clout to keep it. Handicappers would have been reluctant to put their money on either side because in the initial stages of this game there was doubt that proponents of PASPA had the votes to win passage. They might need support from those who had established their state's right to the business. There was no reason for those states to relinquish that right without compensation.

The odds in favor of the passage of PASPA would have risen because of the "power rating" for Senator "Dollar Bill" Bradley, the designated QB behind the legislation, but as the game moved through Congress, odds on "YES" would have dipped. Despite the Senator's expertise with the Constitution, his strategy to use the Commerce Clause to pass the legislation faced opposition from those states that had legitimized versions of sports transactions. Their States Rights would be violated by a federal law that would make their businesses illegal. The power of States Rights confronted the tactic of the Commerce Clause.

Proponents of PASPA countered their opposition with 'political smarts" that attached the legislation to the Lanham Trademark Act. The States Rights advocates had the political smarts to deny them the votes that were necessary to pass the legislation. Stalled in Congress, the odds on passage became "pick em."

Political "smarts" of both contestants would determine the outcome. Compromise was preferable to the proponents of PASPA than defeat. Four-fifths of a loaf was better for them than none. Opposition from the states that had legalized sports transactions led to the "grandfather" compromise that enabled them to keep what they had. The compromise made them exceptions to the other states that were prohibited from the legalization of sports transactions. Both sides could claim victory after the vote.

This victory for States Rights and the Commerce Clause excluded the people in the business outside of Nevada who were denied their Constitutional guarantee of equal protection of the laws. The outcome for them became the domestic version of the foreign policy of containment. Domestic containment was the equivalent of legal segregation. PASPA had made citizens of America who had no voice in the outcome "illegals."

Corporate sports monopolies could celebrate a victory that contained the infringement of their patent rights outside Nevada. Even though corporate interest in gaming had spread beyond Nevada, those corporations would not be able to include sportsbooks in their casinos.

The corporate sports monopolies won this part of the conflict despite the economic climate that had kindled interest in the business from other states. This climate did not have the juice to defeat PASPA despite the fact that Nevada had proven that revenue from sports transactions could add revenue to state coffers.

The opponents of the business would not be satisfied with this "split" decision. Once again they failed to defeat "the people" in the business in Nevada. This time those people were comprised of the political representatives of the economic interests in Nevada as well as those from the other states. This lineup fought and won the battle to keep what they had through the grandfather compromise. States Rights kept the people in the business in Nevada around for another round of this in-running game.

Nevada would remain in the headlights of an opposition that could not be satisfied with the outcome. "Zigzag" would argue that this split decision would not suffice. It would leave the door open for a final solution to the problem, but adjustments would have to be made in order to extend the series into a fourth contest that would attack the business in Nevada from another angle.

Oddsmakers and handicappers in the business would have bet the max that Washington would remain the playing field to finish what remained of the unfinished business for the opponents. The legal business in Nevada remained that unfinished business.

PASPA had forced a change in the lineup of people in Nevada who supported the business. No longer were customers and employees part of that lineup on the playing field in Washington. They were benched in favor of Nevada politicians and the Nevada corporate casinos. This lineup was suited for the climate of this time.

Oddsmakers and handicappers would incorporate the factors that led to this outcome into the "Zigzag" theory. They would speculate about the adjustments that would have to be made for the next contest. But time would be the one factor resistant to that speculation. It would have taken a decade for "YES" to become the prohibitive favorite for the proposition:

Will There Be Another Game in this Series?

The seeds that were planted by PASPA had grown to where opponents of the business could harvest them. The climate had ripened for a contest that pit:

ASIA vs. PASPA

This contest had its roots in a Nevada Regulation that was enacted in 1962. Nevada Regulators documented their lack of integrity with a Regulation that left the door open for opponents of the business to finish what PASPA had started. After PASPA established the legal segregation of the business opponents of the business would use a Nevada Regulation to "free" people in the business in Nevada from the segregation that had been imposed on them by PASPA. They would stretch the lack of integrity of Nevada Regulators to the depths of a prohibition of the business in Nevada.[285]

What appeared to be "over" after the outcomes of the earlier games with Federal regulations met the standard for the axiom "it ain't over til it's over." Opponents of the business found a loophole in a Nevada Regulation that could be used to renew their attack on the business. The Regulation opened the door for the "integrity of the game" to finish what the Commerce Clause had started.

The Regulation opened the door for a "back door" cover by the opponents of the business. That loophole prompted the effort by Senator John McCain (R-AZ) to propose legislation that would repeal the States Rights guaranteed to Nevada by the grandfather clause in PASPA.

"Upon further review..." Senator McCain believed he found a way to make prohibition of the business of sports transactions the law of the land. He proposed the AMATEUR SPORTS INTEGRITY ACT (ASIA) as the way to do it. This legislation had the potential to end of the legal business in Nevada.

---

[285] Thanks to Lisa at the West Las Vegas Library for her input into "stretching integrity."

His adjustment in tactics responded to the previous defeats of the opposition in the in-running games of Regulations. Those attempts to control the business had failed because of the home field disadvantage. A change in the playing field to Washington would enable the opponents to turn a Nevada Regulation that was enacted to protect the business into a Federal Law that would end it.

Nevada Regulators had opened the door to that option in 1962. They defined the "integrity of the game" in a Regulation that prohibited sportsbooks from transactions on contests that involved UNLV and UNR. The Regulation was an attempt to respond to a climate in which sports transactions were considered to be a part of "organized" crime. Concerns about the possibility that organized crime might be able to "fix" outcomes of collegiate athletic contests led to the Regulation.

The Regulation implied that the proximity of UNLV and UNR to sportsbooks in Nevada raised the odds on the possibilities for "fixed" outcomes. Consequences from this "illogic" would appear three decades later when Senator McCain used it to begin the next phase of this in-running game.

Four decades later, Senator John McCain would use the intent behind the Regulation to extend its prohibition of transactions on UNLV and UNR to all collegiate teams. A prohibition of transactions on all college games could have closed the doors to the legal sportsbooks in Nevada.

"Distant" replay would begin this contest of regulations on the Senator's playing field in Washington, D.C. He proposed to extend the lack of integrity by Nevada Regulators through an endeavor that would exploit what they had attempted to prevent.

Regulators had not extended their prohibition on transactions on all amateur teams because they knew it would cripple business at the sportsbooks. They could not foresee that the consequences of what they done to avoid a situation would open the door to the possibility that it could lead to end the business.

Senator McCain used their argument to make his case that all college teams needed the protection of integrity that was afforded to UNLV and UNR. He ignored the proximity of these schools as the reason for the Regulation. Instead he emphasized the need to protect the integrity of all college games as the reason for the need for ASIA. The extension of the prohibition to all collegiate teams would have posed a threat to the survival of sportsbooks. Passage of ASIA would encourage the professional sports monopolies to expand the loophole of integrity to include the prohibition of wagers on their teams.

If ASIA was enacted it might also provide casino corporations the reason they needed to terminate their unwanted stepchild. An extension of the regulation to include all collegiate teams would threaten the economic survival of the business. There might not be enough business to justify the cost to operate a sportsbook in a casino.

The Senator used these possibilities to take advantage of changes in the climate for collegiate sports. NCAA football and basketball had become big business. This corporate sports monopoly sought protection of its product against violations of its patent rights. Senator responded to their interests with legislation that would rescind the exception granted by PASPA to the "grandfather." ASIA would prohibit Nevada sportsbooks from the exploitation of the patent rights of the NCAA.

Although the integrity of the game was included in the arguments for PASPA, it had to take a back seat to patent rights. The economics behind patent rights had to be used in order for Senator Bradley to justify his use of the Commerce Clause to pass the legislation. Integrity would not suffice for legislation based on economic interests. But compromise was necessary to cash in on those interests. PASPA had allowed for a compromise between the contestants that led to "grandfathers." ASIA left little room for compromise.

Nevada Regulators had to set aside the hypocrisy of their predecessors in order to contest the challenge to the business from Senator McCain. They became "the people" who contested the strategy that attempted to exploit the hypocrisy of the Regulation.

Oddsmakers would have made Nevada Regulators the prohibitive favorite in this contest with Senator McCain. His power rating would have been lower than the one for Senator "Dollar Bill" Bradley, the QB for PASPA. "Dollar Bill" was able to keep the contest on his home field in Washington. Senator McCain relinquished that home field advantage. Even though he initiated the challenge from the floor of the U.S. Senate, Nevada Regulators responded from Carson City.

Their home field advantage would have bestowed a power rating of 100 on the Nevada Gaming Control Board after the Chairman announced the commitment to keep their "grandfather" alive. They would not abandon the effort of Nevada politicians that had led to the grandfather victory in PASPA. Nevada politicians had to protect the monopoly that had been granted to the corporate casinos in Nevada.

Nevada Regulators had to respond to the hypocrisy of their predecessors. They repudiated the Regulation that had governed the business for decades. In June of 2000, the Chairman of the Nevada Gaming Commission announced his intention to repeal the Regulation that prohibited wagers on amateur teams in Nevada on January 1, 2001.

Senator McCain would not be able to use that Regulation to justify ASIA. Regulators proved once again that home field advantage belonged to Nevada when the threat to their business was posed through challenges to regulations. "These people" in Nevada owned their playing field. Senator McCain was not able to keep them from doing what they had to do.

After the repeal of the Regulation, Nevada Regulators handed the ball off to Nevada politicians who would employ their political "smarts" to continue the effort to defeat ASIA. They became the "people" who would defend this challenge to their business. Nevada Senators Bryan, Reid, and Ensign followed in the footsteps on the path created by Senator Cannon.

Power ratings for this phase of the in-running game would have to be recalculated. The power rating for Senator McCain would have plunged as a result of his choice of a game plan that could not win. The Nevada Gaming Control Board had taken care of his business. He was no longer able to use the Nevada Regulation to justify ASIA. He lost the tool that was necessary to generate the political support in Congress to help him pass the legislation.

While the number for his power rating would have been a matter of debate among people in the business, they would have agreed on the direction. They would have to calculate the importance of the knock-down in order to translate it into a number that reflected the odds on the outcome of this contest. Whatever that calculation might have been, it would have been lower than the power ratings of Nevada Senators Bryan, Reid, and Ensign. Even though they had not delivered the punch, they became beneficiaries of the atmosphere that had changed after Senator McCain lost his strategy to use "integrity" as the justification for ASIA.

The power rating for Nevada Senators would be less than 100 for the Nevada Gaming Control Board. Nevada politicians would not be able to play this game on the home field of Nevada. Without that control over home field, the outcome of this game would be closer to a fifty-fifty proposition. Those odds would change as the game progressed. Compromise and States Rights increased in importance. ASIA left no room for the Senator to compromise with Nevada politicians. Unlike the "grandfather" compromise in PASPA, ASIA boiled down to "all or nothing" for States Rights. Since Senator McCain had established "integrity" as the basis for ASIA, this contest would become one between "States Rights vs. The Integrity of the Game."

The rules that govern politics would have led people in the business to make States Rights the favorite over an integrity that was not part of this political game. The outcome would boil down to whether Nevada politicians had the skills to take advantage of political rules of the Senate that favored States Rights over "integrity."

Senator McCain had demonstrated his lack of integrity through payoffs from the NCAA in exchange for sites in Arizona for BCS Championship games and tournament sites for the "Big Dance." Those payoffs helped to pay for his sponsorship of ASIA. They did not benefit other members of the Senate. Those politicians might be reluctant to abandon the States Right they had given to Nevada through PASPA. They might need to use that right in the future to protect their state's interests.

Speculation about the odds on the contest between Nevada Senators vs. Senator McCain would have been influenced by changes in the power ratings for both sides as the legislation moved through Congress. The ability of Nevada Senators to use their political smarts to delay a vote on the legislation raised their rating. The inability of Senator McCain to enlarge his base of support for the legislation after he lost the battle of integrity with Nevada Regulators lowered his rating. The time it had taken for him to present ASIA to the Senate for a vote had also lowered interest in the legislation. His integrity had lost its luster.

The in-running game had progressed to the point where people in the business would be able to speculate about odds for the proposition:

Will the Senate vote on ASIA?

Whatever those odds might have been, handicappers would have been inclined to put their money where their mouths were on "NO." Nevada Senators had demonstrated their ability to prevent a vote on the legislation.

Senator McCain would have been favored to win a vote on the floor of the Senate, but Nevada politicians had worked the playing field to create a situation that would enable them to prevent a vote on ASIA without a filibuster. Odds would have risen against the likelihood that ASIA would reach the floor of the Senate for a vote. Oddsmakers would have made "NO" a favorite with a number that would deter handicappers who would have agreed.

The outcome was determined by factors that went beyond numbers. This home field added the factor of the clout behind the Constitutional protection of a States Right. Nevada politicians used that clout to attract allies to support the constitutional right they might need in the future for their states.

The integrity of this game could not be stretched by Senator McCain. There was no room for him to make a "grandfather" compromise as there had been with PASPA. Whatever might have been "owed" to Senator McCain by other Senators was not enough to risk a challenge to their States Rights just to support ASIA.

The defeat of ASIA ended the in-running game between opponents of the business and Nevada. Opponents of the business were forced to accept the boundaries PASPA had established for the business. The effort to impose the economic interests of the corporate sports monopolies on Nevada had ended. The Commerce Clause had stretched the politics of integrity as far as they could be stretched. The border of Nevada was established as that limit.

Corporate sports monopolies were forced to live with the corporate sportsbook monopolies they had helped to create in Nevada. The protection of States Rights allowed those sportsbooks to continue to exploit the patent rights of their opponents. They became "business partners." Both could live with an outcome that prohibited the legalization of the business beyond the borders of Nevada.

The victory celebration by those people would not end this in-running game. Even though the contest between Congress and Nevada was over, a climate had emerged that ensured there would be future contests in this in-running game. The end of the contest between Washington and "the people" in Nevada had not ended the one with "the people" in the business outside Nevada. This contest began in the "Information Age."

Technology helped to create the ground rules for a contest that began with the effort by Senator Jon Kyl (R-AZ) to close doors on new ways for people in the business to do what they want to do. Senator Kyl proposed legislation that attempted to prohibit the opportunities for people in the business to make transactions with sportsbooks in other nations. This phase of the in-running game would pit:

IGPA, UIGEA, IGRCPEA, IGRTEA
v. PEOPLE IN THE BUSINESS.

While Senator McCain targeted the business of sports transactions in Nevada for prohibition, Senator Kyl began an effort to target all transactions from America for prohibition. The Internet Gambling Prohibition Act (IGPA) would prohibit sports transactions via the Internet to nations that licensed internet casinos and offshore sportsbooks. IGPA extended the prohibition on sports transactions to include all casino games.

While Congress remained the playing field for this contest, the opponents from previous games became teammates. They united behind the need to protect their monopolies. Corporate casinos in Nevada switched sides to become partners with the corporate sports leagues. Corporate gaming in Nevada performed this "one eighty" in order to protect the monopoly on sports transactions that had been bestowed on them by PASPA.

Segregation had created a monopoly. The political representatives of this monopoly would not fight for the liberation of the people in the business outside Nevada as they had for the people in Nevada. They supported internet legislation because it would rein-force the prohibition against legal transactions with sportsbooks other than those that were owned by the monopolies in Nevada.

There was no opposition from people in the business to these corporate monopolies. Residents of Nevada had no reason to organize. "Illegals" outside Nevada were not "free" to organize.

Jack Abramoff was hired by E-Lottery to defeat the legislation. E-Lottery had staked its future on the sale of lottery tickets over the Internet. The effort was successful. Even though people in the business had no representation, the playing field proved to be hazardous even for Senator Kyl; however, that loss did not quell opposition to the business. Seven years after the defeat of IGPA, Senator Kyl, along with others, began another contest. The Uniform Internet Gambling Enforcement Act (UIGEA) expanded the playing field of this in-running game beyond the Commerce Clause and States Rights. This playing field extended

Washington into the homes of Americans. The legislation challenged the constitutional right to privacy.

UIGEA also expanded the playing field to include a contest between America and nations that legalized sports transactions. UIGEA set the stage for a conflict over whether America had the right to prohibit transactions with sportsbooks other nations had licensed. UIGEA would deny all people in the business in America the right to engage in free trade with them.

This playing field was one-sided. There was no sideline or dugout for opponents. The power rating for Senator Kyl would have made a comeback after he used this advantage to help navigate UIGEA through Congress as an attachment to the Safe Ports Act. However, passage of the legislation did not lead to victory. Unlike the outcome of the effort by Senator Bradley with PASPA, UIGEA could not escape the shackles of its Committee assignment. There was opposition to the regulations that would implement the legislation.

The power rating for Senator Kyl would have fallen off the index after he handed the ball off to bureaucrats and politicians who were unable to formulate regulations for the legislation. UIGEA proved to be easier said than done. Problems with the enforcement of this legislation through Regulations separated UIGEA from previous federal attempts to control the business. Neither PASPA nor ASIA required regulations to enforce the prohibition imposed on states by the federal government.

The Information Age moved this contest to the Internet. UIGEA extended the prohibition to all Americans. It extended the prohibition to all casino games. It also changed the focus from the people who made transactions to the means they used to make them. But enforcement of the prohibition could have led to legal challenges based on the right to privacy. Because of the complexities of enforcement, the Regulations became mired in controversy. There was resistance from those who would be assigned the responsibility of enforcement. That responsibility would be assigned to businesses and government agencies. They contested that responsibility because the regulations would be difficult to enforce. While the language of the legislation could tell people what they would not be allowed to do, those who would have to enforce that edict did not want the responsibility to have to keep them from doing it.

These opponents of UIGEA were joined by The Poker Players Alliance. The legislation treated them the same as people who engage in sports transactions or people who play other casino games. Poker players did not accept the illegal status that was also imposed on them. They were above those "partners in crime."

International organizations and nations that had legalized sports transactions and other casino transactions also joined this opposition. They argued UIGEA violated "free trade" agreements that had been made between the U.S. and other nations.

Not one representative from the business of sports transactions joined the opposition, not even when disagreement arose over whether the Wire Act of 1961 should be included in the regulations. Opponents of sports transactions were reluctant to relinquish this control they had over the business. They were concerned that if the Wire Act were included in UIGEA it might detract from its utility as a tool to challenge sports transactions. Their opposition to the inclusion of the Wire Act in UIGEA was solidified by the outcome of the challenge to the Legislation by Jay Cohen, the owner of an offshore sportsbook.

Mr. Cohen had to return to America in order to challenge the law. He ignored lessons people in the business had learned the hard way. The last place for a verdict that would allow him to do what he wanted to do was a courtroom in America. The legal system that guaranteed his day in court also guaranteed him prison time. The system that was responsible for the enactment of the Wire Act could not be repudiated in the setting of a courtroom that was part of the system.

This outcome would be highlighted for futures on the future. While the Wire Act could be circumvented by people in the business, the law could not be overturned in a courtroom. The system that created the law would have to be challenged.

The verdict against Jay Cohen ended the debate over whether to include the Wire Act in UIGEA. Sports transactions would remain the exclusive domain of this legislation. The Wire Act could be enforced without regulations. Opponents of sports transactions won the contest to exclude the Wire Act from UIGEA.

At this stage the contest would have been declared a draw. The business had been saved from further prohibitions by a coalition of interest groups who had no interest in sports transactions. This "no decision" on regulations for UIGEA opened doors to the games of politics. Congressman Barney Frank (D-MA) began his effort to change the game from the prohibition of internet transactions to their regulation by Congress. He proposed the Internet Gambling Regulation Consumer Protection and Enforcement Act (IGRCPEA) as an alternative to UIGEA.

The Congressman became a representative of "the people" in the business of sports transactions. His legislation would allow them to do what they wanted to do over the Internet. This phase of the in-running game became a contest between IGRCPEA vs. Corporate sports monopolies. Experiences with PASPA and AISA would have made this legislation an underdog because it would legalize sports transactions. "NO" would have been the prohibitive favorite for speculation about:

Will IGRCPEA Pass With Sports Transactions Included?

People in the know would have bet their lives against this proposition. Congressman Frank became a representative of the people in the business in a contest against the NFL. The Congressman learned the hard way he would not be able to include sports transactions in his legislation. In order to keep IGRCPEA alive, he caved in to opposition from the NFL. The Congressman removed sports transaction from the legislation. His "cave-in" kept sports transactions separate from the other Internet games.

The NFL was able to retain the home field advantage in Congress for all of the corporate sports monopolies. This outcome would be highlighted for speculation about the future of the business. Without the opposition from Nevada politicians, the business had to rely on a Congressman from another state who did not have the clout to play on their field.

But even without the inclusion of sports transactions there was opposition to internet legislation from government agencies and businesses that would have the responsibility to enforce the law. Visa, MasterCard, the Federal Reserve, the Treasury Department, as well as others opposed the imposition of the duty.

None of these opponents of the legislation supported the right of the people to make their transactions. They opposed what it would take for them to enforce the prohibition on their transactions. They knew more than the proponents of the legislation about what it would take to keep people from doing what they want to do.[286]

---

[286] Industry reacts to Ways and Means Committee Hearing on Internet Gambling". Poker News Daily 10/6/11

Despite the lack of political support, people in the business of sports transactions received support from international organizations and businesses. The World Trade Organization, E-Lottery, the nation of Antigua, and the European Commission became allies. This coalition challenged America's attempt to prohibit sports transactions to nations that licensed the business. Those nations and organizations argued in favor of free trade. The politicians who began this game of internet prohibitions and regulations did not have the clout to finish it. They left the door open for other politicians to try to continue this game from other angles. Representative Bob Goodblatte (R-VA) became a spokesman for the opponents of all internet legislation. His opposed all transactions because gambling is immoral.

Representative Jim McDermott (D WA) sponsored the Internet Gambling Regulation and Tax Enforcement Act (IGRTEA). His legislation would add a 2% federal tax and a 6% tax on deposits imposed on people who gamble over the Internet. Supporters of the legislation argued that the legislation could generate revenue for government. They speculated that the regulation of transactions over the Internet would generate revenue as well as lead to the creation of more than 30,000 jobs.[287]

These arguments did not satisfy banks and the gambling corporations that would be responsible for the administration of this tax. They refused to attend the hearing on the IGRTEA. They rejected the attempt to assign responsibilities the tax would impose on them.

Whether the details can be resolved could generate speculation about whether any of the legislation before

---

[287] Thanks to former colleague "Mr. Robinson" for his observation that "people do what they want to do debate on the legislation. They rejected the attempt to assign responsibilities the Tax would impose on them.

the Ways and Means Committee becomes law? However, people in the business of sports transactions would be reluctant to waste their time to calculate odds and handicap a matter that had been decided for them. More than a decade after Senator Kyl began this contest, the NFL proved it retains the clout to veto legislation that would permit people in the business to make legal transactions.

Even without the Regulations that enforce the Internet prohibition, sports transactions from America to other nations are illegal. People in the business are also legally segregated from the world.

Game Summaries

This in-running game began in the climate of organized crime. The ten percent tax on transactions and federal regulations were tactics used by opponents of the business to exercise control over sportsbooks in Nevada. If successful, they could have crippled the business.

Opponents of the business were defeated by the guile of people in the business. They found ways to get around the tax and the regulations. The people extended this game to where time would expose the futility of these tactics.

Opponents of the business adapted their offensive to the climate in which big business assumed control over sportsbooks. The opposition moved the playing field from Nevada to Washington in order to create a home field advantage for themselves; however, there were limitations in that advantage. States Rights and the political smarts of Nevada politicians preserved the business in Nevada through the "grandfather" tactic that was preserved by the defeat of ASIA.

The end of the contest with Nevada led to adjustments by the opponents that fit the playing field created by the Information Age. They proposed federal laws and regulations that reaffirmed the illegality of sports transactions over the Internet.

Opposition to the regulations came from those who would have to enforce the legislation, not the people in the business. The NFL had the clout to remove sports transactions from the laws and regulations that might approve internet transactions on other casino games.

This contest over regulations opened the door for other contestants. The Information Age had become synonymous with the climate of globalism. The contest over sports transactions was not the exclusive domain of America. Other nations joined the opposition to laws and regulations that would restrict free trade between America and their legal sportsbooks.

The in-running game that began with taxes and regulations for turf clubs in Nevada had evolved had into a contest between America and the world. The series of contests was a result of adjustments that were made by the losers of the previous contests. Adjustments by the losers were essential to continue this series.

They had applied the principles of the "Zigzag" theory. The inability of the opponents of the business to win the contest on the playing field of Nevada led them to move it to the halls of Congress. The inability to end the business in Nevada led to a game plan that would ensure the legal business would not expand beyond the border of Nevada.

Even though opponents of the business won that segment of the in-running game, they had to extend their endeavor. They could not allow the tools of the Information Age to lead to a "back door cover" for people in the business. They had to enact legislation that prohibited transactions via the Internet with sportsbooks in other nations. While the regulations have not been implemented for transactions on other casino games, sports transactions from America will be prohibited with those nations.

The "Zigzag" theory would argue that adjustments will have to be made by the people in the business in order to continue this in-running game for freedom. This adjustment can take advantage of the change in the global economic climate that has kindled interest in money from the business for states in need of additional sources of revenue for their budgets. This change in the climate has opened the door for the possibility to continue the in-running game.

Speculation about futures on the future for this phase of the game might have to incorporate the insights from:

"WAY BEYOND THE FRINGES"

"Before we get to options for the future we have to begin with where we are," said the Senator from the State of the Union. "We have reassembled here in order to resume the discussion of an issue most Americans would not consider important. The Professional and Amateur Sports Protection Act (otherwise known as PASPA) would not make any list of issues that are important to America other than on those of us who are here. We need to convey its relevance to the rest of America. We can make that case in the context of the problems PASPA has created for what the Founding Fathers envisioned as freedom in a representative democracy. The ability to resolve those problems will be one barometer of the future for our form of government. While most Americans might not regard the legal segregation of sports-betting as important..."

"Sports transactions, *not* sports betting," a member of the audience interrupted.

"Permit me to correct myself," the Senator responded. "While most Americans would not consider the legal segregation of the business of sports transactions important, we can show them that it is. If we do, it would set a precedent that could be applied to the other so-called big issues of our times. We must show that the problems that have been caused by those who oppose this business is an example of the way government has become manipulated by business interests that have enough money to buy what they want. The history of the opposition to the business of sports transactions stands out as an example of the way money can stretch the distance between Americans and their government. We must try to help to shorten that distance so this country becomes the representative democracy the Founding Fathers envisioned in the Constitution.

"That's why we're no longer number one in the world," a person shouted from the audience.

"We might not even be in the top ten anymore," another responded.

"Do not eject them," the Senator said to the security guards. "They have the right to freedom of speech in this room. Their public feelings on the issue before us have been excluded for too long."

"We've never had a voice outside Nevada," a member of the audience shouted.

"I know and that's one of the problems," the Senator responded. "Before I turn this meeting over to the Senator from the State of the Unrepresented, I want to leave you with observations that will bring some of my notes from past meetings to the present.

"First, that 10% poll tax imposed on sports transactions in Nevada amounted to taxation without representation. People in the business followed the example of our revolutionary predecessors in dealing with those types of taxes. Senator Kefauver chose to ignore lessons learned from the past. The will of the people prevailed over his political expediency.

"The Professional and Amateur Sports Protection Act amounts to an exploitation of the Commerce Clause, turning it into the claws of commerce that turned all the "dollar bills" who supported it into million dollar babies. Even Rhodes Scholars succumb to those temptations. So much for whom representative government represents."

"With regard to ASIA, I concluded that the State of Arizona is still laughing all the way to bank for what Senator McCain did for the coffers of his state. Payoffs from the Big Dance and the Big Games continue to reward him and his constituents. That deal made him look like a genius until he chose to remain at the craps tables instead of taking his business to the sports-books where even he would stand a better chance at winning.

"Enough, enough," said the Senator from the State of the Unrepresented to the audience that had risen with requests for more. "I will try to bring everything up to date in order to make it possible to reach a consensus that brings all of us together for the future. To get there we must try to transcend the ideological stalemate over the role of government in our lives. That stalemate has made it almost impossible to do anything about the special interests that control the agendas of our nation."

"The odds on that outcome would be off the boards in Las Vegas," said the member of the National Association of Segregated Handicappers and Odds-makers (NASHO).

"Your business may be off the boards in Las Vegas if we don't," the Senator replied. "Since you are the first to respond to my comments in a way only a member of your profession could do, I will begin this discussion with you. Please tell us about your organization."

"Thank you for the time, Senator," the member responded. "NASHO is an informal organization of people in the business. We held our first meeting just recently to discuss the efforts of the State of New Jersey to repeal PASPA and what it might mean for the future of our business. While NASHO is based in Las Vegas, our organization is concerned about all of the problems that affect our business in America."

"How many people are in your organization?" the Senator asked.

"Just a few...all of them from Nevada."

"Just a few members from Nevada," the Senator repeated "...out of the hundreds of thousands or maybe millions of people who engage in the business. Do we even know how many people engage in the business of sports transactions?"

"No, Senator. No one has even tried to count of the number of people in the business in Nevada. People outside the State would be reluctant to come out in the open about what they do. They saw what happened to Jay Cohen when he exposed himself. Maybe you can ask one of the branches of the federal government to take this on as a study wherein people are counted, but remain anonymous. Those numbers could help our cause."

"I welcome your suggestion, but tell me why you have only a few members from Nevada where the business is legal?" the Senator asked.

"I'll try, even though it might not make sense to people outside the business. First of all, people in our business tend to work alone. Privacy is important. They don't work at desks in an office setting. Sportsbooks aren't conducive to thoughtful conversation. There aren't many opportunities to discuss anything more than 'who do you like?' Another problem is time. People are reluctant to take time away from what they do in order to spend it on issues that don't allow them to put up or shut up. The daily routines of oddsmaking and handicapping, along with watching their games, tends to take up all the time people can spend on the business.

"And, as long as they can do what they want to do, they don't have an interest in spending time thinking about the freedom of people in the business outside Nevada. Legal segregation has created a divide that keeps our people apart. When you're free to do what you want to do, it's hard to get people interested in the big picture of freedom for everyone, especially when you believe there is little you can do anyway.

"And last, but not least, the corporations that own the business in Nevada have the power to censor the people who work for them. People who would have a lot to say are not free to speak for themselves on record about the bigger picture of the business."

"A lot of what you said sounds like excuses to me. Let me try to rephrase the question. What could people in your business in Nevada do to change the situation if they had the time to spend and were willing to spend the time?" the Senator asked.

"The easiest part would be for them to just to start thinking about some of the current issues. The time is right because there's a lot going on right now. People in New Jersey voted in favor of legalization of the business. Politicians have proposed legislation that would make transactions legal in the state. They also expressed a willingness to challenge the constitutionality of PASPA before the Supreme Court. One politician said he would propose a bill before the House of Representatives that would legalize the business in the state. Those actions might send a message to people in other states. They might want to join or follow New Jersey. And the people in Nevada could help by sharing their experiences in order to help them move forward."

"Would it be possible to estimate how much money legalization of the business could bring to the budgets of government?" the Senator asked.

"We have the figures from Nevada. You might be able to help us if you could make the potential for revenue from sports transactions a priority for one of the federal agencies to analyze. They could include the total amount of money the federal government has collected from the .025% that remains from the ten percent tax on owners of sportsbooks in Nevada. They could provide estimates of money that might come from New Jersey and other states and that could add fuel to the fire. I'm sure the NFL would not be interested in a discussion of those figures, but I don't think they could veto the research that would shed light on the topic."

"You might have something there. Dollar figures always attract attention. I will follow up on your suggestion," the Senator said.

"Perhaps estimates of the amount of money that America loses to illegal bookmakers and to offshore sportsbooks might put a dent in the armor of the people who oppose the business. We need to publicize what we do know about the legal business from Nevada. We could make them known around the country in order to emphasize the business angle," said the member of NASHO.

"Your suggestion would help to shed light on the topic. Now can you tell us how the people in the business in Nevada might benefit from the desegregation of their business? Can you tell us why it would be in their interest to get involved? I'm talking about the people who make the transactions, not the owners of the businesses, the politicians, or the bureaucrats," the Senator said.

"One thing right off the bat is the freedom it would create for everyone to shop for numbers and make transactions anywhere in the world without being concerned about threats from law enforcement. Maybe we could help bring back individual owners of sportsbooks—the so-called bookmakers who are now illegal. They would create competition for the corporations. That competition might attract more people to our business."

"Now that we've got the ball rolling, let me stop with you for a moment in order to open this discussion to the main opponent of your business." The Senator turned to address the representative of the NFL. "The discussion so far has been about some of the consequences of the segregation from the laws you have helped to impose on America. Have you or the other sports leagues ever taken into consideration the impact of those laws?"

The NFL representative responded. "I can't speak for the other sports leagues. I can only say that the NFL does not believe it is appropriate for people to bet on our events."

"It's not betting," a member of the audience interrupted.

"Please, let the representative continue in the words their organization has chosen to use. This forum respects everyone's freedom," the Senator said.

"I would give them all the freedom to speak as long as they didn't have the power to back it up with all of the laws that serve their interests," the member of the audience responded.

The representative from the NFL had to ignore the catcalls in order to continue. "We believe the American people support us on this issue; however, we are always open to suggestions that could make the situation better for America."

"When this whole thing began in the last century, your opposition to sports transactions stressed the immorality of gambling and the potential for fixed outcomes of your contests. I haven't heard your organization use those reasons lately to justify its opposition to the business. Do you believe those reasons justify the legal segregation of a profession?" the Senator asked.

We welcome the technology that has made it more difficult for gamblers to fix our games. That technology has helped to deter them. But we always remain on the alert for sports gamblers who want to try to fix an outcome."

"The legal industry in Nevada helps you maintain that integrity," the member of NASHO said. "Sportsbooks are always on the lookout for a fix. They're the ones who would pay the price of a fix. They provide you with information on line movements that might raise suspicion. Why don't you give our business credit for helping to raise the level of the integrity of your games?"

The NFL representative ignored the remarks. "A recent survey shows that the belief in the integrity of our games is at an all-time high; however, we can't assume the problem has been solved."

"If the morality of gambling and the integrity of your games are no longer as important as they once were, why do you continue to oppose the legalization of the business throughout America?" the Senator asked.

"The NFL remains adamant about the exploitation of our business by sports-betting. Owners of those businesses are free to conduct their business at our expense. We are business people. We have the responsibility to protect our products. We will continue to oppose any use of our products without our approval."

"What about your exploitation of our business?" asked the member of NASHO. "Your announcers and analysts use our business. They use our numbers, our terminology. No one in our business ever asks you for compensation from something that helps the ratings for your business. Exploitation is a two-way street."

The Senator had to ask the audience to remain seated and cease their applause. "What if there was a way for them to compensate you for the use of your product?" Would you change your position about the need for PASPA to protect your interests?" the Senator asked.

"Why would we support the repeal of a law that works for us everywhere except Nevada? And even at the sportsbooks in Nevada we have the power to stop them from using language that is our patent right. We can sell products for the Super Bowl at the sports-books, but they can't use that name to promote betting on our game."

"I repeat my question. What if there was a way for them to compensate you for the use of your product? Would you change your position about the need for PASPA to protect your interests?" asked the Senator.

"How could we have that discussion? Who would we talk to? "They don't have anyone who speaks for them."

"Indeed. How could you?" The Senator turned to the NASHO representative. "You don't have anyone who speaks for your interests, do you?"

"I know I don't speak for the business. No one person does. Our history shows that we spoke as one when the interests of the business in Nevada were threatened. Nevada is the only place in America where people in the business could band together. People on both sides of the counter joined forces to defend the turf clubs from the ten percent tax. The Nevada Gaming Control Board allied with Nevada politicians and casino corporations to defend the business when it was attacked by the PASPA and ASIA. Once upon a time people in the business in Nevada organized around the Nevada Association of Race and Sports-book Operators. NARASO lobbied for the business in Washington. Unfortunately, NARASO didn't last long."

"How could that lobby speak for all Americans in the business if it was the *Nevada* Association instead of the *National* Association?" Wasn't that part of the problem?" the Senator asked.

"You're right. The divide between people in the business in Nevada and the rest of America has made it impossible to have one voice that serves our interests. We don't even have that voice for the people in Nevada because there is no competition with the corporate owners of the sportsbooks."

"There is no voice because the system prevents it," the Senator said.

"But then times might be a changin'," said the NASHO representative. "NBA Commissioner David Stern has opened the door to the possibility. If the NBA and the NHL see advantages to their businesses from the legalization of our business, that could put a dent in the armor of solidarity of the corporate sports monopolies. Maybe the time is right for one or two of the leagues to make a break from the NFL."

Even if it does, why would the business in Nevada concede the profits from its monopoly? What advantage would there be for Nevada to change the system?" Aren't the monopolists in Nevada also part of the problem?" the Senator asked.

"You're right. I wonder if America has ever faced a problem like this one?" the member of NASHO said.

"Right now we have to strip ourselves of the delusion that anyone can speak for the business," the Senator said. "Maybe we could entice the NBA to start us in that direction. Maybe they could appease the casino monopolies in Nevada with an offer to extend their monopoly to the rest of America through phone accounts." That would give them an initial advantage to solidify their business before others could catch up. Also, the corporations from England who may take over the sportsbooks in Nevada might be able to make the deals with the sports leagues the corporate casinos can't make."

"Well, at least we have come up with one possibility. Maybe there's some hope after all. "I wonder if it would be any easier for the NBA to make that deal if there was an appeal of PASPA to the Supreme Court?"

The Senator turned to the representative of the Justice Department. "Isn't it obvious that a law that creates legal segregation is unconstitutional? How can people in one state be free to do what nobody else in America can do? Why should people outside Nevada be treated as criminals for doing the same thing that people in Nevada do legally? Isn't it embarrassing to you that the federal government has to enforce this law? Has anyone in your Department ever thought of challenging the constitutionality of PASPA?"

"You bit off more than the whole Department could chew with all those questions," the representative said. "One thing I can say for certain is that we do not intend to interfere in a process that must be initiated by the states. Several of them have expressed an interest in pursuing that route. We will leave it to them to challenge PASPA. But I wouldn't bet that the issue of segregation will be resolved by them."

"I would bet against it," a member of the audience shouted.

The representative of the Justice Department continued. "The Courts might find reasons to rescind PASPA, but just for New Jersey because they had been one of the grandfathers. But even if they decided in favor of New Jersey, the other states that weren't grandfathered might still be denied that right. Courts might decide the issue on a case-by-case basis or the Supreme Court could decide the issue for all of America in one case. There's a lot of room for speculation that would make it a great game for the boards in Las Vegas."

"If we posted one would you get down?" the NASHO member.

"Do it and you'll find out. That would be our version of the Super Bowl," the lawyer said.

"Big Game, not Super Bowl," a member of the audience shouted.

"You're right. The NFL has already proven they have the patent right on the use of that language in Las Vegas," the lawyer said. "My bet would be that the Courts will uphold the politics that led to the creation of this system. They are likely to reject an appeal that would allow another state to do what Nevada does. I would be inclined to go with a decision that keeps it the way it is,"

"What about the legalization of the business on Indian reservations?" I read about a study prepared by a law firm that concluded the Supreme Court would likely uphold the legality of sports transactions that were made from Indian reservations. Is that possible?"

"We think that appeal would be unlikely because of the time and the cost it would take to bring this issue to the Supreme Court. The business isn't that profitable to warrant what it might cost a casino on an Indian Reservation to try to win a case. They're probably looking for someone else to pay the freight, then they could benefit at someone else's expense. I'd bet they'll wait and see."

"What about an appeal from individuals or an organization that is based on their legal segregation from the rest of America?" the member of NASHO asked. Is it possible a law school or private law firm could make a pro bono appeal on behalf of individuals in the business?"

"Now that's a tough one. I don't know if the so-called victim in this case could establish themselves as an entity that could be protected from legal segregation. I mean, who are these people? Are they an occupation, a profession, or just people who bet on sports? If they established a legal status for what they do, the Courts might give them a chance to make their case."

"What about an appeal from a person who has established professional credentials in the business? Could one person challenge legal segregation?" asked the member of NASHO.

"I don't want to get into that question. You will have to consult with a law firm or law school to get that answer."

"Can you envision a law school at Ohio State, LSU, Alabama, or Kentucky doing what you suggest? Do you think they would dare challenge the NCAA? The NCAA might terminate their Division 1 status," the Senator said.

The audience responded with additional names that included the Top 50 collegiate football and basketball programs. The names included institutions with so-called higher academic standards such as Stanford, Duke, and Northwestern.

"Maybe a Division Three law school might take a chance. What would they have to lose?" the lawyer said.

"Just the trillion-to-one shot they have to be invited to the Big Dance or to the BS Championship Game," replied the member of NASHO.

"I hope you can find someone who would be willing to explore that option. I'll include that possibility in our report on the State of the Union," the Senator said.

"Let me turn back to the representative from the Justice Department to ask about the challenges to this situation in America from other nations and international organizations. How will they impact this situation?" the Senator asked.

"They might regret messing with us. I heard rumors that members of the military industrial complex suggested we use drones to enforce our laws in other countries. Wipe out one or two sportsbooks to send a message," the lawyer said with a chuckle that could not hide the regret that accompanied the words.

"I'm sure the corporate sports monopolies would be willing to pay for it. That would pay their membership into the military industrial complex," a member of the audience said.

"I hope what you say could only be possible in a novel," the Senator said. "Let's hope sports are included in the internet regulations. Is that possible?" the Senator asked the representative of the Justice Department.

"Not unless the NFL backs down from their opposition."

"Don't even ask," the NFL representative said before the Senator could ask.

"Offshore sportsbooks, violations of free trade, fines from the World Trade Organization, federal confiscation of deposits for transactions, regulations for money transfers from here to there make us look like one of the zaniest nations on this planet. Who knows what new technology might do to make it even screwier?" said the lawyer.

"It could get even nuttier if the professional sports leagues expand to other nations where sports trans-actions are legal. Will people in those countries be allowed to make transactions on their games? Will the leagues allow people in those nations to steal their patent rights? Would the leader of the free world allow that to happen? Would Americans allow people in other nations to have the freedom we are denied in 'the land of the free'?" the member of NASHO asked.

"Let's move on to something that might make more sense," the Senator said. I'll ask the represen-tative from the Treasury Department to join this discussion. "Do you think it would help if the case were made for the benefits that could come by raising the leftover from what was the ten percent tax? The federal government still collects the .025% tax from corporations that own the sportsbooks in Nevada. If the business was legal everywhere, we could make the case that the revenue from an increase in the tax would help to address the budget deficit."

"It would be hard to argue against it, especially since it wouldn't come from the wallets of the people," said the representative from Treasury.

"We wouldn't benefit from that tax," said the NFL representative.

"You have more benefits from your conferred monopoly status than any tax could ever render," the Senator responded. "You have no competition. Other businesses can only dream about your benefit."

"They would even like to control our thoughts about their business, if they could," said the NASHO member "...and you still want more"?

"Your monopoly has more power than the constitutional guarantee of States Rights. You have the power to take away the right of forty-nine states to conduct a business that you've made legal in only one and in doing so, you have taken away the power those states must have to make the constitutional guarantee of States Rights the law of the land," said the Senator.

"Right on!" a member of the audience shouted. "We're talking about the rights of all of us who live in those States. We're the ones who make it a state's right and we're the ones who have been sentenced to the sidelines for this game."

"Your points are well taken," said the Senator. "The people who are the subject of the Constitution have not been a part of the politics that created this situation. They are not represented in this so-called democracy."

"Maybe the Commissioner of the NBA opened that door for us when he said that the expansion of legal transactions on his business may be just around the corner," said the member of NASHO. "Maybe the politics of representation will start after a divide is created among the sports leagues. Maybe we in the business can make it happen by offering benefits to those who are willing to make that break. Maybe we can offer them PASTA as an alternative to PASPA."

"PASTA?" the Senator asked.

"The Professional and Amateur Sports Transaction Act could replace PASPA as the law that governs the business. We touched the tip of the iceberg with the mention of raising the leftover of the ten percent tax on licensees. We could use that revenue to offer a commensurate tax deduction for the sports leagues that side with us," said the representative from NASHO.

"So the revenue that was generated for the government from the small increase in the tax on the licensees would enable us to offer a tax deduction to the sports leagues that agree to support PASTA. Both would benefit from the expansion of the business," the Senator said.

"And we could add more to the PASTA," said the member of NASHO. We could offer the Leagues "board certified" members of the business to analyze their games on sports networks for free."

"Board certified?" the Senator asked.

"People we certify are the best among the handicappers and oddsmakers in the business. They could replace the big mouths in the media who contribute to global warming with all of their hot air."

"You could offer them money, your expertise... what else?"

"The business could offer the TV networks the opportunity to send their ratings to the moon through the opportunity for viewers to make transactions from their homes while the game is in progress. Technology has made it possible for people to make in-running wagers. That kind of interaction would put sports entertainment in a class by itself."

"Is any of this really possible?" the Senator from the State of the Union asked the member of NASHO. Can any of this happen? Before I prepare the report on the State of the Union I need help with the odds on these possibilities. I'd appreciate it if you could calculate the odds on the success of an appeal of PASPA to the Supreme Court based on States Rights. And while you're at it, how about the odds on the success of an appeal based on the legal segregation of the members of the business? And if that isn't enough, before we begin anything in Congress, could you please show us the odds on the chances for PASPA to become PASTA? What are the odds that Congress would repeal the law of the land?"

HANDICAPPING THE FUTURE

Those questions are addressed in the next in-running game. The "Zigzag" theory will be the basis for speculation about whether adjustments can be made that would reverse the outcome of the previous contest. Nevada and the other grandfathers had exercised their States Rights to retain their right to legal sports transactions. However, PASPA precluded that right for all of the other states. This in-running game will focus on whether that situation can be changed.

This contest is made possible by the changes in the global economic climate. The "trickle down" from the economic recession reached the playing field that PASPA had ruled for more than two decades. There had been no incentive to change the law of the land until the global recession impacted the budgets of states that began to look for additional sources of revenue.

This need for additional revenue prompted politicians from the State of New Jersey to begin their endeavor to change the law of the land in order so that they could legalize single game sports transactions. New Jersey Congressmen announced their intentions to introduce legislation in Congress that would either make New Jersey an exception to PASPA or would lead to the repeal of PASPA by Congress. New Jersey State Senator Raymond Lesniak added a third alternative. He decided to contest the constitutionality of PASPA before the U.S. Supreme Court. The Senator began the process with the introduction of legislation that the State of New Jersey can use to petition a federal court to declare PASPA unconstitutional. It is expected that the loser of this contest will appeal the decision to the U.S. Supreme Court.

All of these initiatives contest the right of the federal government to prohibit single game sports transactions in New Jersey. They will argue that New Jersey has the constitutional right to decide whether that business should be legal. New Jersey politicians will attempt to replicate the efforts of the political representatives from Nevada who saved the business of their sportsbooks from the proponents of PASPA and ASIA.

In addition to these efforts by New Jersey, there is fourth option that could also remove PASPA from the playing field. In this contest, "We, the people" can make an appeal of our legal segregation to the Supreme Court. This appeal would contest the prohibition of individual liberties that ensued from the legal segregation of people in the business that was imposed by PASPA.

FUTURES ON PASPA

Four contests will be posted on this futures board.

1. Will Congress grant New Jersey an exemption from PASPA?

2. Will Congress repeal PASPA?

3. Will the Courts decide in favor of the petition from New Jersey that PASPA is unconstitutional?

4. Will the Courts decide in favor of a petition from "We, the people" that PASPA is unconstitutional?

"When" each outcome might be decided will be added to the speculation about "Will" it happen whenever it is possible.

No. 1: WILL CONGRESS GRANT NEW JERSEY AN EXEMPTION FROM PASPA?

The anthem that began this game was the announcement by Congressmen from New Jersey that they would introduce legislation in the House of Representatives to challenge the prohibition on single game sports transactions in New Jersey rendered by PASPA.

This legislation decided the fate of that business for New Jersey in 1992. Politicians from that state had voted for the compromise that established the legal segregation of their "grandfather." They had been content to live with the prohibition imposed by PASPA until the economic recession of 2009 created the need for additional sources of revenue for their state.

Voters in New Jersey decided in favor of a proposition that would legalize single game trans-actions in their state. After the vote, New Jersey Congressmen announced their intentions to resurrect their "grandfather" that had expired. They proposed to introduce legislation that would either grant New Jersey an exemption from PASPA or would allow New Jersey the freedom to legalize the business through the congressional repeal of PASPA.

Either piece of legislation would render a second chance for New Jersey. New Jersey had squandered the first chance in 1992 when they failed to take advantage of the door left open by the grandfather clause in PASPA. Although New Jersey had been one of the "grandfathers" included in PASPA, this "grand-father" expired after state legislators failed to meet the eighteen-month deadline established by PASPA to enact the measures that were necessary to legalize the business in the state. A bill to make that possible in 1993 did not make it out of committee.

Handicapping the outcome of this option will benefit from an examination of the factors that led to the outcome of the previous contest between Nevada and the proponents of PASPA. Those factors that led to the victory for Nevada would make "NO" the "right side" for speculation about whether Congress would grant an exemption from PASPA for New Jersey.

New Jersey legislators would have to secure the number of votes in Congress that were necessary to provide their state with that exemption. The numbers game for this contest differs from the one that determined the outcome for Nevada. Nine states besides Nevada had used their States Rights to legalize sports transactions before PASPA was enacted. All of them supported their States Rights to legalize their business.

Those numbers were enhanced because the right of these states to enact this legislation opened the door to support from other states. The Constitutional guarantee of States Rights transcends the particular issue of sports transactions. It would be in the interest of every state to protect a right they might have to exercise in the future to protect their interest on another matter.

In the first contest over PASPA, there was a coalition of interests that had enough votes to veto PASPA. Proponents of the legislation had to make concessions to them. They created "grandfathers" in exchange for the votes to enact the legislation. If New Jersey Congressmen decide to go it alone with legislation that would create an exemption for their state, the odds against them would be prohibitive. Oddsmakers would place an "X" before both "YES" and "NO" on the outcome of this option. They would not post odds on a game whose outcome was "fixed."

"Zigzag" would argue that no adjustments would be possible to change the outcome for New Jersey that had been rendered by PASPA. The economic climate of the recession might have to worsen into a depression in order for New Jersey to have the support from other states that was necessary. Without that change the factors that had led to the enactment of PASPA would hold sway two decades later. The likelihood of this outcome would change the focus on the future of PASPA to OPTION TWO.

No. 2. WILL CONGRESS REPEAL PASPA?

After the proponents of ASIA failed to extend the prohibition on single game transactions to Nevada, PASPA did not come into play again until Congressman Barney Frank attempted to circumvent the prohibition through IGRCPEA. His legislation would have legalized sports transactions with offshore casinos and sportsbooks over the Internet.

The NFL sacked him. They would not allow the legislation to reach the floor of the House of Representatives until the sports option was removed. The League showed it had retained the clout to protect its business with a veto over legislation that would have legalized sports transactions over the Internet. This outcome would serve as an example of what is likely to happen to New Jersey's attempt to repeal PASPA.

The "Zigzag" theory would argue that the New Jersey Congressmen would have to make adjustments in order to have a chance to win this contest. Without an assist from an economic recession that turned for the worse, Representative Frank would have had to add PASTA to his legislation in order to attract the support that was necessary to obtain its release from Committee. Greased palms translate into numbers. He might have tried to entice a corporate sports monopoly to side with him through economic incentives in exchange for their support. Rebates to the leagues from the expansion of the business might have persuaded some of them to at least consider an end to their opposition. Offshore sportsbooks could have added their incentives. The Congressman might have been able to convince them that it would be in their interest offer their version of the former ten percent tax on transactions from the U.S. in order to entice congressional support for the repeal PASPA.

The offer could have been sweetened if it had been made through the World Trade Organization (WTO). The WTO might have found the ways to rescind or refund the penalties imposed on the United States for violations of free trade agreements. As part of the package the WTO might have negotiated "foreign aid" to the U.S.

These and other options could lead to a fracture of what may be a fissure in the alliance or corporate sports monopolies. Statements from the NBA Commissioner David Stern about the inevitability of legal sports transactions in America opened the door to the possibility. It may be an indicator that the NBA is amenable to accommodations in exchange for an end to its opposition to the business.

One thing is certain. Doing nothing to attract support for the cause ensures defeat. The same holds true for the effort by New Jersey Congressmen to repeal PASPA. They must make adjustments in order to have a chance to win their games.

They must offer incentives in order to attract the support that is necessary to change the situation. They must do what Congressman Frank should have done. Without those incentives to support New Jersey, oddsmakers would make "NO" the prohibitive favorite for Option Two.

Even if that is the outcome, it might not end the attempts to repeal PASPA. Previous in-running games have shown that it might take a decade or more for the environment to change to one that might be suitable for the repeal of the legislation.

In the meantime, speculation about Options One and Two may become irrelevant if the courts decide whether or not PASPA is constitutional. The time clock for that playing field can shorten the time for when a decision will be made on the future of the business. Speculation about when that may be can be included in the analysis of OPTION 3.

No. 3: APPEAL OF PASPA BY NEW JERSEY TO THE COURTS.

New Jersey State Senators began this contest with their challenge to PASPA before a Federal District Court. Their petition was denied. The Judge ruled these legislators did not have the legal right to ask the Court to declare PASPA unconstitutional. The Court said the Governor would have to file the petition through the State's Attorney General's Office.

New Jersey legislators responded to the decision through a referendum that presented the issue of the legalization of sports transactions to New Jersey voters. They voted in favor of the proposition to legalize the business at casinos. Afterwards, the Governor announced his intention to support legislation that would legalize the business. New Jersey had complied with the decision of the Federal District Court to take the steps that were necessary to make an appeal of PASPA before the District Court. Whichever way the District Court decides their case, it is expected that the decision will be appealed to the Supreme Court by the side that loses. Neither New Jersey nor the corporate sports monopolies would settle for less. This appeal would pit the States Rights of New Jersey against the Commerce Clause of the Constitution. Speculation about the outcome would focus on the legal precedents established by the history of judicial contests between the Commerce Clause and States

Rights. Speculation would also include the previous decisions by members of the Courts on this issue.

Handicapping that employs the tools of our business will be used to supplement this legal analysis. Experience with the calculations of home field advantage is one of those tools that can help with a forecast on the outcome of this appeal.

The proponents of PASPA have held on to their home field advantage in Congress for two decades, but the economic interests of the corporate sports monopolies that were protected by Congress would be reviewed on another playing field. Justices whose palms had not been greased would determine whether the previous decision by Congress was a "fixed" outcome.

Sponsors behind the legislation who helped to grease the palms of their legislators would not have this advantage in the courts. The terrain for this playing field is less suited to "for sale" signs. That would raise the odds in favor of a decision based on a principle other than money.

The numbers for this playing field differ from those in Congress. Numbers can help to create a home field advantage. Instead of the 435 members of the House of Representatives and the 100 members of the Senate there will either be three Justices on the Appeals Court or nine Justices on the Supreme Court who will be the arbiters of "upon further review."

Fewer numbers will level the playing field. Those who oppose PASPA do not have the clout that is necessary to have access to all of the backrooms of the power brokers in Congress. On this playing field before the courts both legal teams will have equal access to the justices through their presentations. There will be fewer variables for speculation. Fewer uncertainties increase the odds in favor of a forecast that is "on the money."

Handicappers would anticipate that the lawyers for PASPA will incorporate in their argument all of the reasons that led to the passage of the legislation. That will include the history of precedents that established the Commerce Clause of the Constitution as a way to extend federal control over the states.

The lawyers will also show that the issue of the grandfather clause in PASPA had already been addressed by the Court. A Federal District Court had already rejected the argument against the constitutionality of the grandfather clause that had been made by the State of Delaware in its petition against PASPA.

Delaware is one of the "grandfathers" included in the legislation. This "grandfather" had legalized parlay transactions on the NFL before PASPA was enacted. Delaware was granted the legal right to continue with those transactions.

Two decades later an interest in revenue from sports transactions prompted Delaware Governor Jack Merkell to contest that grandfather restriction before a Federal Appeals Court. The Governor asked the Court to allow Delaware to legalize single game transactions on the NFL, NBA, MLB, NHL, and the NCAA at the racinos in the State.

The Appeals Court ruled that the legalization of sports transactions on individual games by Delaware would violate PASPA. The decision upheld the constitutionality of the grandfather restrictions of the legislation. Delaware appealed the decision to the U.S. Supreme Court. The Court rejected the appeal without comment.

This outcome impacts the grounds for an appeal by New Jersey. Instead of a challenge based on the constitutionality of the grandfather clause, the legal team decided to contest the constitutionality of PASPA.

New Jersey will argue that on this issue the Tenth Amendment of the Constitution prevails over the Commerce Clause. The legal team will attempt to make this a contest about which level of government has the right to control the business of sports transactions. They will make it a contest about the constitutionality of PASPA, *not* the use of the grandfather clause.

The legal team that defends PASPA against the appeal by New Jersey will argue that Congress had decided the issue of constitutionality when the legislation was enacted. They will argue that the Court should follow precedents from similar contests between states and the federal government. Most of those precedents concluded that whatever Congress had enacted should remain the law of the land until Congress repealed the legislation. A majority of those precedents concluded that it was up to the politicians in Congress to undo what their predecessors had done.

If the Appeals Court is consistent with the precedent they established with Delaware it will reject the petition by New Jersey. If the grandfather clause is constitutional, the assumption would be that the Act itself is constitutional. This conclusion would be based on precedents that concluded the commerce clause was constitutional in cases where the jurisdiction of the Federal Government had been imposed on states.

If New Jersey decided to appeal this decision of the Federal Appeals Court to the United States Supreme Court, State officials would be forced to ignore the words of Delaware Governor Merkell. He said, "...only a small fraction of appeals are actually heard by the Supreme Court". That small fraction of one out of ten would also apply to an appeal by the State of New Jersey.

Oddsmakers would make New Jersey a prohibitive underdog in a contest with the Supreme Court. The Court would be favored to reject the appeal without comment. The Court would be expected to conclude as it had in the case of Delaware that PASPA was a matter for Congress to address.

Implicit in this decision would be the question of why it had taken New Jersey almost two decades to make the appeal. The Justices would have reason to question why it had taken that long to challenge legislation that was deemed unconstitutional.

The legal team for New Jersey would have to employ people in our business in order to help them offer explanations. Then they would be able to argue that the climate in which PASPA was enacted did not include the technology that could have discredited one of the arguments that was used to justify the legislation. Instant replays were not available to refute the argument that PASPA was necessary to protect the games from outcomes that could be fixed because of sports transactions.

They could add that the State did not know when the technology would also improve the ability legal sportsbooks to detect "suspicious" behavior that would enable them to sound alerts to everyone in the business. At the time PASPA was enacted the State did not have the examples to make the argument that sportsbooks reinforce the integrity of the games.

The case would be made that these challenges to PASPA had to await the development of the technology that could refute the arguments that were used to support the legislation. At the time the legislation was enacted New Jersey could not have foreseen that the technology of the Information Age would refute reasons for the legislation that were acceptable in a climate where the business of sports transactions was made to be a part of organized crime.

The legal team for New Jersey would not need the voices of people in our business to refute another argument for PASPA. They could make the case that the Information Age made it possible to expose the culprits who are responsible for the lack of integrity in the game. While the arguments in favor of PASPA pointed at people in the business of sports transaction, the Internet, and the media ignore that yawner in favor of primetime features of the lack of integrity enacted by people in the sports businesses. They are the culprits who detract from the purity and wholesomeness that was never inherent in the games in the first place. Public exposure to what transpires behind the sports scenes proves they are no different from people in other professions who impugn the integrity of what they do.

But even if members of the Court accepted these arguments they could still demand an explanation for another failure on the part of New Jersey. They could ask why state legislators did not challenge this violation of their State's right when the legislation was enacted. The fact that New Jersey waited until the economic climate changed to one where the state now had a reason to contest PASPA would undermine a challenge based on States Rights. New Jersey did not acquire a right in 2012 it did not already have in 1992.

Politicians from New Jersey would be able to assist the legal team with an explanation. They have the expertise that would enable them to explain in political terminology why New Jersey failed to act because it was in the interest of the State to remain silent.

They could show how the conflicts between the sports leagues and Nevada had frightened New Jersey legislators into silence. Their opposition to PASPA might have presented a threat to the future of NFL games played at Giants Stadium in East Rutherford. The NFL could have challenged their opposition to PASPA with a threat to move from New Jersey if sports transactions were made legal in the State. Until the MetLife Stadium became a done deal, New Jersey would not risk a challenge that could undo it.

The case for the State might also be helped by excuses that equate with political expediency. Those arguments would try to make the Justices sympathetic to the situation in which politicians from the State were unable to contest one of their own who was responsible for PASPA. At the time, the value of Senator Bradley to the state exceeded the value of legalized sports transactions. After the Senator left office they could afford to make a challenge to the legislation he had imposed on the State. Politics had kept them silent.

Handicappers would bet that the Justices would distance themselves from all of these arguments that dodge the obvious. If States Rights supersedes the Commerce Clause in 2012, it superseded it in 1992 when the legislation was enacted. A change in the economic climate of the time does not change the constitutionality of the legislation. Since New Jersey legislators had relinquished their States Rights in 1992, the Court would likely tell the State to take the fight back to Congress where it began.

Oddsmakers would make "NO" the prohibitive favorite for a proposition on whether the Supreme Court would hear the case; otherwise, handicappers would storm the bastions to get down on a "lock."

If the United States Supreme Court were to defy those odds with a decision to hear the case, oddsmakers would be reluctant to post the proposition:

WILL THE SUPREME COURT DECIDE IN FAVOR OF NEW JERSEY?

They would have to make "NO" the prohibitive favorite in order to deter people from the proposition. The outcome of the appeal by Delaware would lead to that decision because the Court would have otherwise rejected the appeal without comment.

Handicappers would have to explore the possibilities that had led to the decision before they put up or shut up. They might hesitate because of the uncertainties about the political bent of each member of the Court on this issue. The majority might have concurred that this case could offer them a chance to make a point with their decision that extends beyond sports transactions to the big picture of politics. Their decisions might be based on the possibility for a score for their political sponsors.

It might also be possible that a decision in this case would help to make a statement that provides ammunition for either side of the battleground over Tenth Amendment rights versus proponents of federal jurisdiction.

Statements could also be made by the Justices to benefit either side of the debate between liberals and conservatives. Proponents of so-called "big" versus "small" government could use the decision for their purposes.

Proponents of Keynesian and "free" market economics might be able to incorporate the decision in arguments on their behalf. These and others would be open for speculation by handicappers as reasons that led to this decision by members of the Court, but the key to the reasons might be a psychoanalysis of each member of the majority. The reasons might not be evident to any handicapper without this "inside info."

The appeal by New Jersey does not preclude the possibility of another from a different angle. Instead of an appeal based on the Tenth Amendment, "We, the People" can challenge the constitutionality of our legal segregation.

"We" have an opportunity to "put up or shut up" on the opportunity to make "freedom and justice for all" more than just words. This in-running game about the future of the business will come to an end if "We" can win Option Four.

No. 4: APPEAL OF PASPA BASED ON LEGAL SEGREGATION.

This appeal can make the constitutional contest a double-header. Besides the contest between States Rights and the Commerce Clause, "We, the People" can initiate a contest that pits the right of Americans to practice their profession against the sports leagues that oppose our right. The boundary they created through PASPA amounts to legal segregation. This boundary prohibits the right of the "People" to engage in their profession wherever "We" reside in America.

A game plan that utilizes the home field advantage of freedom and justice for all Americans would raise the odds in favor of a judgment that rhymes with the words of the Constitution. "We, the People" can force the Justices to put their money where their mouths are.

The game plan will attack the constitutionality of the legislation that imposes legal segregation on Americans who practice their profession. "We" will challenge the constitutionally of PASPA.

The argument will show that the grandfather tactic was also employed in "Jim Crow" legislation. The grandfather clause was used to enforce racial segregation. The racial segregators used the grandfather clause to deny African Americans the right to vote.

This tactic was also embraced by the proponents of PASPA in order to pass the legislation. The States that opposed the federal prohibition of their businesses made it necessary for the proponents to make a compromise. A compromise was necessary to secure the votes from the soon to be grandfathers that were necessary to pass the legislation. The "clause" made it possible for them to support the legislation. They guaranteed their state's right to their businesses.

There was no need to make a compromise with the other states whose support was also necessary to pass the legislation. There was nothing for them to lose because they had not enacted legislation that legalized sports transactions in their states. They could be "lobbied" for their votes by the proponents.

The losers were the "People" in the business. Their rights were not included in the compromise. The compromise denied them the legal right to practice their profession outside Nevada.

This compromise segregated a business whose practices do not warrant this denigration. The transactions themselves do not pose a threat to anyone. There is nothing about the transactions themselves that would create the need for legal segregation. The boundary is an act of political expediency. It does not protect the rest of America from harm the business in Nevada could cause to the nation.

The reasons that were used to segregate the people cannot withstand the challenge from the facts derived from over a half century of the legal practice of the business in Nevada. The door that was left open by the grandfather clause will be used against the proponents of PASPA to close it. This grandfather will prove that what goes around does indeed come around.

History refutes the arguments that were made to denigrate the profession as a criminal activity. Decades of the legal practice in Nevada proves the profession is an activity that can be regulated by the State as a business.

Despite the allegations that have been made by the opposition, organized crime does not control the business in Nevada. State Regulators have kept people with criminal backgrounds from ownership of the business.

The segregators ignore these facts to make their case that there have been instances in which members of the profession attempted to fix the outcomes of their business. The retort to them is that no profession or business is prohibited because of the possibility that people might attempt to violate the standards of their profession. There would be no politicians, business-persons, journalists, athletes, doctors, lawyers, or clergy if that were the case.

The history of the profession in Nevada refutes the claim that "fixes" are an ingredient of the business. The proponents of PASPA ignore the fact that sports-books would be hurt by a "fix." The sportsbooks are organized to prevent a fix. Their vigilance, along with the scrutiny of instant replay, has raised the odds against a successful fix to where most fixers would be deterred.

The case against PASPA will show that the business in Nevada helps to ensure the integrity of the games. These insurance policies issued by sportsbooks have been exploited by the corporate sports leagues for a half century without compensation and yet the beneficiaries of this insurance have the audacity to argue in favor of the prohibition of the business, except for where their insurance policies are issued. As long as their policies are issued from only one state, they have the best of both worlds. They can exploit the business where it is legal while they prevent the spread of its legality elsewhere.

This prohibition on the spread of the business by the corporate sports leagues has led to the creation of a sportsbook monopoly for Nevada gaming corpora-tions. The monopoly benefits both the Nevada gaming corporations as well as the corporate sports leagues.

This petition will also show the way the changes in the climate for the business forced the proponents of PASPA to reorder the importance of the reasons for the legislation. Their argument that suggested the busi-ness of sports transactions and so-called organized crime was inseparable has been shuffled to the bottom of the deck. Even they know that organized crime has better ways to make money.

Changes in this climate exposed who and what impacts the integrity of the games. The argument that the wholesomeness of the people who engage in the games is corrupted by sports transactions is challenged with regularity by stories that make the headlines. NFL "hit men," child molestation, coaches who lie and cheat, forged college entrance exams, non-graduation rates for college athletes, and drug abuse, among others, have become the clouds that rain on the integrity of the games. Threats to the integrity of the game come from the owners, coaches, and athletes.

The protection of patent rights had been layered beneath these other reasons that were suited for public relations. After those reasons were debunked the sponsors of the legislation were left with the reason that prompted their sponsorship of PASPA. Patent rights were suited for their use of the Commerce Clause to pass the legislation.

This challenge to PASPA will question whether that patent right still exists. The argument will ask the Court to decide whether the patent has expired. Perhaps it belongs in the graveyard beside the one for the pointspread that was never issued to Charles McNeill, the inventor of the pointspread.

This argument will add that the exploitation of a patent right extends to both sides of this contest. The protection of a patent right should work both ways. While corporate sports monopolies argue that the business of sports transactions uses their product without the license to do so, it will also show that exploitation is a two-way street.

The corporate sports monopolies have refused to engage in negotiations with people in the business in Nevada in order to rectify the dispute because it is not in their interest to do so. "We" will show that while these segregators whine about the abuse of their patent rights, they created a double standard that allows their licensees to exploit the patent rights of sportsbooks without retribution. The licensees who use their products find the ways to get around what should be an obligation to pay for the use of the products that belong to the business of sports trans-actions.

Announcers on the networks that broadcast the games of the sports leagues use the terms "big and small" favorites and underdogs. They use pointspreads without a reference or credit to those who created the numbers. They can say "it's over for the under" without kudos to the oddsmakers or sportsbooks who created the pointspread for the comment. Innuendo is a convenient way for them to titillate their audiences with so-called "predictions" about which side will "beat the spread" without a reference to "the spread."

The argument will also show that the exploitation of sportsbooks by the sports leagues extends beyond property rights. The sports leagues depend on the "books" to help them protect the integrity of their patent right. They use information from sportsbooks on "line moves" to alert them to suspicious behavior on their games. The NFL has even called sportsbooks in Las Vegas for reports on the movement of the spreads. Those sportsbooks reassured them about the integrity of all of their games that were posted on the boards *without charge.*

This "goodwill" gesture by sportsbooks was accepted and then repudiated by people in the sports leagues. They prove that their two faces are better than one. Without the imprimatur from the sports-books, the integrity of their games might reach the bottom of the barrel with so-called "professional" wrestling. If sportsbooks were to keep their games off the boards it would raise doubts about their integrity. Hypocrisy has no bounds for the sports leagues who exploit this imprimatur of integrity from the business they prohibit because that business uses their patent right.

Perhaps the courts can decide that an accommodation with patent rights between the two sides can resolve the challenge to PASPA. The Court could force them to reach an agreement over the use of each other's products and the compensation for it. That would resolve the challenge to PASPA. There would be no need to proceed with the challenge.

If the Court does not force the parties to negotiate it will have to deal with another consequence of PASPA. The legislation created a monopoly for the casino corporations in Nevada. The grandfather clause created a monopoly for Nevada casino corporations on the single game transactions that define the business. Members of the court would have more than a mouthful to swallow if they decided to support a law that created legal segregation and in turn created a monopoly for Nevada corporate casinos. Fortunately for the justices, they would not have to explain how the politics of PASPA made "strange bedfellows."

If that isn't enough for the Court to deal with, the argument will also show that the corporate sports monopolies have extended the tentacles of PASPA into the pockets of taxpayers. Taxpayers pay for the enforcement of the legal boundaries created by the legislation. They pay for the protection of a patent right. Law enforcement uses taxpayer dollars to protect their product from domestic and international exploitation. Perhaps this situation will resonate with a Court as a form of taxation without representation.

If this "big picture" doesn't whet the appetite of the justices to declare PASPA unconstitutional, then the issue of "freedom of speech" might become the frosting for them. While people in the business in Nevada are free to talk about what they do, people in the business outside Nevada are not. They have reason to fear the repercussions that could accompany their exercise of free speech. They are aware of the punishments dealt to Jay Cohen and others who have had the audacity to act out their dissent against the system PASPA helped to create. Their sounds of silence are preferable to the freedom to speak. Separate is unequal when it comes to freedom of speech.

The proponents of PASPA will be forced to use their two faces to argue with a straight face that the Constitution can be subverted in all of these ways in order to protect a patent right that may no longer exist. No matter which way the members of a court might lean toward in their politics they will find it hard to keep a straight face if they try to support a law that pierces as many holes in the Constitution as this legislation has done. The Constitutionality of PASPA will test the mettle of integrity of all of the members of a court no matter which way they might lean in their political persuasions.

But even if this argument were to be ordained by legal scholars as one of the "top ten" of all time, a proposition on its outcome could not be posted until after there is a declaration to "let this game begin." When that announcement is made, will the proposition qualify for the boards:

WILL THE COURTS DECIDE IN FAVOR OF "WE, THE PEOPLE"?

The future will be defined by "YES" or "NO."

But the "books" might be reluctant to "post" this "prop." If it were on the boards people in the business might "storm the bastions" in order to "get down on an outcome that expands the right of Americans to be free to practice their profession everywhere in the world.

Perhaps we can begin to create the atmosphere for this endeavor by following the example of the people in the movie *Network*. "We" can show that "we are mad as hell and won't take this anymore." "We" can begin to make it possible for us to be included among "the people" in the Constitution. First class citizenship can be the incentive to use the home field advantage of the Constitutional guarantee of freedom and justice for all.

In order to collect on this "guaranteed lock," we must put our money where our mouths are in order to MAKE THE ODDS BE WITH US. A payout that exceeds any amount ever paid by sportsbooks should be incentive to begin the action now. That "lock" may not be available tomorrow.[288]

---

[288] Thanks to Frances Czuchra for the reminder that all we have is "now."

ABOUT THE AUTHOR

Paul Czuchra moved from Chicago to Las Vegas in 1979. He began his career in the sportsbook industry in the Castaway's sportsbook. From there he went on to become part of a group that made the "Las Vegas Line." He has worked with the most respected Las Vegas oddsmakers and handicappers. He has also written an MA thesis and a doctoral dissertation in Political Science at the University of Chicago.